THE FASCISM
THIS TIME

AND
THE GLOBAL FUTURE
OF DEMOCRACY

BY THEO HORESH

First published by **Cosmopolis Press 2020.**

Special thanks to Elephant Journal for use of articles contained in this book.

Cosmopolis Press
2301 Pearl St. 54
Boulder, CO 80302

Library of Congress Cataloging-in-Publication Data

Horesh, Theo

THE FASCISM THIS TIME AND THE GLOBAL FUTURE OF DEMOCRACY

ISBN

TABLE OF CONTENTS

ACKNOWLEDGEMENTS

It is sometimes said that writing a book is like starting a business. What begins with a clear vision, and is quickly firmed up in a doable plan, produces an endless series of contestations, leading to countless revisions. The end result may seldom be what was expected, but carried out with due diligence, it is invariably better—and far more interesting. It speaks to its consumers in a more visceral way, and when it comes to a subject like this, that means it can do more good.

This book began as a series of insights, fleshed out in articles, and debated in small groups. Face-to-face discussions took place in dialogue with the Trident Philosophy Gang in Boulder, Colorado, where we have met almost weekly for the past decade-and-a-half. Its core members were essential to the development of my views, especially the late Devin Wilson, who could have been one of the great philosophers of his generation; along with Johanna Blumenthal, Joshua Wine Morriston, Douglas Baldwin, Asa Henderson, Nick Montana, David Zindell, Jay B Bargeron, Bill Bishop, Rob Glenn, and countless others.

Meanwhile, Facebook may be playing a major role in the destruction of democracies, but it also presents an extraordinary opportunity to connect old friends with thinkers and activists from around the world. Thus, online discussions took place primarily on Facebook among an especially astute circle of friends, authors, journalists, and activists across the planet. Many stand out over the past six years for their contribution to my thinking, especially Mitch Hampton, Jake Murray, Hani Adi, Jennifer Peters Johnson, William Strother, Matt Turner, Layman Pascal, Greg Abolo, Mike Burch, and Idrees Ahmad.

The original intuitions forming the core of this book were expressed and tested, revised and debated, in what John Rawls described as a reflective equilibrium. But they were also peppered with countless insights emerging from these conversations. Some of the deepest came from my closest friend, Andrew Duff McDuffee, and my partner, Samar Hanna. Their psychological insights brought greater nuance and depth to the book, and our ongoing conversations tempered my views, while helping draw out what was most salient about them. Meanwhile, her love and care helped ground my life and inspire my persistence.

I am grateful to my former mentor, Eric Wolterstorff, for our countless discussions on collective memory and trauma, which laid the foundation for many of the book's most interesting insights. And I am thankful to my late mentor Doug Latham, from decades back, for infusing into my spiritual quest an ethic of realism, service, decency, and responsibility, qualities I can only hope characterize this text. And I would like to thank him for introducing me to the work of Erich Fromm, whose central thesis in *Escape from Freedom* has played such an outsize role in this book. If only his life had lasted as long as his memory.

I am especially indebted to Danny Postel - a model of friendliness, service, intelligence, and justice - for taking the time out of his busy schedule whenever he was called on to help, as did Jamie Mayerfield and Andy Heintz. I am grateful to Vincent Fakhoury Horn, Roger Wolsey, Joe Perez, Imon Ghosh, Andreas Hernandez, Didar Islam, and Yassin Al-Haj Saleh for taking the time to read and review the book. And I am especially thankful for my PhD thesis/ dissertation advisor, Garrett Wallace Brown, for grounding my work academically while humbly supporting my full potential as a writer. It is hard to imagine a better teacher, friend, mentor, and cheerleader.

I am thankful for the proficient, affordable, and beautiful cover design work of Ken Leeder and interior design work of Armen Osipov.

I am grateful to my good friend and production manager, Dave Passiak, for his outstanding work in bringing it all together with patience, warmth, kindness, and persistence. And I am thankful for my loving father, Morris Horesh, who may not like the contents of the book but has long supported my writing.

Needless to say, no one who helped shape my views should be held responsible for their most ill considered manifestations. Like all my books, this one has been a learning journey; hence, my views on its contents will continue changing once it is set down in print. Perhaps the greatest source of learning has come from my engagement with citizens of poorer states, who are more accustomed to the dysfunctions Americans have been experiencing under Trump. Hence, last but not least, I would like to thank all the people in countries around the world who continued resisting fascism and authoritarianism when all seemed lost.

Palestinians and Syrians, Algerians and Sudanese, Hong Kongers and Kashmiris, and every protester and commenter resisting authoritarian rule: over the last four years, you have been my inspiration and sustenance. Thank you for leading the way in making the world a better place.

"Fascism has an enigmatic countenance because in it appears the most counterpoised contents. It asserts authoritarianism and organizes rebellion. It fights against contemporary democracy and... does not believe in the restoration of any past rule. It seems to pose itself as the forge of a strong state, and uses means most conducive to its dissolution, as if it were a destructive faction or secret society. Whichever way we approach fascism we find it is simultaneously one thing and the contrary."

JOSÉ ORTEGA Y GASSET,
Sobre el Fascismo[1]

"Our contemporaries are constantly wracked by two warring passions: They feel the need to be led and the desire to remain free. Unable to destroy either of these contrary instincts, they seek to satisfy both at once. They imagine a single, omniscient, tutelary power, but one that is elected by the citizens. They combine centralization with popular sovereignty. This gives them some respite. Each allows himself to be treated as wards by imagining that they have chosen their own protectors. Each individual allows himself to be clapped in chains because the other end of the chains is held not by a man or class but by the people themselves."

ALEXIS DE TOCQUEVILLE,
Democracy in America[2]

PROLOGUE

"Better to be despised for too anxious
apprehensions, than ruined by too confident a
security."

EDMUND BURKE
Reflections on the Revolution in France[1]

The election of Donald Trump felt to many like that final scene from the *Planet of the Apes,* when riding horseback on an isolated beach, the astronaut who has landed on a world ruled by apes sees—sticking out stark and alone on the quiet shore—the head of the Statue of Liberty, and realizing he has not traveled to another planet, but rather to a future without humanity, gets down on his knees amid the breaking waves and sobs, "You maniacs, you blew it up—God damn you, God damn you all to hell."

We believed it could not happen here, and now we are living with what never seemed possible: fascism has finally arrived on the shores of America. And while most of us go about our daily lives unperturbed, a momentous sense of dread has come to nag at our consciences. We try to ignore the possibility that it may spell an end to American democracy, and with it so many of the freedoms we had so recently taken for granted. Yet, we periodically awaken to the reality with a sense of helplessness and angst, struggling to find an appropriate response to what can often seem a sort of mass psychosis. But mostly, life just goes on as before.

There is a moment of calm that can come before a horrific crisis. We cannot believe what is happening and tell ourselves it is not as bad as we think. We try to normalize the things we are about to confront or find humanity in a violent perpetrator. It is much the same with the victim of a kidnapping as it is with the subject of a tyrant: most people try to normalize their situation in order to carry on living. But often it is worse than they could ever imagine, and the disproportionality of their responses only highlight the dangers.

All this was conveyed to me by an older Syrian gentleman in a Greek island cafe. His city had just been besieged by the Assad regime, which was starving the population to get at the Free Syria Army, and people were killing each other for bread. So, when Isis arrived, and they were "nice at first" as he put it, people accepted them in the hope things would change. But then they began killing people en masse for petty religious offenses and leaving their bodies to rot in the streets. Now he found himself in a refugee camp, awaiting acceptance into an unknown country on another continent. And yet, life rolled on as we sat with his wife and children, slowly sipping coffee.

A period of unnerving calm followed the election of Trump. Many people said we should wait-and-see; that he would shake things up and displace elites; that he was a pragmatist with no clear ideological commitments and could be influenced in the right direction. Now all of that is gone, and almost everyone who was not a supporter has awoken to the reality that they may soon be living in a once and former democracy. The new normal is so surreal that outrage at specific policies and pronouncements will probably fail to get at the tectonic shifts now knocking us off our feet. As this book goes to press, the *Washington Post* reports that America is experiencing the worst pandemic since 1918, the worst economy since 1933, and the worst civil unrest since 1968; they forgot to add, the worst leadership of any major developed state since 1945, and the worst ever in our history. And yet, the greatest danger may lie in the increasing equanimity with which all this is greeted.

PROLOGUE 🌐 | 11

Fascism is anything but normal, but it must be normalized if it is to succeed. It is normalized through its contagious energy, which empowers followers, paralyzes skeptics, wears down opponents, and destroys resisters. Peter Fritzsche's *Life and Death in the Third Reich* highlights the way even people resistant to the regime became swept up by its activities. The Third Reich made itself felt everywhere, and there was no place to resist, but people also welcomed the vigorous sense of national pride accompanying its ascent to power. They were excited over the changes taking place and felt joined together as part of a great nation. Meanwhile, those who might otherwise have resisted gradually found themselves overwhelmed and isolated.[2]

This kind of normalization involves both institutional and personal changes, of which most people remain unaware. Hannah Arendt illustrates this process in her classic, *Eichmann in Jerusalem*, which focuses on the ordinariness of the man in charge of the logistics of liquidating the Jews. At first, he tells himself he is helping them migrate to the new state of Israel and even considers the Jewish leaders he is helping to ethnically cleanse to be his friends. Then when he is told of the "final solution" to come, he talks about the color fading from his life and even losing the will to live. And yet, somehow, he is picked up years later in Argentina after bragging about killing five million Jews. Somehow, he had reconciled himself to playing logistical mastermind to genocide.[3]

Few Americans have ever lived under an authoritarian, let alone fascist regime. We have never watched leaders arrogate power without justification, never witnessed the unapologetic assault on democratic institutions. We have never seen friends and family explain away such outrages, nor read about fellow citizens being shipped to camps where they await deportation. Few of us can imagine how we would respond to all this, and yet much of it has become a daily reality already. The gulag of concentration camps, where kids are separated from parents and placed in densely packed cells without shampoo, toothpaste, or bedding; the president's calls for heavily armed white nationalists to join the police in defending his White House; and his sharing of statements about killing all Democrats are now a daily reality.[4] In the end, we may adapt much as did the Germans, gradually reconciling ourselves to what never seemed possible.

The spectacle accompanying these changes may make it all the more likely.

The fascism this time is less strident and more disorderly, less disciplined and more absurd. The country is more stable than Weimar Germany and postwar Italy, and its institutions are stronger. Scholars of fascism are divided over how to characterize the administration, with most settling for a more narrow definition of fascism that would exclude it. The Trump administration certainly bears a family resemblance to Nazi Germany and Mussolini's Italy in its populism, nationalism, militarism, and ethnocentrism. The irrationalism and nihilism of the administration lend to it a similar tone. And the cult of personality surrounding its narcissistic leader, with aggressive impulses and an abusive manner, could not be more familiar.[5]

But whatever we wish to call the administration, we must take the threats it poses seriously. Almost nobody in Germany would have imagined the extremism of the Third Reich when Hitler entered office in 1933, but his radicalism deepened as he consolidated power. In the end, ordinary Germans embraced the mass killing of Jews, even as they were repeatedly given the opportunity to sit it out.[6] It takes time to wear down institutions and to staff them with your own people, to normalize hate and erode distinctions between fact and fiction.[7] The road to a fascist state may in fact be longer than we tend to think, and it is for this very reason that we should not take anything for granted.

America is not yet a fascist state. Rather, we have a fascist leader, with a fascist following, who has taken over an increasingly fascist party, while presiding over a largely fascist administration, which is gradually taking over the government. But administrations change with elections, so the state itself remains largely democratic, if having suffered repeated blows. Trump has succeeded in putting loyalists at the head of a number of key bureaus, but the government itself possesses over a million employees. Fascist Germany and Italy possessed far smaller states; meanwhile, scholars of fascism generally agree that Italian fascism was never really consolidated. States were far smaller almost everywhere—as measured in the percentage of revenues spent on government programs—in the first half of the twentieth century, and America possesses an especially large state in the twenty-first century simply as a result of the size of its population and its level of wealth. It will be hard to find the loyalists necessary to staff its bureaus, and it will take time to impact the minutiae of its regulations. Thus, the economist Tyler Cowen believes, in an ironic retort to libertarians, that it is actually the government's vastness that will preserve its freedoms.[8] Yet, Trump is eroding institutions faster than almost anyone thought possible.

The greatest concern probably lies with the gradual destruction of democratic norms and institutions, amid widespread social regression. Democratic norms are always fragile, for they are based on widely shared sentiments, passed down from one generation to the next in a chain of succession, which over the course of a few generations might be broken altogether. Democratic institutions rarely last without the love of freedom and sense of inherent equality, which makes people so resistant to authoritarian leaders. But these sentiments were already weakening and are now being assaulted, along with the legitimacy of basic democratic institutions, like freedom of speech and assembly, fair courts and elections.

Trumpist populism is a sort of confused patriotism, which rejects the most essential American values in the name of making the country great again. And it gets away with it because the left, for the most part, refuses to celebrate any vision of its culture whatsoever. Fascists are able to claim the nation to themselves, as the left picks up votes on the multicultural margins, because the left has failed to present a compelling vision of what it means to be American.[9] Something similar seems to be happening across the globe, as liberals abandon the nation in favor of a more multicultural world.[10]

But this time, there is no Roosevelt to serve as a bulwark against fascism; thus, the fascism this time may have to be fought from below, and it may have to be fought globally.

Yet, as the stresses involved in facing what is happening intensify, many will simply turn inward in a perverted attempt to find their bearings, expecting others to continue the resistance, with most lacking the strength to do so without the support of everyone else. It has happened countless times before in nations that succumbed to authoritarian rule, and in the Second World War over an entire continent,[11] but this time it could be the world itself that goes under.[12] Yet, a twenty-first century world in which democracy is pushed to the margins could never begin to redress global challenges like climate change and nuclear proliferation.[13] It is now quite possible that in our weakness before such challenges, we will simply give up and give in.

Preventing such an outcome will require that we commit to using resistance to make ourselves better and stronger. It is a path of personal development few people living in developed democracies have given much thought to, but it is a common path for marginalized people struggling under oppressive conditions. Simply finding the strength to face the forces of oppression is a powerful path of personal development when the stressors you are facing will not go away on their own. For in facing overwhelming odds, we develop capacities we never thought possible. Hence, what begins as a worldly struggle can be transformed into a personal path of freedom, with the resulting freedom being both an external condition and an inner state of mind.

It is time we begin to consider such a path more suitable to the times. It is time we commit to fighting to preserve freedoms that only yesterday we took for granted. It will be an ennobling fight, and we should look for allies among libertarians and conservatives. Some of the greatest resistance to Trump has come from the conservative leadership itself. Conservative thinkers like Charles Krauthammer and David Brooks, who refused to vote for him, deserve our ears.

Conservative leaders like Governor John Kasich and the late Senator John McCain, who have resisted Trump's crudity and inhumanity, deserve our respect. It is now time for all good people to band together against a force of darkness, subverting the moral order, and strand by strand, shredding the social fabric.

If we succeed, we will find ourselves not only better people but a better nation—and maybe, perhaps, even a better and stronger world.

This book had its start as a series of articles, which first began to be published in the spring of 2016. These were soon strewn together into a book whose noticeable gaps were filled in over the course of the next year. The initial ideas fermented, as the articles grew in length and depth, and the original spine began to grow flesh. In the end, its initial intuitions were refined and tested until something emerged that was as innovative as it was predictive. Many of its concepts harkened back to the thirties and forties of the last century when social psychologists like Wilhelm Reich sought to explain the rise of fascism in authoritarian family structures,[14] and Erich Fromm explored the way fascists sought an escape from the burden of freedom.[15] Yet, the fascism this time was different, and it required its own concepts, replete with its own rhetoric, logic, style, and tone. It needed to be situated within a thoroughly globalized and multicultural world. And it was not enough to simply analyze it: anyone serious about the fascism this time needed to resist it, in words and deeds alike.

The concepts at the core of this book hung heavy in the public sphere, where comparisons with Germany in the thirties permeated the air. Yet, scholars of fascism largely rejected them, and journalists soon fell in line. After an initial wave of speculation, both groups generally concluded that Trump was not a fascist but rather a rightwing populist:[16] and for every rightwing populist, it was only logical to conclude that there was an equally dangerous leftwing populist.[17] Yet, there were virtually no leftwing populists outside of Latin America posing serious threats to democratic institutions. And none whatsoever were carrying out the kind of crimes against humanity undertaken by rightwing nationalists like Bolsonaro in the Amazon, Netanyahu in Gaza, Assad and Putin in Idlib, and Trump in Yemen. The global threat was overwhelmingly rightwing and authoritarian, and yet opinion leaders continued speaking in the same insipid jargon of moral equivalence.

They referenced Trump's racism and sexism, his chronic mendacity and assault on reality, but never the way he spoke just like Mussolini, or shared so much in common with Hitler. Scholars in political science took Trump's threat to democratic institutions seriously.[18] Yet, even as he established concentration camps, packed with children separated from their parents, and embraced the starvation of millions of children in Yemen, while encouraging his supporters to physically attack, and sometimes slaughter, his opponents en masse,[19] respectable journalists and academics somehow deemed the fascist label extreme. However, major Holocaust scholars were often explicit in comparing America to Germany under the Third Reich.[20]

It was to set the record straight and call them by their true name, so as to help remove them from power, that this book was written. However, the book itself has its own weaknesses, of which readers should be forewarned. Perhaps the most glaring is that, while its analysis of fascism is global, it is mostly focused on America and Trump. Some of this focus was strategic: in leading what is arguably the most influential state in the world, Trump is arguably the most powerful person on the planet. And since fascists tend to worship power, taking out the most powerful leader among them is likely to weaken the rest. It is for this reason that the book also focuses on Putin, who has empowered fascists in American and Europe alike. But some of the focus is the result of my own limitations. As fascist leaders grew in strength and number, it became increasingly difficult to provide a comprehensive account of their offenses.

Several states also deserved much greater attention. Israel has mobilized a racist and militarized society against native Palestinians.

It has routinely armed the most fascist states in their crimes against humanity, including in the Rohingyan, Bosnian, and Rwandan Genocides. It has been a pioneer in the Islamophobia through which all too many rightwing nationalist and fascist regimes find their common focus. And it has probably done more than any state, except Russia and its all-powerful backer America, to weaken the global rules-based order. However, its social and political power is relatively dispersed, and this made it a poor fit for my narrative, which emphasizes the hierarchical nature of fascism.

Similarly, the Assad regime has long brutalized its population through extralegal thuggery;[21] and the sadism of its prison system, where tens of thousands have been tortured to death, calls to mind the worst horrors of the Holocaust.[22] Moreover, the failure of the international community to put a halt to its abuses, sustained with the help of an increasingly fascist Russia, helped normalize the crimes of rightwing nationalists and fascists the world over. But while the initial uprising against the regime was far more progressive than its critics give it credit for,[23] the reaction of the regime was much less a response to rapid social development than that of fascists in places like Russia, Germany, Italy, India, and America. So, it did not fit as well into my narrative, which emphasizes the way fascists meet rapid social development with a forced regression to patriarchy. Finally, since the skeleton of the book was written before Bolsonaro came to power, the threats he posed were sometimes difficult to incorporate into it.

The challenge lay in articulating timeless features of fascism that were relevant to the present. Yet, in emphasizing some features and downplaying others, my conceptions all too often omitted some of the most salient contemporary examples of fascism. In this regard, it was a lot like the scholarship on early twentieth-century fascism which, in trying to arrive at an irreducible definition of fascism based on its past permutations, missed the obvious signs of the fascism this time. It is nevertheless my belief that the concepts upon which my own notion of fascism is built will prove helpful in analyzing an array of protofascist regimes, much as have those of leading scholars like Robert Paxton.[24]

However, the book suffers from another quirk, which is that a decision was made early on to serialize its chapters in the form of articles. The decision has resulted in a dynamic book, in which each chapter tends to emphasize a different dimension of fascism, which may well make for more interesting reading. Yet, it has made it far more difficult to build a logical and coherent argument. But in providing a psychosocial account of the forces animating and sustaining fascism today, it offers something almost wholly unique; and it meets these forces with an equally powerful account of the spirit of democracy and how it might be mobilized in a global movement. Meanwhile, in speaking a language every bit as sweeping as the forces we are up against, it is my hope that it will inspire as much as it illuminates, and in providing a more salient assessment of the fascism this time, highlight the spirit with which it must be fought.

The conception of fascism presented in this book led to my prediction, before Trump was even elected, that his administration would be more extreme than almost anyone imagined, and that it would become increasingly authoritarian with the passage of time. It led to my prediction that it would take some time to put down the resistance within his party but that he would eventually succeed, and after doing so he would begin taking over the courts and the federal bureaucracy. It led to my prediction that concentration camps would arise on the border of Mexico; that the blockade of Yemen would degenerate into a mass die-off that looked a lot like genocide; that crimes against humanity would explode across the world; that at least a dozen, and quite possibly dozens of, democracies would degenerate into autocracies; that the world order led by advanced democracies would be largely destroyed; and that a global arms race would ensue.

The book argues that all this is either currently in motion or has already come to pass, and that if Trump stays in office it will get worse. Readers can decide for themselves the extent to which these predictions were accurate, but we would do well to consider how the predictive power of this model stacks up against those of leading scholars of populism and fascism. These scholars generally predicted that while Trump may possess authoritarian tendencies, he will not destroy democratic institutions or attempt to seize power. They typically argued that he did not possess the same level of cruelty as early twentieth-century fascists, thus we would not see a repeat of the kind of horrors they inflicted. And they made clear that he was not making use of extra-legal force, as did the early fascists. Of course, a brief summary such as this cannot do justice to the nuances of their views, and Holocaust scholars were a salient exception among them,[25] but it starts to get at how badly most of them got it wrong.[26]

As this book goes to press, much of the world is in lockdown in an effort to suppress coronavirus infections. And while it has hit some of the freest places the hardest, four of the most fascist administrations in America, Brazil, India, and Russia are currently experiencing the highest numbers of infections and deaths. Meanwhile, the rightwing nationalist administration of Boris Johnson in the U.K. is close behind and experiencing the highest death rates among all but the tiniest countries with the densest and most mobile populations. It is a fitting denouement to an era that was sure to end in destruction. The fascism this time may not have been responsible for the spread of the coronavirus, but it certainly made the rate of infections worse through its attack on the international institutions that might have coordinated a global response. There is no doubt that the suppression of information and the delusions of leaders in states like India, China, America, Russia, and Brazil allowed the virus to spread faster and further. But across the world, it has been the actions of individuals who refuse to face the challenge of living in a globalized world, retreating instead into a world of fantasies, that has sustained its spread. And while the vast bulk of this book was written before the outbreak of the pandemic, and does not reference it as a result, the global cataclysm it represents is in accord with its predictions: fascism always ends in destruction; thus, the globalized fascism of today was bound to end in global destruction. The only question is how long it will last—and how much havoc it will wreak in the meantime.

The first section of the book explores the nature of the fascism this time and how it differs from the last. The second deepens the exploration by looking at its components in greater depth. The third proceeds to look at the democratic institutions and vulnerable minorities that the fascism this time threatens. The fourth looks at the conditions sustaining the fascism this time, along with those that might contribute to its demise. And the fifth looks at how we can better meet its challenge through stronger movements, consisting of wider coalitions, organized with others around the world, and seize the moment to transform the day. The fascism this time is global, so the resistance must be global as well. The fascism this time possesses state power, so the resistance must be organized from below. Finally, the fascism this time has all too often hypnotized us, so the resistance is going to have to seize our attention and inspire our hearts. It is my hope that this book will play its part in turning the tides.

THEO HORESH,
Leeds, U.K.

"Fascism in power is the open, terroristic dictatorship of the most reactionary, the most chauvinistic, the most imperialistic elements of finance capital."

COMMUNIST INTERNATIONAL,
1935[27]

"... fascism draws its internal cohesion and affective-driving force from a core myth that a period of perceived decadence and degeneracy is imminently or eventually to give way to one of rebirth and rejuvenation in a post-liberal order."

ROGER GRIFFIN,
The Nature of Fascism[28]

"(Fascism is) a form of political behavior marked by obsessive preoccupation with community decline, humiliation or victimhood, and by compensatory cults of unity, energy and purity, in which a mass-based party of committed nationalist militants, working in uneasy but effective collaboration with traditional elites, abandons democratic liberties and pursues with redemptive violence and without ethical or legal restraints goals of internal cleansing and external expansion."

ROBERT O. PAXTON,
The Anatomy of Fascism[29]

INTRODUCTION

FIRST TIME AS TRAGEDY,
SECOND AS FARCE

"Men make their own history, but they do not make it as they please; they do not make it under self-selected circumstances, but under circumstances existing already, given and transmitted from the past. The tradition of all dead generations weighs like a nightmare on the brains of the living. And just as they seem to be occupied with revolutionizing themselves and things, creating something that did not exist before, precisely in such epochs of revolutionary crisis they anxiously conjure up the spirits of the past to their service, borrowing from them names, battle slogans, and costumes in order to present this new scene in world history in time-honored disguise and borrowed language."

KARL MARX,
Eighteenth Brumaire of Louis Napoleon

Karl Marx once noted that all great historical events repeat themselves, only the first time as tragedy, the second as farce.[1] Seldom could the maxim be so poignantly applied than to the fascism this time. Whereas the first fascism channeled the energies of vigorous German and Italian youths, Trumpist fascism vents the resentments of marginalized retirees. Whereas the first fascism projected the image of an ordered march into the future, Trumpist fascism is backward-looking and incontinent. Whereas the first fascism united the nation through rituals and symbols, Trumpist fascism is slovenly, discordant, and buffoonish.

Trump is to Hitler as Groucho was to Karl, and Bolsonaro, Duterte, Assad, and Netanyahu do not fare much better.

Early twentieth-century fascism channeled the restless energies of newly formed nations, which had just lost big in the First World War. It sought to break the gridlock of unstable and corrupt democracies through the iron hand of an authoritarian strongman. And it sought through force to fend off the communist menace. It moved to the rhythms of the industrial age, and subsumed individuals to a greater social machine. In this sense, it was a product of its time.[2]

But wherever rightwing populists seek to strengthen the nation through racist exclusion and militarist expansion; wherever leaders and followers fuse themselves in an unconscious effort to bolster their flailing sense of self-importance; wherever an assault on democratic institutions comes coupled with a cult of personality and the denigration of women; we see the hand of fascism at work. It is a protean creed, whose doctrines dress in drag to elude detection,[3] but its structure is much the same everywhere.

Fascism made its debut in Italy toward the close of the First World War, under the steely-eyed leadership of Benito Mussolini. Italy was a young nation, but a half-century old. Its institutions were weak, its democratic parliament riven with conflict. Its national identity was unformed, its youth spent in the shadow of great empires. Italian fascists drew from a class of educated and elite nationalists and looked to the future. They were known for their flamboyant but sharp sense of style. They wanted to take their seat among nations and bring order to their underdeveloped society. They also did a lot of cocaine and beat up their political opponents—and they came to power in a coup, sanctioned by church and crown. Yet a powerful myth of greatness, set forth from the tongue of a magnetic leader, has a way of blocking out the harsh light of reality.[4]

German fascists were also young and forward-looking, fusing an unruly use of extralegal violence with the façade of traditional patriarchy. They frightened elites but comforted the middle class with the illusion of order. And much as in Italy, conservative elites welcomed their vigor in the fight to restore the monarchy.

Looking back, we tend to imagine Hitler's actions as springing from programmatic discipline. However, the historian Richard G. Evans emphasizes in his *Coming of the Third Reich* that Hitler had no program except to make Germany great again—and he lied constantly.[5] Never underestimate the power of reification, the concretization of abstract ideas, which mistakes the fictions of our minds for the facts of existence. Perhaps all authoritarian leaders rely on the reification of their insecure followers but none so much as the fascist. The symbiosis between leader and follower would not be possible without the willingness to collude in their delusions of grandeur.[6]

Fascists were everywhere a mess of contradictions.[7]

If Trump appears more the flaccid, old clown than the vigorous fascist youth, perhaps it is because he is applying old answers to new challenges. Racist nationalism may find a following in a teeming global village, but its program is impotent because it has languished too long in fantasy. Rightwing populists are marginalized by blaming their problems on everyone but themselves and creating excuses to scapegoat minorities. They are thus linked to the fascists of yore, who scapegoated communists and Jews, and sought renewal through ethnic purity.

Magnanimous progressives like to blame the rise of the fascism on neoliberalism, and its attendant economic insecurity and inequality.[8] But fascism has always drawn supporters from a wide socioeconomic swathe of the population.[9] And Trump's base does not care so much that he has traded the populist rhetoric of his early campaign for a cabinet of billionaires and tax breaks for the wealthy. Meanwhile, fascism has appeared in both neoliberal America and socially democratic Brazil; and fascist movements have been stunningly strong in stable social democracies like Germany and Sweden. Moreover, former Soviet successes like Poland and Hungary, which liberalized gradually, have seen rightwing nationalists and fascists take power.

In contrast, others like Ukraine, which experienced the worst shocks of liberalization, have pushed these movements to the margins. And then there is Israel, where ethnic supremacism and militarization began generations ago under socialist rule but were intensified as the neoliberal and nationalist right gradually consolidated power. There are just too many anomalies like these to blame neoliberalism alone for this latest wave of fascism. Like Hitler and Mussolini, Trump disarmed progressives with populist rhetoric, while his followers played along, unconcerned with the primitive magic of economics. What mattered to them was what always matters most to fascists, which is to feel themselves great again—nation be damned.

While the fascist solution worked as poorly then as now, at least its first instantiation appeared powerful. Whereas Trumpist fascism wears its absurdities on its sleeve, the first fascists were able to maintain the illusion of strength. The illusion was sustained through radio, whose hypnotic messages could be spread en masse to tens of millions of people at a time.[10] Trumpist fascism uses the same outlandish propaganda, but it does so in the information age, where millions of commenters scrutinize every pronouncement. If Trump seems more the clown than Hitler, perhaps it is the ease with which the emperor can be stripped naked and his purposes turned inside out.

And therein lies the rub: rightwing populism may be every bit as fascist this time around as last,[11] but its bad faith is so obvious as to make it look comical. And the comedy embedded in the membranes of this tragedy is so apparent it has become a rather macabre source of entertainment. It is often said of this presidency that it is a reality show custom made for an age of entertainment. American culture has increasingly taken on the trappings of a reality show,[12] and now its politics has finally succumbed. Political leaders must now play the part of entertainers and sustain their support through constant stimulation.

This may seem a far cry from the iron will of Hitler or Mussolini, and yet fascism was always a distraction from reality. It substituted myths of greatness for economic programs, ethnic scapegoats for policy analysis, showmanship for leadership, bold decrees for moral fortitude. It was in its drift into fantasy that fascism would meet its demise. Fascists had a tendency to overreach, not least in their failure to distinguish fact from fiction, but sustaining the fiction will be harder in the information age.

Trump's supporters will never be able to lend him the same allegiance as the original fascists did their leaders if only because his ruses will be constantly exposed. Hence, their allegiance will remain lazy and provisional, with his biggest supporters avoiding open confrontation, lest they are laughed off the face of the earth. In the end, Trump will fall like so many tyrants before him—and he will almost certainly do so faster. The only question that remains is how much damage he will do in the meantime.

This book distances itself from political events and pronouncements, which have been better covered by journalists and analysts elsewhere.[13] It eschews careful historiography of much fine scholarship on fascism,[14] which can overlook present dangers amid the minutiae of past horrors. While it draws heavily on these historical tragedies, its main focus lies in not repeating them in the present. And it shies away from the comparative analysis and systematic definition of fascism, which has been exhaustively studied by experts in the field,[15] opting instead for a psychosocial view, more reminiscent of early writings on fascism, like those of Hannah Arendt, Erich Fromm, Wilhelm Reich, Max Horkheimer, and Eric Hoffer.

There is a tendency among scholars of fascism to define it so narrowly that it is largely irrelevant to the present course of history. Almost no one expects liberals today to hold the same views as nineteenth-century liberals, who would have been shocked by the size of the state advocated by libertarians, let alone liberals. Almost no one expects socialists today to hold the same views as early twentieth-century socialists, who would have favored a far higher degree of state control and class antagonism. We expect them to be different because times have changed. Yet, an increasing array of studies in political psychology suggest that the general impulses behind their political participation,[16] and the organization of their movements, are much the same as they were in the past.

Fascist movements can be identified by their toxic brew of populism, nationalism, militarism, and authoritarianism. But their most worrisome trait lies in the aggression they mobilize against outsiders. Fascist movements are organized around charismatic leaders, whose loyal and aggressive followers scapegoat minorities and shut down dissent,[17] enforcing a conformity that is gradually extended from movement to party, from party to polity. It is a disease that rots the social fabric through the mind-numbing repetition of meaningless pronouncements.

Fascist movements tend to appear in advanced societies amid economic displacement and the breakdown of democracy. They are populist in that they blame elites, but their economic agenda tends to vanish upon attaining power.[18] Their core impulses are conservative, but they differ from traditional conservatives in their disparagement of established institutions,[19] libertarian conservatives in their disregard for basic freedoms,[20] and moderate conservatives in their disdain for reason.

Fascist movements are often characterized as conservative or populist,[21] but this overlooks their regressive nihilism.[22] Fascist movements are dangerous because they harness nationalist aggression against outsiders, but their greater danger may lie in their turn against reality.[23] Fascist movements reject science and rationality because they are experienced as a threat, but since the world cannot be turned off, they try to tear it down instead. The impulse is, at the same time, nihilistic and socially regressive. Fascists seek to go back to a more bounded set of conventions, but their developmental retrenchment is doomed to fail. It all looks a bit like grown men trying to repeat what they missed in elementary school. Yet, fascism can also appear simply evil, for the nihilism it mobilizes tends to culminate in genocide, and when fascism goes global, it threatens not simply vulnerable minorities, but the world itself, whose vast complexity, and the life it sustains, remain incomprehensible, to narrow and contracted minds, living out a regressive fantasy of omnipotence.

Designating contemporary movements as fascist is commonly treated as irresponsible and extreme. An insult to obsessive-compulsive disciplinarians, a smear against mass movements, a universal term of abuse, it is often said that fascism is one of the most overused terms in the English language. But if fascism is abused through overuse, its underuse and neglect are a greater cause for concern. Holocaust historian Timothy Snyder points out that since Americans have never experienced fascism up close, it has never been granted the same urgency as in Europe. Americans neither understand what it looks like in practice nor how it undermines democracy, and we lack the vocabulary to name it when we see it.[24]

Fascists have typically risen to power in unstable democracies before consolidating absolute control. The Nazis received the greatest share of votes in 1933 when Hitler was appointed Chancellor, but within a matter of months he had declared martial law and started throwing communist rivals in concentration camps. Mussolini came to power after a short experiment with democracy, which was largely dysfunctional. Putin was elected for the first time after a decade of unstable and corrupt democracy in Russia, just as the country was coming out of a massive economic recession.[25] And Trump has come to power after a short decade of virtually unlimited campaign contributions, which have severely corrupted both major American political parties.

The turn to fascism this time comes at a worrying historical moment. Not a single region of the world has been spared a series of tsunamis that may together threaten the survival of democracy itself.[26] Information is increasing with the proliferation of research on most everything. Immigration is increasing with the ability to travel almost anywhere. Inequality is increasing from automation happening nearly everywhere. And globalization is increasing because it is all so interconnected. These forces are globally pervasive and show little likelihood of abatement. Together, they challenge people across the globe to make sense of a vastly more complex and overwhelming world than the one into which they were socialized, whose challenges must be confronted if human civilization is to flourish.[27]

If the fascism of the twentieth century was about young nations coming together and defining their place in the world, the fascism this time is about shutting down the show. Information overload inundates us with complexity. Immigration transforms us into a Babel of differences. Inequality pushes most everyone to the margins, and globalization makes it next to impossible to resist. Together, these forces constitute a seemingly unstoppable juggernaut. The term juggernaut is instructive, signifying the inexorable sublimity of insurmountable forces. It was brought to the West in the fourteenth century by a Franciscan missionary, who claimed worshippers in India would throw themselves beneath the wheels of a great carriage, honoring the Hindu God Vishnu, amid a vast procession crushing everything in its path. The first fascists experienced just such a juggernaut in modernity, the fascists this time in postmodernity. But in both instances, they have sought to counter progress with their own unstoppable march, and the danger is that they will have the momentum of history on their side this time and destroy every democratic institution standing in their path.

THIS IS HOW FASCISM COMES TO AMERICA

*"... faced with insoluble economic problems and
an increasingly revolutionary working class, the
bourgeoisie now fell back on force and coercion,
that is the say, something like fascism."*

ERIC HOBSBAWM,
The Age of Extremes:
A History of the World, 1914–1991[1]

THIS IS HOW FASCISM COMES TO AMERICA

"Perhaps it is historically true that no order of society ever perishes save by its own hand."

JOHN MAYNARD KEYNES,
The Economic Consequences of the Peace[2]

Fascism is born everywhere humanity seeks to be in chains. It appears on the scene when people, weary of the burden of freedom, seek to throw it off and submit to a leader who promises to set things right. The leader portrays himself as a father of the nation, whose primal power is beyond question, and the followers he gathers mythologize his vitality, bolstering themselves through joining in his power.[3]

Fascist leaders appear in confusing times with easy answers. The confusion may be brought on by the dislocation of economic recession or inequality. But it might also stem from rapid social development, which spurs experimentation. Women leave home and enter the workplace, gay people come out of the closet, artists explode conventions, and everywhere, a spirit of innovation reigns. Rapid social development can generate personal growth and make everything seem possible, but it can also foster the kind of contraction seen in old men, who end their days in irritation and disgust with everything new. Rapid changes can be disorienting, and many will long for the security of the old order.

It is in this effort to raise the drawbridge and seal the gates that the fascist reveals his true motives. Fascism seeks to go back to a time when everything was simpler, but also to a lower level of development in which everything was less complex. It is in this sense regressive, and the historian of fascism Eugen Weber notes that the fascist leader is always a man and that his movement is always a reaction to the rising power of women.[4] Fascism is in this way a forced regression to patriarchy, and the fascist masks his regression with panache.

The structure of its ascent can be glimpsed in both Nazi Germany and Fascist Italy. A populist strongman builds a movement of the lower-middle classes that attacks the establishment, emphasizing the failure of democracy and civility, claiming force can accomplish what failed by consent. He attacks feminists and effeminate elites, minorities and immigrants, socialists and intellectuals, and claims he can make the nation great again.

Hitler fought the communists in the streets and barroom brawls for a decade before attaining power.[5] Mussolini started at the grassroots, growing a movement among disaffected leftists, which quickly drifted rightward.[6] Both relied on the threat of extralegal force and cultivated a myth of their greatness. And while quieter and more subdued, and the discrete successor to an otherwise democratic leader, Putin also relied on a mythologized machismo,[7] and the extralegal force of nationalist youths,[8] who terrorized demonstrators and gay people.[9]

Traditional conservatives try to brush off these strongmen and downplay their dangers, but fascists possess the vitality needed to win. Reluctantly, conservatives join the fascists, believing they can keep their leaders on a leash and harness their energy to maintain power. Thus, King Emmanuel made Mussolini prime minister after his Blackshirts marched on Rome and deposed the liberal government. President Hindenburg made Hitler chancellor after he got the most votes in 1933. The oligarchs backed Putin and Republicans got behind Trump—but none were kept in check.

Meanwhile, liberals, centrists, and social democrats try to form a grand coalition to beat back the barbarians. Anything seems better than the fascists, so they join in an uneasy coalition, like the French Popular Front of Jewish Prime Minister Léon Blum in 1936. It was a short-lived government that ultimately failed, but they staved off fascism by bringing socialists, communists, liberals, and centrists into a grand coalition.[10] It has been much the same since Macron was elected to the leadership of France in 2017, and Canada experienced the same strains under Justin Trudeau before settling on a coalition government that is pulling him to the left.

The challenge for such coalitions lies in staying together. Each opposed to the other, the parties can appear the very caricature of corruption and inefficiency painted by fascists. Consider the campaign of Clinton 2016: centrist enough to win over some Republicans, not progressive enough to win the left, the campaign fell victim to every stereotype of weak and corrupt liberals—and as the center wobbled, fascists picked up steam. Meanwhile, the Corbyn campaign in the United Kingdom may have swung too far left to keep the center, which sabotaged his campaign with trumped-up charges of Antisemitism.

Twentieth-century fascist movements were usually formed in opposition to the communist left. But leftists tend to desert the liberal-social-democratic-center for its compromises and corruption. For fascism arrives at a time of national displacement, and as the philosopher and longshoreman Eric Hoffer noted, people join mass movements when they feel isolated and marginalized, hopeless and displaced. Hence, the same forces driving people into the arms of fascists draw them into the hands of leftist mass movements as well.[11]

If the left is strong enough to pull away a substantial portion of the social-democratic center, or if the liberal-center is too weak or corrupt to justify its antifascist stand, the coalition falls; and as the center disintegrates, a longing for stability sets in, and the fascists take power. It is for this reason many have blamed the left for the rise of fascism. They may be the most repulsed by its regression, but they can be a wrecking ball that smashes the last lines of defense when they press too hard for deeper structural changes.

Conservatives quickly discover fascists are willing to say anything to attain power, but seldom do the conservatives withdraw support.[12] Rather, they ride the bull through the streets of history, pretending to restrain what they never really grasped—riding the bull if they are lucky, for all too many are trampled in the melee. No one controls fascist movements, least of all the fascists, who are driven by impulses beyond their control. A generation may pass with them smashing norms and institutions before they fall from grace, amid a national spasm of regret—but then again, the fascism this time may be different.

Neither Putin nor Trump is a traditional fascist. Putin is too measured, Trump too bombastic. Putin was a quiet successor to a democratically elected leader, Trump a billionaire reality star. But if Trump fits the bill in his open bigotry and threat of extralegal violence, Putin does so in his destruction of democratic institutions and imperialism, and his mind-numbing machismo. Their initial alliance looked a lot like that of Hitler and Stalin, which lasted until Hitler invaded Russia. It was the last thing Stalin imagined; some say Hitler was the only person he trusted. The invasion was the highlight of the Second World War in terms of death and destruction.[13] But the prospect of a Trump-Putin pact suffered the combined effect of a backlash against Russian meddling in Trump's election and Republican concerns the affair would backfire. Still, Trump has demonstrated an obsequious fondness for dictators like the Philippines' Duterte and Kim Jong Un, which could lead to a new axis upon which the world might soon turn—for the fascism this time is also, unfortunately, global.

FASCIST, POPULIST, TYRANT, OR CLOWN

"Far more crucial than what we know or do not know is what we do not want to know."

ERIC HOFFER,
The Passionate State of Mind:
And Other Aphorisms[14]

It is commonly said that the first casualty of war is truth, but the dictum is better applied to autocracies. Perhaps the most insidious way autocrats control their subjects is through the systematic under-mining of truth. Dictatorship is called democracy, violence is masked in the name of security, lies are dressed up as facts. Hence, Confucius once said that if he were ever made ruler, he would begin with a rec-tification of names—redefining things as they truly are.[15]

Definitions matter because words can deceive us at the roots of our thinking. If our senses tell us we are being lied to and yet we convince ourselves we are being told the truth, we might come to doubt our ability to discern fact from fiction. If our senses scream fascist and yet we convince ourselves we are seeing a populist, we might resolve the cognitive dissonance through the denial of political categories altogether, lumping every deviation from the norm into the same confused mass.

The question of definitions is pertinent to whether we call Trump a mere populist or fascist. Populists mobilize the masses against out-of-touch elites, promising to improve their lot; fascists mobilize the powerful against threats to their assets. While populists speak dangerous truths dumbed down for the masses, fascists lie in the name of truth-speaking. The fascist is racist, the populist egalitarian. The fascist is a bully, the populist a defender of the bullied. The fascist is hateful, the populist inspired.

Fascists tend to be master propagandists, but they are also shameless liars. The lies are used to advance their direct goals, like Hitler's consolidation of power following the burning of the Reichstag, which was falsely blamed on a communist plot. But they also use lies to obliterate the distinction between fact and fiction, for a citizenry that no longer believes in truth is a population ripe for submission. Think of the way Assad simply labeled nonviolent demonstrators terrorists in the early stages of the Syrian Revolution and later blamed his own worst crimes on the rebels.[16]

While leftwing populists never seem to make it to power in advanced democracies, where more sober social-democratic parties can better redress the needs of the poor, rightwing populists do. But the rightwing populists who make it to power look a lot like fascists. Conservatives, by definition, seek to protect the status quo, making a conservative populist something of an oxymoron. And this probably explains why the whole idea of rightwing populism in something of a neologism, barely making an appearance in political theory until the last couple of decades.

The most influential books on the new populism are telling. Jan Werner-Müller's *What is Populism?* manages to provide an incisive description of it while nevertheless eschewing almost any historical examples. This allows him to simultaneously divorce the new populism from its historical roots and any association with fascism. But populism has historically pitted the poor and marginalized against wealthy elites, while the populism Müller describes turns the formula on its head, pitting the wealthy and marginalized against liberal elites. And he ignores the fact that once in power, rightwing populist followers have not cared much that their leaders did not go after wealthy elites.

However, while scholars of populism like Jan Werner-Müller[17] tend to ignore its history, outside of philosophy[18] and humanities departments,[19] with rare exceptions,[20] most scholars of fascism tend to focus on it.[21] The social sciences generally treat political ideologies like liberalism, conservatism, and socialism as perennial proclivities of the modern political mind. They recognize that each has become more pragmatic with time and that each has learned from its failures. Fascism alone is treated as an historical anomaly, and major scholars of fascism are almost uniform in their insistence on it.[22]

Part of the reason lies in the utter failure of early twentieth-century fascism. Its failure meant that few leaders wanted to associate themselves with it,[23] and few people wanted to think about it. European societies had to get along, so they pretended fascism was dead, even as leaders like Hitler and Mussolini enjoyed high favorability ratings decades after their demise.[24] Instead of treating the psychosocial dynamics leading to its rise as perennial, fascism was treated as a historical aberration, and the genocide it spawned as a unique, almost cosmological event.

The Holocaust was treated as unique partly because of its sheer brutality: it arguably annihilated more people than any genocide since those of Tamerlane in the late Middle Ages.[25] But it was also the first genocide to be studied in depth, and Israel and its supporters often used it to justify their own human rights abuses, carried out in the name of safety.[26] However, it was also treated as unique because few knew how to make sense of the fact that so many ordinary people had carried it out,[27] nor could they face up to the fact that genocides continued to crop up all around them, while few spoke out.[28] Isolating it in the mind made it easier for people to face their compatriots, whose own behavior was sometimes eerily reminiscent of the fascists who carried it out.[29]

As fascism came to be treated as a unique human evil, it also came to be used as an all-purpose insult to be thrown at people opposed to social change.[30] Fascism was always an amorphous affair. As a leading scholar of fascism Robert Paxton notes, its ideological expression differed markedly from its early movements; its early movements from its first years in power, its first years in power from its mature expression.[31] Fascist leaders tended to be demagogues, who told people what they wanted to hear, and they tended to be liars, who deceived the masses in order to gain power.[32] And there were only a couple of prototypical fascist regimes that stayed in power for more than a few years.[33] So, it was easy for demagogues to muster up whatever image of fascism served their political purposes. Meanwhile, popular images of fascism focused on its mechanistic conformity and cultish devotion to authority, which is only just beginning to be apparent among followers of Trump.

While early writings on the matter, like Wilhelm's Reich's *Mass Psychology of Fascism*[34] and Hannah Arendt's *Origins of Totalitarianism*,[35] were generally psychosocial, later writings sought to bring greater precision to a description of its causes and effects. But the precision demanded a historical accounting for which the social-psychological analyses were far too amorphous. And the hunt for some irreducible fascist minimum, and the precision it required, a "generic fascism" in the words of Roger Griffin,[36] shifted the focus away from what was most salient about it. Yet the salience of fascism lay not in its political programs or its ideology but rather its uses and abuses of power, which tended to culminate in mass crimes against humanity.

And while there was always more to fascism than populism, populism had always been essential to it. Rightwing populists lash out at immigrants and minorities to divert attention from the economic plight of their followers. Hence, their movements require a constant string of lies and fresh infusions of hate to keep up the diversion. The anger and abusiveness tend to attract authoritarian followers, who line up behind strongmen with whom they bully the weak.[37] The authoritarian nature of these movements means leaders are often vested with boundless powers.[38] It is the same in the Philippines under Roderigo Duterte as it is in Russia under Putin; in India under Modi as in America under Trump.

It is therefore extraordinary that while scholars of fascism in history and political science departments have been almost uniform in their rejection of a link between the rightwing nationalism of today and early twentieth-century fascism, major Holocaust historians like Timothy Snyder and Christopher Browning have often treated Nazi Germany as a template for what is to come.[39]

The historian, Richard G. Evans, suggests in his magisterial *The Coming of the Third Reich* that Hitler had no program except to make Germany great again. Everything else seemed thrown together and improvised,[40] much as in the case of Trump. Rightwing populists and fascists do not tend to have political programs, but rather slogans. The slogans allow them to mobilize the masses and use them for their own purposes. With no clear agenda, their followers become ripe for manipulation.[41] The process was detailed in the personal diaries of a German Jewish professor of linguistics, Victor Klemperer. "Nazism permeated the flesh and blood of the people through single words, idioms and sentence structures." These expressions were then endlessly repeated and taken on "mechanically and unconsciously."[42]

No major Western nation has arguably ever made a populist head-of-state through elections since the middle of the nineteenth century, except the Germans with Hitler and America with Trump. If we include Italy among the major Western states of Germany, Britain, France, and America, then we can add Silvio Berlusconi. However, while Trump and Berlusconi look clownish, Hitler and Mussolini appear fierce and disciplined. Perhaps the image is mythologized,[43] perhaps it comes from reading history backward, seeing in their crimes the product of relentless planning. But while it is often said of Mussolini that he made the trains run on time, Trump just gives us an endless train of make-believe.

And yet, Trump often looks less like a fascist and more like a clown impersonating a tyrant. Having never really worked for a boss or board in his life, he has never known what it is like to answer to a superior. Having never occupied an elected position, he does not seem to understand democracy. He began his presidency issuing decrees and commanding the press like a tyrant, but his constant string of ill-considered social media posts suggests he is too incontinent to be classed with men of steel like Mussolini. No American president has ever tied so many members of his family to his administration. No American president has ever had so many financial conflicts of interest. No American president has ever asked a rival power to interfere in his election. And no American president has ever been so heavily criticized by both liberal and conservative thinkers for their lack of qualifications—except perhaps Andrew Jackson, who carried out the most thoroughgoing ethnic cleansing of native peoples in American history, and opened up the core of the Deep South to settlement. That was America's last populist president, who entered office long before the rise of fascism.

How anyone could have mistaken a billionaire bully like Trump for a populist is a mystery that will plague future historians. Whether we regard him as a tyrant or a clown seems more a question of perspective. Hitler also looked liked a clown to many Germans before he became führer. Perhaps every out-of-work tyrant looks a bit clownish, and every clown who commands an army looks a bit like a fascist. That a multicultural, information-age society could even ask whether it is more appropriate to label its president a fascist, populist, tyrant, or clown in the twenty-first century is a testament to the enduring folly of humankind.

THE FORCED REGRESSION TO PATRIARCHY

*"Intolerance of ambiguity is the mark of an
authoritarian personality."*

THEODORE W. ADORNO[44]

Fascism is a premodern reaction to postmodernity. It meets the
premature dissolution of social norms with the heavy hand of authoritarianism, the sudden fracturing of settled forms with the illusion
of law and order. It meets surrealism with classicism, atonal composi-
tion with military marches, and the liberation of women with a return
to the kitchen.[45] But while fascism may romanticize the past, what it
actually presents is a brutal alternative to rapid social development.
Fascist orders may be patriarchal, but they are far from traditional.

It is no accident that Republicans chose, out of what the conservative columnist George Will referred to as their most capable field of
primary candidates since 1980, the crudest and most sexist domina-
tor among the pack. Republicans chose their most abusive bully and
lined up behind him as he broke all social and political norms to tear
down perhaps the most powerful woman in the world. They chanted
"lock her up" not simply because they viewed her as a criminal but
because they were reasserting their patriarchal right to power.

Patriarchies are generally understood to be hierarchical orders
dominated by men. Premodern societies are typically patriarchal,
with males dominating politics and the family. Gender roles are circumscribed and human freedom is limited, but with economic devel-

opment, all of this tends to change. Development provides the security needed to explore options, fostering expression and the liberation of women.[46] It also tends to foster democracy, which frees individuals from traditional orders.[47] Stable democracies are rarely patriarchal, but the regression to patriarchy is common for failed democracies like Poland, Russia, Turkey, and Hungary.

Sometimes social development is just too fast, too chaotic, too disorderly, and ultimately doomed to fail. In the aftermath of defeat, in the dislocations of great recessions, at the tail end of an economic miracle, traditions can melt away, making everything seem possible.[48] But it is at just such moments that higher development all too often fractures and fails. The postmodern movement would not appear until long after the heyday of fascism. Still, its precursors can be found in the social and artistic innovations of the "roaring twenties," which saw literary forms dissolved in Joyce's *Ulysses*[49] and sexual norms exploded in Margaret Mead's *Coming of Age in Samoa*[50] and D.H. Lawrence's *Lady Chatterley's Lover.* It saw the emergence of *Art Deco* and *Bauhaus* in architecture; the popularization of jazz and the rise of cinema. Like the postmodernism of the late-twentieth century, the erosion of forms accompanying these developments left all too many people feeling unsettled and shaky, as if walking along a slippery slope at altitudes too high to travel.[51]

The artistic and intellectual innovations of the early twentieth-century can make those of the early twenty-first appear unimaginative and conventional,[52] but innovation is not enough to sustain freedom. True freedom takes work to sustain, and it is everywhere reliant upon settled institutions,[53] like freedom of speech and assembly, the rule of law and the right to vote. These were unstable in Italy and Germany following the First World War, as they were in Russia at the turn of the millennium, and Central Europe today. And where democratic institutions are unstable, freedom tends to be suspect; where accompanied by widespread disorder, a visceral appeal to tradition often emerges to shut it all down. And with the past exploded and social progress unsustainable, fascists have nowhere to turn but to a reimagined past, decked out with all the paraphernalia of the future from which they run for their lives.

Fascism cannot be properly understood without some consideration of this reversion to patriarchy. Eugen Weber has written that fascism always emerges in response to the rising power of women.[54] Nazis entered office after a long decade of democracy in which women gained the vote and children won legal protection. The patriarchal family broke down in Weimar Germany, amid an open gay scene in Berlin, and a flourishing of the experimental arts,[55] to which the Nazis responded with a dominant father-of-the-nation, who sought to re-establish patriarchy.[56]

A similar reversion to patriarchy could be witnessed in Russia following their failed flirtation with democracy in the nineties. Russian journalist, Masha Gessen, documents the rise and fall of a thriving gay rights movement, which quickly emerged after the fall of the Soviet Union. But a decade of corruption and economic dislocation led the nation to seek security in a strongman, who would recriminalize homosexuality, initiating a homophobic campaign, which would see gays and lesbians terrorized by gangs of young men, and scapegoated for Russia's social failures, as the new leader struck the homoerotic poses of a muscle-bound warrior.[57]

America may be on the cusp of similar developments. Women are continuing the slow decades-long rise in the workplace. A younger generation of women is increasingly assertive and confident of its ability to succeed. The movement to end sexual harassment is overturning workplace norms. Gays and lesbians are coming out of the closet; gay marriage has been institutionalized; the transgender rights movement is bringing the scrutiny of gender itself, long an academic and feminist preoccupation, into mainstream debate.

But conservatives have reacted with a backlash, reviving a virulent form of patriarchy, which sanctions unrestrained masculine impulses and the denigration of women by powerful men. And the masculinization of cultures has been all-pervasive. Movies eschew sentiment in favor of action. Male stars increasingly look like slabs of meat. Video games are ever more brutal, the beard is making a comeback, pick-up artists have turned the manipulation of women into a popular science, and the language and concepts of a once marginal men's rights movement have gone mainstream.[58]

Meanwhile, liberals are carrying out their own paradoxical crackdown on sexual freedom. The criminalization of relatively minor infractions of sexual norms; the severe crackdown on borderline cases of sexual harassment; the pathologization of late-adolescent expressions of sexuality; the privatization of perversion through a new pornography in which anything goes, but nothing can leak into the real world; the conformist turn in male fashion, popularizing shorter hair and more colorless clothing; all point to a rising distrust of sexuality and curtailment of libidinal freedom.

Many of these changes will liberate women from male domination, but many could fast be turned against them as well. The containment of male sexual aggression is easily confused with a more traditional prudery that has arguably been more oppressive to women. While the sexual revolution of the sixties and seventies played its part in the rise of the new American fascism, through the sanctioning of unrestrained expression of often antisocial impulses, the effort to contain these excesses may ultimately come at the expense of greater libidinal freedom. But the revitalization of social hierarchies, coupled with the rise in economic inequality, poses even greater dangers.

Whether the reason lies in biology or cultural conditioning, men tend to locate themselves in hierarchies of other men.[59] Conditioned to find their place, they typically maneuver through such hierarchies with alacrity, thus faring better than women in more hierarchical societies. Most try to hold their own in the pecking order, but alphas aim for the top, and fascists attempt to overturn traditional hierarchies altogether, setting up their own alternative orders, behind which their followers might line up.[60] These newer orders tend to be punishingly vertical, as in the new Republican Party, where stepping out of line now ends careers, for their principal organizing mechanism is the ability to bully others.

The bullying has been perhaps most extreme in recent years in Syria, where the social development preceding the descent into fascism may have been weakest, and the genocidal aggression through which it was expressed the most brutal. Prior to the revolution, gangs of beefy young men on hormones, working closely with the regime, terrorized the population, extorting money and services. As the revolution got underway, these same "Shabiha," or ghosts as they were called, began carrying out the worst atrocities, mopping up after the formal military left the scene. Meanwhile, the regime began carrying out a sadistic regimen of torture that would ultimately result in tens of thousands of its opponents' deaths.[61]

Fascists do not try to prettify their actions but rather use them to hammer liberals and minorities into submission, for domination is essential to cowing the opposition and assimilating the weak. Women are vulnerable to this kind of intimidation, for they are seldom as well-schooled in the art of oppression as men. But patriarchy is oppressive to men as well, for it places them in a gender straitjacket, which starves them of emotional expression. The early twentieth-century social-psychologist Wilhelm Reich believed fascists rely on this kind of sexual and emotional repression to foster a masculine aggression that can be directed against outsiders.[62] But whatever its purpose, it is bound to pervert male psychosocial development.

Republicans have long sought to re-establish a traditional order that puts women back in the kitchen, but Trumpist fascism represents a more visceral form of domination. Studies have shown that while support for McCain and Romney was loosely correlated with more chivalrous views of traditional gender roles, support for Trump is correlated with outright hostility toward women. The barrage of presidential decrees with which Trump began his presidency may have been a show, but it sent an ominous message that he would hold nothing back.

It is for this reason that the women's march and the movement to end sexual harassment have been so important. They send a message that whatever this administration does, women's hard-won freedoms will be preserved; and the freedom of women means the freedom of men to express themselves more fully. Freedom is the death-knell of fascism, for free peoples do not take to hierarchy,[63] and without the capacity to sit at the top, the fascist leader is just a bloviating pig. Fascism can be fought in many ways, but perhaps the most rewarding will be through the full expression of everything we love and cherish.

NIHILISM IN THE CULT OF THE FASCIST KING

"The totalitarian mass leaders based their propaganda on the correct psychological assumption that, under such conditions, one could make people believe the most fantastic statements one day, and trust that if the next day they were given irrefutable proof of their falsehood, they would take refuge in cynicism; instead of deserting the leaders who had lied to them, they would protest that they had known all along that the statement was a lie and would admire the leaders for their superior tactical cleverness."

HANNAH ARENDT,
The Origins of Totalitarianism[64]

If fascism involves a deliberate regression to patriarchy, it is not the patriarchy of traditional societies. Traditional patriarchy tends to be settled and conservative. It forswears social change in favor of continuity, and as emphasized by both the Chinese Confucius[65] and the English Burke,[66] it honors the ancestors for the institutions they have built. Yet, the regressive drive of fascism dictates a forceful closure to new information, and an often violent attempt to disrupt the social order.[67] And this demands a level of devotion that can appear quite cultish.

The cultishness of fascist movements shows up in their devotion and unthinking obedience to leaders. It is ever-present in their punishment of nonconformists and mistrust of outsiders. And it reveals itself in their dominance hierarchies and antirationalism. Fascist movements structure themselves around the same sorts of pathological leaders as do cults, and they create the same alternative systems of valuation, which differ markedly from more widely shared norms.

Fascist movements and cults share the same tendency to sanctify insanity. The mental instability of leaders that is readily apparent to outsiders looks to insiders like marks of greatness; the pathologies that so trouble outsiders look to insiders like signs of salvation. Irrationality is reinterpreted as inscrutability, social transgression as transcendent wisdom, and the crudest moral regressions look to followers like honesty born of integrity. Almost nothing the leader says or does can shake their faith, because his pathologies are reinterpreted as signs of greatness. Followers may know his bizarre lies and half-literate ejaculations are pure lunacy, but they play along because it excuses their inadequacies. For what they were seeking was never the great man they claimed to emulate but rather the same adolescent imp that had been shocking the rest of us all along.

How do we know that almost nothing the leader says or does can shake their faith? Because we have seen it over and over again: think of Trump's famous claim that he could shoot a man on Fifth Avenue and get away with it. How do we know they reinterpret their leaders' pathologies as signs of greatness? Because we have repeatedly seen them do so: think of the way he can publicly lie several times a day and be labeled a truth-teller. But how do we know that they do so because of their inadequacies? While there can be no definitive proof of what motivates people from the inside, their attacks on the educated are an implicit recognition of the schooling they lack, their misunderstanding of policy an admittance of their political ignorance. Their choice of inarticulate and stupid leaders, over more intelligent ones who might better represent their interests, suggests a willingness to sacrifice their interests in order to avoid confrontations with intelligence. Meanwhile, their proclamations of cultural breakdown betray a lack of social skill in maneuvering change.

The tendency is perhaps most extreme in the fascism this time, where followers find themselves inadequate to the tasks of a complex and globalized world; where lacking the social skills to cope with multiculturalism, and the self-control needed to check their prejudices, they stew in resentment,[68] and long to protect their privilege. It is in this way that they arrive at their bizarre salvation. By exalting the least virtuous man among themselves, they excuse the least virtuous impulses inside themselves, normalizing their social incontinence, and transmuting it into strength. The sleight of hand is accomplished by changing norms from the top down. If the leader expresses their prejudices and displays their inadequacies without apology, it normalizes behaviors they cannot help but act out. If they praise him for doing so, they instantly transmute their vices into virtues.

But the sleight of hand only works when the narcissism is complete. What Donald Trump, Jair Bolsonaro, Roderigo Duterte, and Adolph Hitler all share in common is their immunity to censure; and it is precisely the nonchalance with which they have greeted criticism that has shored up their insecure followers. When Bolsonaro tells a leader of the opposition that she is too ugly to rape on national television, the sheer pathology of it is so difficult to absorb that followers must reinterpret it. When Duterte compares himself to Hitler, threatening to kill the same number of drug users as he did Jews, the surreality of the suggestion demands interpretation. But the process of indoctrination into a cult takes time, and the practices that seem most shocking in the early days are soon assimilated into a new normal.

Of course, there are differences between fascist movements and cults. Cults tend to be smaller and more encompassing. They regulate every aspect of their members' lives and entrain their activities to those of the group. The members of cults tend to share in work and meals, sleep and worship. Cults seek to obliterate the personal preferences of their members, and they tend to be more religious. Instead of attacking ethical norms, they foster new, more expansive moral codes. Instead of encouraging moral regression, they try to engineer moral development through strict conformity to moral innovations. While fascist movements tend to indulge the moral weaknesses of their members, excusing violence and encouraging cruelty, cults tend to press individuals to be better in extreme and perverse ways. And it is all the more so with the fascism this time, which appeals to the morally degenerate, whose will to power has been spent, and whose ideals have been worn down with the years.

The fascism this time is less rites and more the kind of spectacles elaborated on by Guy Debord,[69] more postmodern than a flight into the future.[70] Immersive rallies are more entertaining, leaders more likely to play the fool. Racist hate tends to be retractable, norm-breaking masked as humor. But if the fascism this time is a mishmash of Hitler and *South Park*, it is all the more resilient and therefore immersive. For like a big tent religion, it creates space for heresies in an effort to preserve itself in the long run.

The fascism that brought Trump to power was always readily apparent. It fueled his racist conspiracies and brought unity to his orgies of hate. It animated the violence with which protesters were greeted at his rallies and inspired his praise of dictators. The mistake all too many liberals made was to seek some core interest animating this madness.[71] Far from wanting to drain the swamp, Trump's supporters were happy to see it made worse; far from wanting to take on elites, they are cheering on their victory.

For as Pankaj Mishra suggests in his contemporary classic *The Age of Anger*, fascism is not really about politics. Rather, it is about shoring up the weak identities of its adherents by creating an alternative system of values that might finally give them a place at the top.[72] If Trump can do no wrong in their eyes, it is because by making the least virtuous man in the world its most powerful, they have overturned the moral order. And like some giant uprooted tree, all the dirt and filth that was studiously kept hidden from view has now found itself uplifted.

Fascism cannot worm its way into the imagination until it has turned everything on its head, for it only makes sense when everything is looked at upside down. Truth is a lie, facts are fiction, science is magic, rudeness is grace, confusion is clarity, ugliness beauty, impulse discipline, shallowness profundity. The function of fascist leaders does not make sense until they are seen not as serving the interests of the people but rather as benefiting from their service; and the function of their boasting cannot make sense except as mutual congratulations. And so when the fascist smashes the organs of state, he is seen as a great builder; when he places the people at risk, he is seen as their protector. The most virtuous is transformed into a pariah, the least virtuous granted the seat of honor.

And as the moral order is inverted, and the pent-up energy of the domino chain knocks down everything in its path, the ultimate source of evil is suddenly revealed to be the chosen one.

Meanwhile, as the sky thunders down to earth, reason is left boxing in the shadows. Its proclamations are rendered senseless when everything has been turned on its head, for when the premises are scrambled, the logical foundation is shattered. And it is just this primitive magic, where everything is turned inside out, and we are forced to walk on our hands, that reason is ultimately transmuted into insanity. And as it goes about setting things upright, it is taken as the destroyer. For to see things clearly, where others look through funhouse mirrors; and to speak correctly, when everyone else is living a lie, is to overturn the furniture where the fascist wanted nothing more than to finally find a home, after years spent drifting unmoored.

And while Karl Marx had much the same to say about money,[73] the difference is that while money renders values interchangeable, fascism carries them to their grave. And while capitalism rides to the masquerade, seeking an endless string of possibilities, fascism revels in breaking up the party. For fascism was never more than an occasion for nihilism, and the nihilism spoiled the party because it was never invited in the first place. But whereas capitalism had put everything on the market and paraded its goods to proclaim its grandeur, fascism sets about razing the mansion. For it is only in its ashes that it finds its fulfillment. And if left to its own, it will only burn itself out when the last tree is set aflame for the pleasure of the last man, who blames his woes on the virtuous whom he had long ago devoured.

And if fascism has turned the tree of life on its head, and left its followers clinging for their lives, no amount of coaxing and cajoling will get them to come down, because they are precisely where they want to be, and staying there depends on their loyalty. While the urge to overturn the moral order may be cultish, and the desire to reshape one's fate through the crafting of another may be familiar, it is all more tongue in cheek this time around. But the fascists this time are now more exposed than ever, and these heady heights make it hard to hold on.

FASCISM IN THE SHADOW
OF THE ETERNAL PRESENT

*"The frightened individual seeks for somebody
or something to tie his self to; he cannot bear to
be his own individual self any longer, and he tries
frantically to get rid of it and to feel security again
by the elimination of this burden..."*

ERICH FROMM,
Escape from Freedom[74]

F ascism thrives in an eternal, mythologized present, where the burden of past constraints cannot encroach on the fantasy of power.

Social norms, political conventions, established institutions, and expectations of decency are all thrown off in mass rallies where followers fuse themselves to the will of the leader to feel themselves a part of something greater. Fascist rites are reminiscent of Dionysian orgies and spontaneous mobs, where impulses reign supreme, and the herd regresses to an undifferentiated mass of quivering impulses. While early twentieth-century fascism may have produced well-organized mobs of neatly dressed automatons marching in goose step to a vision of the future, early twenty-first-century fascism presents a slovenly crowd of obese retirees giggling over their own offensiveness. Yet, both inspire followers to be swept away by the crowd.

Vladimir Putin, Donald Trump, Jair Bolsonaro, and Benito Mussolini each differ in their own ways, but each attracts uneducated followers, who conform to the will of a big man. They each pride themselves on flouting the rules and threatening extralegal violence. And they each shock elites and worry liberals so as to strengthen their sense of virility. Why else would Trump brag about the size of his penis except that his followers might want to partake in their leader's greatness? Why else would followers in Britain and the Philippines back unapologetic philanderers, unless they are playing out their fantasies through the lives of their leaders?

The fascist follower is weak and insecure;[75] he is unprepared for life in an overwhelming world, and so he seeks security in the greater will of the leader.[76] How do we know this? Because everywhere we find him sacrificing his ideas to conform with those of the leader. He is a lifetime free trader who suddenly turns protectionist; a religious traditionalist who is all of a sudden unbothered by marital infidelity. And like the wild dog at the head of the pack, the ringleader permits them to be savage. They live through his experiences as if they were their own. And by magically swallowing the big man's mojo, through a curious sort of sympathetic magic, the fascist follower imagines himself growing his own.

But for the transference to succeed, the leader must make himself appear larger than life. Why else would he lie so often and so outrageously? He is the richest, the smartest, the most potent.[77] Shameless bragging makes him seem the biggest truth-teller as well. Who else would show the coming emperor in all his naked glory? Fascist braggadocio is part of a magical rite in which small followers feed on the bigness of their fascist father. The stronger his image, the more they might give themselves over to his will; the same process can be found everywhere fascists reign. Everywhere, fascism presents a regression to preconventional barbarism, where loyalty to the leader comes to be viewed as the highest moral aspiration.

Hence, the fascist inflates his ego to gargantuan proportions. No matter that his hands are small and he is unfit for office, his supporters are entranced, and sustaining the trance requires that the past be obliterated so the future might be laid bare. The real magic of fascism lies in the present moment, where the self can dissolve in the long march into a fantasized future, for in it the anxieties of a weak and insecure existence can finally be relieved.

There is a nihilism to the movement supporting Trump, a gleeful offensiveness and revelry in destruction. It often seems as if his followers are not really concerned with the outcomes of their actions, do not even care whether he is telling the truth. There is something uniquely human in this compulsion to self-destruct. Lemmings do not actually gather together in mass rallies to jump off cliffs, like Thelma and Louise, in a nihilistic blaze of glory, but sometimes people do.

Freud called it *Thanatos*—the death drive.[78] As social anxieties build, many long to be part of the frenzied herd, where they might forget their cares and throw off reason. Self-destruction can energize the hopeless; destroying the works of others can make a person feel powerful.[79] And this death-wish is a sentiment that can be sensed equally in the movement to elect Trump, in the glorification of Putin's machismo, and in the English yearning to abandon the world.

Trump is the reality show-host to a mass neurosis that is taking America and the world over the edge.

The fascist moment is not the same *present* spoken of by Eastern spiritual teachers, but it is similar, and access to it may rest on many of the same social conditions. Whereas the spiritual present transcends the ego, the fascist present submits it to the movement; whereas the spiritual present dissolves the human-built world, the fascist present disdains it as worthy of destruction; whereas the spiritual present is pure awareness, the fascist present is mindlessly unconscious. The spiritual present is transformational, the fascist present regressive. The spiritual present is luminous and sublime, the fascist present anxious, alienated, compulsive, and condensed.

It is hard to think, hard to carry the burden of projects from the past into future fulfillment, and immersion in the present eases the strain. But the present moment is a space of possibilities, and in times of great change, it is a place of refuge. And yet, we are not simply taking refuge in the present; everything seems to be pressing us into a claustrophobic moment.[80] Information overload condenses reality into an eternal present, for when the whole historical record is written, every year takes on a special meaning, every place its own significance, and it all dissolves in imponderable specificity. Social media condenses conversations into an eternal present, for when everyone is debating, the social body is sucked into the whirlpool of streaming disorder. Meditation condenses experience into an eternal present, for the senses become opened and the self connected to everything.

A space of possibility has been opened in the public sphere, a magical space in which truth and reason have been thrown off. It is a space open to other ways of knowing, yet it is also a space in which the mob has been set free. There is a hedonism, not so different from fascist revelry, to the spiritualized notion that nothing matters but the present moment. And while it is a hedonism more likely to result in love-making than war-making, a hedonism more likely to deepen empathy than the breakdown of democracy, it is a hedonism that has played some part in paving the way to fascism. There is a shadow to the eternal present, and like most shadows, it is the last thing we want to see.

THE CRISIS IN THE AMERICAN LIBIDO

*"A free society is a community of free beings,
bound by the laws of sympathy and by the
obligations of family love. It is not a society of
people released from all moral constraint–for that
is precisely the opposite of a society. Without moral
constraint there can be no cooperation, no family
commitment, no long-term prospects, no hope of
economic, let alone social, order."*

ROGER SCRUTON,
The Limits of Liberty[81]

Trumpist fascism has its roots in the libidinal drives unleashed in the sixties, when a generation promising free love and equal rights began a half-century journey that would end in rebellion against the most rudimentary forms of restraint. What began as the right to speak out against racism ended in demands for the right to be racist; what began as the right to make-love-not-war ended in the insistence on the right to love war-making.

Fascism inverts the *abuse* of freedom into the *freedom* to abuse.

Consider what Republicans mean when they speak of *freedom*: it is almost always the right of the father to abuse his family, the businessman to underpay his employees, the state to suppress its minorities, the gun owner to intimidate his community. It is the freedom of the man to express his sexism, the white woman to express her racism, this generation to trash the environment into which the next will be born. Of course, they do not say that this is what they mean by freedom, but it is implicit in the freedoms they seek to preserve. Somehow the same process by which women won the right to no-fault divorce ended in the right of sociopaths to purchase assault weapons without background checks.

Hard-won freedoms were abused, and the abuse of freedom inverted its meaning. Individuals atomized by the pursuit of their unbridled interests sought to build an order without restraint and, in the process, surrendered their freedom for the illusion of power. It may seem paradoxical to suggest the violent disorder of a Trump rally has its basis in the unrestrained expression of the sex-drive, but perhaps this is due to an indulgent and permissive conception of freedom that is unusually prone to subversion, which Sigmund Freud cautioned against almost a century ago.

The libido, as conceived by Freud, was an amalgam of primal and sexual drives, which threw off reason and gloried in its own expression, but at its root it was simply the unmitigated pull of love.[82] Like most Freudian notions, it was an abstraction that has been superseded by other more precise psychological concepts. But it is useful for the purposes of this essay because the power of the concept lies in its amorphousness. Libidinous drives had a way of mutating as they were suppressed, so while the raw energy of the sex drive threatened social harmony, and with it the freedoms sustained by an ordered society, it could also be sublimated into productive activity. Freud wrote about it in his one great work of social philosophy, *Civilization and Its Discontents,* where he explained how libidinal drives are sublimated to maintain peace in the family and order in society, but that the social peace comes at the cost of suppressing our deepest drives, a suppression that all too often results in neurosis.[83]

If over half a century has passed since the sexual revolution of the sixties, and America has yet to integrate the libidinal drives it unleashed, perhaps it is because, as the godfather of neoconservatism Irving Kristol suggested, those energies were so much more powerful than almost anyone imagined.[84] The Baby Boomer generation undermined not just the late-capitalist order of postwar America but in many ways modernity itself.

Trumpist fascism has its roots in the failure of the sixties counter-culture to integrate the libido. The long-standing distinctions between nature and culture, mind and body, self and other, and us and them were all obliterated by a generation wary of a social order that burned itself out in the ovens of Auschwitz and the ashes of Nagasaki. Several movements came together in the late-sixties and early-seventies of the last century to constitute a revolution so vast in scope that virtually no one grasped its contours and meaning. The environmental revolution challenged the distinction between nature and culture; the sexual revolution undermined the distinction between mind and body; the spiritual revolution dissolved the distinction between self and other; the anti-war movement tore down the distinction between us and them. And each of these revolutions together constituted a mass movement, stretching across the social and political spectrum, to reintegrate all of the most basic human drives and passions that might be called libido.

It was left to a Nobel laureate economist, Robert Fogel, to dub the transition the "Fourth Great Awakening," the last of the great religious awakenings in American history. Each lasted several decades. Each deepened American religious commitments. Each brought to the fore a range of previously unconsidered social issues. And each would transform the nature of American society. According to Fogel, this awakening would be about self-actualization made possible by the leisure time provided through higher economic development. The social transformation of which he wrote encompassed an otherwise contradictory amalgam of movements—socialist and capitalist, sensual and spiritual, liberal and conservative. It was as if everyone had tired of the old rules. Sex, drugs, and rock 'n roll each played their part in this crusade, but so also did meditation and holistic healing, environmental advocacy and evangelicalism, the antiwar movement and the Reagan Revolution.[85]

The transformation was commonly treated as a case of higher development, through which more educated and freer people achieved greater control over their lives. Higher psychosocial development was in this way a concomitant of higher socioeconomic development,[86] enabled by a new mode of production, variously dubbed the information-age, post-industrialism,[87] and post-capitalist society.[88] But the very same developments were also often looked upon as indicative of a cultural degeneration,[89] which saw the hollowing out of vital institutions and bonds of trust necessary for the perpetuation of any free society.[90] The so-called higher psychosocial development was unfortunately characterized by an indulgent preoccupation with self and a lack of concern for others that was all too often narcissistic.[91] And those preoccupations would make it easy to mistake pre-conventional self-indulgence for higher development, with the result being that social regressions could go undetected for so long that the house would be falling before anyone thought to prop it up.

The historian Jacques Barzun portrayed a long decline that is still unraveling in his splendid work on modernity, *From Dawn to Decadence*.[92] The movement could be said to have had its beginnings in the Romantic Era, after the French Rousseau undermined the foundations of civilization itself, introducing the idea of the noble savage,[93] and poets like Wordsworth and Goethe challenged the rule of reason, calling for greater sensitivity to the wisdom of intuition. Later in the nineteenth century, Sigmund Freud subverted the predominance of reason altogether in articulating the processes of the unconscious mind.

According to the historian Elie Kedourie, romanticism was essential to the first philosophical expressions of nationalism in late eighteenth-century Germany. Advanced in learning, and lacking in opportunities for advancement, young philosophers like Johan Gottfried von Herder and poets like Heinrich Heine sought to equalize society through the concept of the nation, wherein individuals might be fused through a relationship to their shared ancestry and the soil.[94] The kernel of this notion would later prove essential to twentieth-century fascism, but even in its most benign forms, nationalism always involved membership in an imagined community,[95] making it precariously reliant on the forces of emotion.

By the late twentieth-century, the subversion of reason would become commonplace. Popular culture would mock its soullessness. Linguists would note the competition and violence behind intellectual argumentation.[96] Postmodernists would eviscerate its pretense of universalizing imperialism.[97] Feminists would challenge the masculine symbology surrounding the concept itself; people of color, its association with whiteness. The criticisms seemed to come from every corner, culminating in the idea that reason is a pretense, with the result being that every institution that rested on impartial reason was also drawn into question, with democratic institutions being the primary victim.

At the dawn of the twenty-first century, the world itself has been transmuted into a whirling mass of impulses without boundaries. Films mock the schoolmarms and bureaucrats seeking to preserve order; political rallies promise to tear it all down. A hedonism that suggests we can do what feels good and what feels good will make all things right has become pervasive. But what few seem to be asking is how a new social order capable of holding such powerful drives might be established. The task is far from impossible, but America is failing to integrate the drives it has unleashed. It is a crisis of the American libido that could continue for decades, and it has been increasingly exported abroad.

THE NEW AMERICAN FASCISM

*"He who is unable to live in society, or who has no
need because he is sufficient for himself, must be
either a beast or a god."*

ARISTOTLE,
The Politics[98]

A mericans tend to be entranced by the ideal of a radical autonomy that might allow them to break away from everything standing in the way of their free expression. The ideal shows up among
the transcendentalist left and the entrepreneurial right, inspirational
sports stars and Hollywood films. American history is largely an account of people breaking new bounds in almost every institutional
and cultural sphere.[99] But it is also an alienating history of dissociated
individuals failing to protect themselves from one another and the
contingencies of existence,[100] and the new American fascism may be
its most extreme expression.

It has its roots in a perverted libertarianism, which argues that
free people have few moral obligations and those that are imposed
upon them tend to do more harm than good. This doctrine, which is
now pervasive in rightwing discourse, and reached its bluntest philosophical expression in the writings of Ayn Rand in the mid-twentieth
century, implies that only selfish people can be trusted, because only
selfish people are honest about their true motives.[101] It is a dangerous
doctrine which leads its adherents to line up behind selfish and cor-

rupt leaders, but its greater danger lies in its denial of fundamental truths about the nature of human existence, a denial which undermines democratic institutions and basic social relations alike.

Human beings are social animals who must determine their futures together.[102] Every political question involves decisions about who we are and where we are going. The questions of how to start and stop a conversation, or what we owe to friends and family, are arrived at through such shared negotiations. The negotiations happen through semiconscious processes of give-and-take, which multiplied over countless instantiations take on the aura of social rules and norms.[103]

Democratic processes mediate the way we reason through these decisions, setting the ground rules for moderating among conflicting values, providing the forums through which challenges can be aired. Whether in the family or the legislature, the school or the church, we are constantly challenged to negotiate how we live together, and democratic procedures give everyone a say in how this is accomplished. The way we conceive of our connection to the rest of humanity is essential to the political values and beliefs at the heart of these decisions. If each of us is dependent upon all the rest, then we owe them something of our own good fortune; but if each of us is the product of some autonomous self-generation, then the poor and marginalized must be held responsible for their fates. However, believing ourselves immune to the influence of others does not make it so.

All things are interlinked, human societies most intensively so. We cannot get along without others, nor do our views arise in a vacuum. Rather, everything about us is premised on the books we read, the people we know, the places we live, and countless other streams of knowledge inundating us from all directions. Everything about who we are is tied to the worlds in which we find ourselves immersed. American conservatives and libertarians are only able to sustain the illusion of their autonomous self-generation because they deny these fundamental truths of social existence.

The idea that we must depend on others to forge a collective future implies a loss of self-control, which many find threatening. If who we are is the result of interactions in a world beyond our control, aspects of our lives will always prove elusive, and there will always be parts of ourselves from which we feel alienated.[104] And if this is the case, we will need to think more deeply about how a far more vast and deeply interfused world makes us who we are.

This can be irritating to the impatient and self-centered, but it is threatening to the egocentric and insecure. They want to get on with their lives, but the world presses in on them from every side. They want things to be as they are, but things are never quite what they seem. Things are especially difficult in an increasingly complex world, where events in one place are all too often tied to those in every other.[105] And this interconnectedness is especially difficult for American conservatives, who have for decades now shunned complex explanations in favor of the obvious.

Traditional conservatives see themselves as the product of institutions that began long before their births and persist long after their deaths.[106] They see themselves as embedded in a world into which they have been thrown. It is not a world of their choosing, but it is the world in which they must make their way as best they can. And this makes them peculiarly reliant on existing institutions, with the state being central among them.[107] American conservatives today are an entirely different animal, for whom the language of fascism usually fits better; but the language of fascism can also obscure the radical individualism driving their extremism.

They tend to be frustrated by the collective decisions to which they feel bound. Somehow they played a part in creating the world that is pressing in on them, but they are not sure when and how they agreed to it. Some of the agreements they made involve how we should communicate, some the rules of the economy. But these are experienced by the radical individualist as alien and oppressive, like the impositions of some occupying power, and it is for this reason that they want to tear it all down.[108]

Aristotle noted almost 2,500 years ago that human beings are political animals. We are rational animals whose reason is integral to making the world in which we live with others.[109] The businesses and roads, technologies and infrastructure, that surround us are the product of shared decisions. Most everything we encounter is the product of institutions whose roles have been developed by voters and consumers, bureaucrats and executives. Everywhere we go, we find ourselves constructing with others a world we must ultimately share.[110]

The political art of negotiating how we live together is shot through with morality. Every political decision is a moral decision, for political leaders must weigh the needs of multiple constituencies and the greater public good in every decision. People expect politicians to act in their shared collective interests because this is precisely what they are supposed to do, but American conservatives are likely to look skeptically on public service. Moral leaders cannot be trusted because moral leaders are living in denial of their basic selfishness.

But to give up on politics is to give up on one another and ourselves: since politics regulates how we live together, abandoning politics means abandoning our shared fate and humanity. The result tends to be a cynicism that, while directed at political elites, is largely an irritation with human existence itself. If we cannot reason with others and work together to construct the world we must share in common, then we cannot be fully human.

The problem is only exacerbated by social media, which has widened the political sphere while hollowing it out. Now everything about how we live together is up for question, and we are pressured to form an opinion on it all. Reason is being replaced by advocacy, but much of the anxiety pervading political debate stems from the ignorance on which it is premised. We are paranoid because we are uninformed, reactive because we lack confidence, burnt out because the world appears alien and frightening.

Whereas reasoning with others can teach us how to live together, selfish advocacy can tear us apart. Much of the stress of modern life is the result of living in irresolvable tension with others. The tensions result from fundamental disagreements over the nature of our shared existence, but they are also the result of everyday political disagreements. If the tensions of today appear more irresolvable than those of yesterday, perhaps it is because too few of us believe in the process by which we might renegotiate the most basic rules governing our behavior.

If rightwing politics looks increasingly like a circus, perhaps it is because rightwing nationalists and populists are not actually engaging in democratic politics so much as a rebellion from the shared burden of freedom.[111] It is at root a rebellion from the angst of having to work out their fate with others, and the angst is increasing as the world becomes more complex. There is more to know, more to consider, more to feel, and more to decide; the net result is that all too many are left overwhelmed and longing for escape.[112] And it all comes to a head in the democratic process.

Even when everything is functioning smoothly, democratic participation can be a struggle. Ground rules need to be clarified, compromises made, and decisions arrived at.[113] Democratic decision-making tends to involve endless hours spent in meetings arguing, clarifying, listening, compromising, backtracking, reconsidering, agreeing, and disagreeing. But it is infinitely more challenging when you are uninformed and unprepared, because the world in which you are living is so overwhelming you cannot grasp its meaning.

This explains why conservatives get so anxious when it comes to politics.

The conservative hatred for government seems more a hatred for democracy. They hate democracy because it brings up irresolvable existential tensions around what it takes to live with others. They cannot bypass these tensions because they are fundamental to their humanity. They cannot admit to them because democracy is so essential to the Americanness into which they retreat. Hence, they project their dissatisfaction with the structure of existence onto politics, making their very participation in it an act of self-hatred.

In attacking the system, they are attacking their nature as political animals, and the more they engage, the more their frustrations increase. Try as they may, they cannot get away, and the more they thrash against the basic condition of their existence, the more deeply they become ensnared. It is a fertile field for the growth of fascism, because fascists worship the strength of the individual, even as their own voices are drowned out in the mass. It is only the fascist leader who possesses the right to express himself freely, so followers are relieved of the burden of forming and expressing opinions in a confusing and overwhelming world.

The fascist can neither live with others nor live with himself, so he obliterates both at the altar of society. Through an audacious act of nihilism, he frees himself from the moral responsibility of formulating defensible views and from ever having to explain them to others. But whereas others once freed of responsibility might choose hedonism, the fascist submits to a strongman, assumes his views, and lives through his actions.[114]

To cover up the crime, he claims to be the greatest of individuals, even as he mimics the exact language of his leader. This mass conformity in the service of a mythologized individualism is unique to fascists. But whereas the fascists of old masked their conformity with vigor and strength, the fascism this time masquerades as independent and free. This allows fascists to blame the downtrodden while escaping their most basic social responsibilities. But slaves to a master who cannot even control himself, they cannot escape their own absurdity.

SECTION II

THE MORAL ORDER HAS BEEN INVERTED

"Nothing perhaps illustrates the general disintegration of political life better than this vague, pervasive hatred of everybody and everything, without a focus for its passionate attention, with nobody to make responsible for the state of affairs— neither the government nor the bourgeoisie nor an outside power. It consequently turned in all directions, haphazardly and unpredictably, incapable of assuming an air of healthy indifference toward anything under the sun."

HANNAH ARENDT,
The Origins of Totalitarianism[1]

THE MORAL ORDER HAS BEEN INVERTED

*"The wretch, concentred all in self, living, shall
forfeit fair renown, and doubly dying, shall go
down; to the vile dust, from whence he sprung,
unwept, unhonored, and unsung."*

WALTER SCOTT,
The Lay of the Last Minstrel[2]

Darkness has set in over the world. The crude braggart, the undisciplined liar, the hateful bully, and the sexual violator is now the world's most powerful man—and the consequences are rippling through every thought about what it means to live in the world. We are now challenged to come up with a language to describe the outrage and alienation few would have ever imagined prior to it happening, and we may find we can explain a whole lot more by speaking in terms of an inverted moral order.

All across the world, murderers and thugs have risen to power. Vladimir Putin and Bashar Al-Assad have been winning in their genocide in Syria. Rodrigo Duterte has already killed roughly 12,000 and threatened to kill millions more in the Philippines, where he brags about the extrajudicial murders of purported drug users, left dead in the street, heads wrapped in carpeting tape, with signs accusing them of their crimes, for which the people shower him with love.

Everywhere, it seems the liberal and tolerant, the compassionate and sincere, are losing while racists and nationalists rise to the top. It is the stuff of myth and legend, *The Lord of the Rings* and *Star*

Wars. Nigel Farage and Marine Le Pen are tearing apart the European Union in openly racist campaigns. China and India are led by conservative nationalists, Egypt and Turkey by macho authoritarians, who rape political prisoners while playing at their civility. The moral order has been inverted, and now the least virtuous man is its most powerful, while under him sits an ever more ghoulish band of thugs.

Liberals do not tend to think in terms of such a cosmic moral order.[3] Rather, we tend to think in terms of consequences: something is good if it brings about good consequences.[4] Bringing about good consequences often requires bold moral action, but it is good things that are brought about by such actions, not some metaphysical sense of justice. And because we think in terms of consequences, when we turn our minds to politics, we talk a lot about policy and institutions.[5] Hence, liberals confronted with the potential impeachment of Trump tend to ask whether the policies and institutions would be any better under Vice-President Pence. If not, then why speak of impeachment?

But this fails to explain what is so wrong with Trump.

We all know on some level that the world is not just—but we tend to imagine a just order in which the good prosper and the wicked suffer, the wise rule and the ignorant follow. And the closer we come to this order, the more we tend to feel settled and secure. We feel settled and secure because we know we can trust our leaders, if not to do what is right, then at least to try to bring about some good. The trust reverberates through business and society, law and the family. The perception of a just world order helps us to function and get on with our lives, but without it our lives are pervaded with the existential anxiety that results from the thought that anything can happen.[6]

As we all know from work, a good person at the top can change everything. If mistakes are made, then at least they are honest; if they do the wrong thing, then at least they believed in it—thus, we can forgive our leaders and live in peace with power. Our lives may not be perfect, and our leaders may often fail us, but goodness is praised and decency honored, and we are all more civil and able to open up. The result is better lives and relations and hope for a future we can forge together. The world may not be as we want it to be, and it may fail to live up to our ideals, but when we can trust our political opponents to at least do what they believe to be right, then we can settle into accepting that at least some vision of the good will prevail.[7]

However, there are no moral principles, and no vision of the good life, that might justify the actions of Trump,[8] which is why he has to lie about almost everything he does. Universalizing his principles would result in a world of liars and bullies, each threatening the next, until we were all at each other's throats, or else cowed into silence. It would be a crueler and less compassionate world, and it would quickly descend into war. And if everyone behaved the way he did, there would be no guarantee his supporters would even come out on top, for everyone would play by the same dirty rulebook.

Support for Trump also contradicts Rawlsian principles of justice.[9] No one would not want to be born into the kind of society he is creating if, in doing so, they might wind up at the bottom. The consequences would not be worth it, whatever the rewards. For life at the bottom would mean being a toddler in an overcrowded cell, separated from your parents, without access to shampoo, toothpaste, bedding, or flu vaccines. But few would choose to be born into the society he is creating over other comparable societies if they were to wind up on top as well,[10] for there are versions of capitalism from which they might profit without the cruelties and disorder. It is only as the particular beneficiaries of his movement and largesse that people want to be part of the world he is creating.

And despite all the enthusiasm from evangelicals, support for Trump also goes against the golden rule. No one would want the minorities he attacks to do the same to them if they were in the majority, nor for their political opponents to govern by his standards. No one would wish for their children to do business with such a cheat or a member of their family to date someone so sexually exploitative. Trump is the man the Bible warned us about. He gloats about his power while mocking the disabled; preys on the weak while bragging about his strength; tears children from their mothers and tells their defenders to leave the country. He preens and gloats, bullies and mocks, all the while starving millions of children to no end whatsoever.

There is a lot to criticize on the left, whose ideals often ignore realities. And there is a lot to value in conservatism, which wants to know how things will work before enshrining them in law.[11] But Trump lacks the discipline, discretion, decency, and decorum conservatives claim to value.[12] He breaks the norms they struggle to preserve, shatters the institutions they claim to defend.[13] He disparages the constitution, slanders his own office, and talks of dating his daughter—and we all know what Trump does on dates. No wonder not a single major conservative intellectual supported his first campaign for the presidency, while countless others, like Robert Kagan, George Will, Bret Stephens, David Brooks, Max Boot, David Gerson, and Thomas Sowell actively opposed him; and no wonder his advisors and close friends speak so ill of him.

Former Secretary of State Rex Tillerson called him a "fucking moron." Former Chief Economic Advisor Gary Cohn called him "less a person than a collection of terrible traits." Former Chief Strategist Steve Bannon accused him of "treason" while comparing him to "an 11-year-old child." Former National Security Advisor H.R. McMaster said he was "an idiot with the intelligence of a kindergartner." Former Secretary of the Treasury Steve Mnuchin and former Chief of Staff Reince Priebus simply called him "an idiot." His former personal lawyer John Dowd called him "a fucking liar." And former ghostwriter of his bestselling *Art of the Deal,* Tony Schwartz, described him as "a horrendous human being who seeks only to become a dictator."

Trump can seem an abomination not merely because of his lies and his racism or his hatred and ignorance. These are all real enough but fail to get at the intensity of our gut reactions. There are things more morally blameworthy than racism, things more dangerous than ignorance, after all. Trump behaves like a rash and intemperate child, proclaiming his greatness, ranting against adversaries, and insulting anyone who threatens his power. He brags of violating women, then when they confront him claims they are not attractive enough for him to violate. He stirs up hatred against minorities, then claims they love him. This is not simply racist or sexist but something more akin to sociopathy. But pathologizing him also fails to get at just what it is we find so wrong, for it medicalizes what is really a moral problem.

Trump shows all the signs of a tyrant, but when the most powerful man in the world is a tyrant, we need a stronger language than that of mere racism, sexism, and sociopathy. The language of a just moral order is theological and better suited to conservatives. Liberals tend to rankle against it, and for good reason. It is easy to manipulate to illiberal ends, for such cosmic notions of moral order make it easier to condemn deviant behavior without ever saying why it is wrong. But it may describe better than anything else just what seems so wrong with Trump's power.

Liberals the world over must now fight an inverted moral order that casts down the virtuous and uplifts tyrants, punishes goodness and rewards evil. The inversion of the moral order will ricochet through every institution and relation in our lives, for it subverts the incentives typically governing social life. Whereas the good usually profit in their relations, even amid their sacrifices—gaining in friendship what they lose in business, gaining in networks what they lose in assets—the inversion of the moral order scrambles these incentives, transmuting ruthlessness into a social skill and dominance into a virtue. Suddenly, we find ourselves praising qualities we know to be a threat to everything and everyone we hold dear, because they are necessary to survive under an inverted moral order, and what matters most in such an order is that those with whom we are close rise to the top.

This is strong language, and most of us do not use it because it denies the free choice of political adversaries. Over the course of our lives, each of us will settle upon a set of political values and beliefs that others may find dangerous: that is the nature of pluralistic societies in which we are each free to form our own comprehensive visions of the good life.[14] But seldom do we revel in how we might harm not only our adversaries' goals, or even our adversaries themselves, but the moral norms we all share in common. The harm this might do to the sense of a just moral order, sustaining a just political order, is immeasurable. It will leave us alienated and at cross purposes with others, pervaded with anxiety and prone to conflict. If the world after Trump looks a lot more intense and dangerous, it is because we are living under an inverted moral order.

If the language of an inverted moral order does not appeal to you, consider the even stronger language of evil. The language of evil implies not simply a willingness to harm others to benefit oneself but a certain pleasure that is taken in committing the harm.[15] While the sadist takes pleasure in harm, evil spreads it and revels in its diffusion. Satan is seen to be the great corrupter because he finds in the spread of his evilness the very pleasure of his existence, and those who adopt his ways cannot help but share in the glee. This language is probably too strong to apply to Trump. He may be a bully, who revels in the destruction of his adversaries, but he does not seem to savor it in the way we might expect from someone we would call evil, like the former leader of the Central African Republic, Salah Eddine Ahmed Bokassa, who is said to have eaten his adversaries and served them up to dinner guests. And yet, the language may also capture a lot that is missing in talk of his racism and sexism, and when we later turn to the millions of children Trump is helping starve in Yemen, we might find it most apt.

Trump and his supporters now revel in their badness and gain strength through flaunting it, and there is something evil in this revelry. It is not simply liberals and minorities who oppose it, but rather good people the world over, whatever their political values or level of personal development. And the good people who become his allies, like many evangelicals, quickly find themselves and their movements corrupted. Trump is a seducer of the otherwise decent, who threatens to destroy everything he touches, and this moral corruption that rots everything in its path is precisely what we mean by evil.

This is precisely what people living in Europe and America in the Second World War found so frightening about the ascendance of Hitler. Fascism is frightening because it overturns the moral order, bringing evil men and women to power, and spreading that evil among the population at large. Its progenitors are placed in a special class because theirs is an evil that few can rival. And unlike liberals, conservatives, nationalists, and social-democrats, they seek to set up their own order, where their evil has free reign. While they must often make compromises with the status quo,[16] they tend more often than not to subsume it under their own order, undermining its moral strictures and values, and in the process, corroding it from within.

But whether or not we choose to go so far as to call what Trump is doing evil, it is to this process of their moral degeneration that Americans would now do well to turn their attention.

THE NIHILISM BENEATH THE RHETORIC

"Destructiveness is the outcome of unlived life."

ERICH FROMM,
Escape from Freedom[17]

I t is simply not possible in a community of nations, whose power is carefully balanced, where some states can destroy the world many times over, for the most powerful among them to be led by an impulsive narcissist with sociopathic tendencies, without the grave risk of thermonuclear annihilation. Human relationships are simply too fragile, the stresses of high office too great, the propensity to band together in war too unconscious, and the balance of power too precarious, not to take seriously the possibility that an unhinged Trump might very well ignite a train of events that would lead, in the end, to thermonuclear annihilation.

But with rightwing nationalists and fascists with genocidal tendencies at the head of a nuclear-armed India, China, Israel, Russia, and North Korea, the chances of thermonuclear annihilation increase exponentially. The leaders of each of these states are arguably more irresponsible and aggressive than any of the Soviet leaders who spent much time in office following the death of Stalin.[18] And Nixon looks like a genuine peacemaker when placed beside Netanyahu or Putin.

Since early in the primaries before he was elected, people have argued that if Trump were to win, he would be hemmed in by a system of checks and balances, a mainstream cabinet and advisers, an unsupportive Congress, and his own incompetence, and that this would keep him from carrying out his most diabolical schemes. But Trump has rapidly worn down those checks and balances, and it often seems as if his most destructive impulses are his most revered.

It is often argued that Trump appeals to people the global economy left behind.[19] They were left behind by rising inequality and undermined by the same politicians they helped elect.[20] They lack the social skills to fit into a multicultural society and the mental agility to cope with complexity.[21] They grew up expecting more and now feel their culture has been hijacked. This may or may not be true, but why a New York billionaire, with no ties to the heartland, who is inarticulate and dishonest, with no record of public service? Trump's agenda is hazy, his policy proposals thin, and he is clearly out of his depth. The idea that they think he can save them insults their intelligence. They may love him, may want him as their leader, but it doesn't mean they think he can run the country. A less sympathetic view suggests they were seeking a dominator-in-chief, a "winner" who can tell it like it is and do so forcefully. From this vantage, Trump's humiliation of primary candidates signaled to them authority, while his wealth proved competence. They did not want an effective candidate to articulate their agenda but rather an authority figure to line up behind. And this too may be true, but why Trump?

Virtually all his primary opponents were more articulate, experienced, and politically competent. And some, like Cruz and Christie, were practiced bullies. These men knew how to wail on liberals and humiliate opponents. But perhaps Trump supporters wanted something more than another authoritarian bully. Perhaps they wanted something far less rational, something of which they were far less conscious. Herein lies the danger: Trump's irrationality, his incessant bullying, his lack of a serious agenda, his willingness to break all the rules, his ability to play on the fears of a crowd, and his blatant authoritarianism, all appealed to something deeper than the need for authority or even a savior. And as we have seen, what he appealed to was their primal drives, long held in check by the same liberal society from which they had been outcast and were now rebelling.

Suddenly, Republican voters were free from the shackles of having to justify a contradictory agenda; suddenly, they could throw off the cloak of respectability. Now all the hatred needed no justification, the nihilism need not make sense. Far from articulating their hopes and fears, far from giving them something with which to identify, Trump freed them from the need to explain themselves. And perhaps this above all else was the greatest pressure they felt from liberals, intensified like never before from constant warfare on social media, made all the worse by a competent and popular black president, and driven home by the smugness of a woman even some of her biggest supporters found hard to trust. Liberals made them feel like losers and they wanted to be winners without having to win, and they had just the magician for this spectacular feat.

What liberals seem to miss is that Trump is an articulate spokesperson of his followers' needs precisely because he is so inarticulate; he is the best representative of their agenda because neither he nor they know what they want. Trump possesses that rare capacity, common perhaps only to television newscasters and fascist demagogues to look like they are in charge while blathering nonsense. If it sometimes seems that he grows more popular the more unhinged his pronouncements, perhaps it is because his popularity rests on his striking capacity to make no sense. For this frees his followers to vent their unconscious, and this is where it gets really scary.

Their leader is now doing this on the international stage, and his opponents are now foreign adversaries. But you cannot smack down Ayatollah Khamenei without Iran erupting in nationalist fervor; you cannot go after Kim Jong Un without either placating his ego or receiving a military reply. What was once a fragile global order is suddenly boiling over into a cauldron of petty rivalries, replete with people in the streets and the drum beats of war.[22] Whatever isolationism Trump may espouse, he is inflaming nationalist passions every time he opens his loose sphincter of a mouth.

And he is normalizing the kind of brinkmanship that might take other nuclear-armed states to war as well. Trump entered office amid a tectonic shift from a unipolar order, wherein America was the sole dominant force, to a multipolar order in which several powers now compete for dominance. Realists in international relations have long considered multipolar orders to be peculiarly dangerous.[23] And while a skillful realist like Otto von Bismarck or Richard Nixon can often manage such an order while preventing warfare from breaking out among the great powers, the forces unleashed by Trump have overturned the tables of what might have been a careful game of poker, wherein each player aligned their interests with the carefully managed bluffs of the other players.[24] The chances this will result in a nuclear holocaust are probably thin. But he is taking us to the brink and, standing over the abyss, reveling in his power, as he ignites the world in hate. Now we are contemplating a level of destruction his followers never seemed to imagine, and of which they still appear scarcely able to conceive.

THE LOGIC BEHIND TRUMP'S LIES

*"There is no hope for the frustrated in the actual
and the possible. Salvation can come to them only
from the miraculous, which seeps through a crack
in the iron wall of inexorable reality. They ask to be
deceived."*

ERIC HOFFER,
The True Believer[25]

Criminal gangs and militias often force prospective members to commit heinous crimes before being accepted. Drug gangs have been known to force their members to kill innocent civilians to demonstrate their willingness to murder indiscriminately. Yet, the killings also demonstrate their prospective members are not with the police while defining them once and for all as criminals. Several African militias have taken this logic a step further, abducting children and forcing them to kill their parents. For once you kill your father, you cannot go back to your village and must substitute leader for father and submit to his command.

Voting for Trump involved a milder rite of passage, which nevertheless operated according to much the same logic. To vote for him was to assent to his agenda, but also his racist and sexist rhetoric. This quickly came to define his supporters as racists and sexists in the eyes of friends and family. It was a transgressive act against minorities and women but also basic norms of decency. The day they voted for Trump was the day they came out of the closet en masse. Now the more he lies, the deeper they are implicated in his offenses, like members of a gang, who have gone too far to turn back.

A similar process appeared to take place in the United Kingdom. Not everyone who voted to leave the European Union did so for racist reasons, but the leave campaign was beset with racism. So, even those who imagined leaving would bring more money to the National Health Service, or wanted a more accountable government, got swept up in a racist campaign. However, the campaign also stripped the pretense from their desire for national sovereignty: they may have believed they merely wanted a return to their old culture, but for many getting there meant getting rid of foreigners. Yet the foreigners they wanted to get rid of were all too often Indians and Pakistanis, whose families had been citizens for generations. Hence, their vote not only redefined the culture but their own identities as well. Suddenly, they found themselves the victors of a racist campaign, which was as much about defining the nation as leaving the continent. And the definition of the nation it highlighted was white and English, as opposed to multicultural and British, a wider identity that had long included Scottish, Irish, Welsh, Indians, and Pakistanis.[26] This made it easier for them to throw themselves into the more racist campaign of Boris Johnson a few years later. Johnson described black people as "pickaninnies" with "watermelon smiles," gay men as "bum boys," Muslim women wearing face coverings as "letter boxes." His call for a "no-deal Brexit" was an implicit call to get rid of immigrants, even at the risk of economic collapse. For almost any deal with the E.U. would involve the continued right of Europeans to work in the U.K. Gone was the illusion that leaving would bring more money to hospitals; gone was the belief that it would improve the economy. Suddenly, countless millions found themselves supporting an inveterate liar, poised to carry them into a deep recession. Johnson did not want to make Britain great again, but rather make an otherwise great nation English. Yet, the United Kingdom had never been an ordinary nation-state. England was a premodern state with little sense of national unity, Great Britain an empire spread wide across the world, and the United Kingdom a federation, later bound into the transnational confederation they were now poised to leave. Thus, in voting for his party, his followers wedded themselves to racism, grounded in an illusion, sustained by his lies.

Yet, coming out in favor of Trump was even more extreme. Trump relishes defining his supporters against what he has often referred to as his "enemies," which seems to include most anyone who challenges his agenda. This only pushes them further into a cultish movement, whose cost of leaving grows with each offense. To support Trump in his most delusional and irrational assertions is to gain membership in a new elite. To stand by him as he utters his most racist and sexist offenses is to lend to your fragmented self a newfound stability.

It does not matter so much that electoral experts found virtually no cases of undocumented immigrants voting in California's election, for instance; that the claim was so outrageous it led to an identity crisis among journalists accustomed to never calling their sources liars; that even Fox News challenged it; that the administration could not even concoct an argument to justify it. It did not even matter that by the end of his first year in office, the *Washington Post* had conducted a study that concluded he lied an average of five times daily, and by his last year in office, it had risen to twenty times daily, for a grand total of over 20,000 lies.[27] The more outrageous the lie, the more it bound together supporters and pushed them to be loyal.

All of this was on vivid display when Trump commanded his first Press Secretary Sean Spicer to hold an aggressive news conference in which he attacked the press and lied about the size of the inauguration crowd. Trump questioned Spicer's loyalty, in what would soon become a ritualized trial by fire for cabinet and press secretaries alike. Yet, in pressing his lies publicly, Spicer assured him of his loyalty, further implicating himself in the effort to deceive the public. And this made him more reliant on his boss, for it set a wedge between him and more mainstream Republicans. That he was later fired, like so many other members of his team who had stuck their necks out for their boss, only highlighted the extent of his loyalty.

If you can get someone to support you in your most irrational lies, you will have won their allegiance twice over: you win their support, and you win their solidarity, because in supporting you, they become members of your irrational subculture. And in the age of social media, shared participation in an irrational subculture is the ticket to a reinforced identity.[28] For the more the members of an irrational subculture are challenged, the more tightly they band together, fabricating their own sources of information, and bolstering their own weak arguments—just what the members of mass movements need most.[29] Thus, Trump's need to bolster his fragile ego through ever more outrageous claims does the same for his supporters through participation in his conspiracy to defraud the public. Similarly, supporting a no-deal Brexit that will tank the economy makes you not simply a conservative voter but a member of an elite army who will win at any cost.

Yet, Trump may be up to something still more perverse. Erich Fromm believed that fascist leaders were locked in a sadomasochistic symbiosis with their followers. Sadistic leaders needed masochistic followers because they made them feel powerful: masochistic followers needed sadistic leaders because they made it easier to escape the burden of freedom.[30] But in a brilliant twist, a close friend of mine, Andrew Duff McDuffee, suggests that Trump is deliberately doing what's wrong and saying it's right because he likes degrading his followers, who are forced to come to his defense. Meanwhile, his followers love it because it can be exciting to obey and be degraded, like the raging fans at a staged wrestling event.

Whether they go so far as to embrace their degradation may be questionable, but they most certainly do embarrass themselves in defense of their leader. Hence, we should expect them to avoid rational discussion, for the most reasonable and civil exchanges may challenge their identities the most. When confronted with such discussions, we should expect them to freak out, lash out, play nice, and delete—anything to halt the challenge. And this is exactly what they have been doing, which is why they have retreated into their own epistemological bubbles, where in the words of the Russian journalist Peter Pomerantsev, "nothing is true and everything is possible."[31]

The nihilism of this movement is often quite flippant. All too often, they seem utterly unbothered by their contradictory claims, and unconcerned with their ineffective actions; and it sometimes seems they delight in provoking a backlash, even when it undermines their standing. But this too paradoxically protects their identity. If you can destroy something that makes you feel bad about who you are, then you defeat an existential threat and reassert your sense of self—all the more so if in doing it, you can tell yourself you simply do not care. The point is rather how it makes you feel, and if you can convince yourself you do not care, when you are being dragged through the mud, you will have attained if not freedom, then at least a release from responsibility.

Trump has inverted the hedonism of the counter-cultural seventies—if it feels good, do it—into the first principle of reactionary nihilism: if it makes them feel bad, you can feel good doing it. In the process, he has made a virtue of his own contradictions, annihilating any semblance of principle left in his party, and any sense of decency to which his followers might adhere. Trump's supporters have been challenged by a culture they do not understand and in which they struggle to function. But by banding around the most irrational bully, they can convince themselves of an alternate reality in which the most feel-good assertions are true because they will make them true by force of will. It is upon this same mythos that fascist movements have long relied, but it is a bubble that can be popped by the hard realities of the complex world in which they will find themselves stymied at every turn.

THE BUBBLE IN AMERICAN EGOS

*"... just as early industrial capitalism moved the
focus of existence from being to having, post-
industrial culture has moved that focus from having
to appearing."*

GUY DEBORD,
The Society of the Spectacle[32]

There is something miraculous in Trump's ego. It is not simply
that, contrary to the laws of physics, his head seems to grow
bigger the more hot air is released from his mouth. It is not even that
he can brag about his penis in a nationally televised debate and somehow show no shame. No, the miracle lies elsewhere and is deeply
rooted in American business culture. Like a car that runs on vapors or
a city in the sky, his ego seems to grow where there is nothing there
to sustain it. It is a classic bubble, built on a vapid confidence, which
grows because it is growing, and feeds on its success. It is a learned
behavior, taught by self-help gurus, with disastrous consequences
for culture and economy alike. You too can inflate your ego to such
proportions that the people around you can no longer tell fact from
fiction and, therefore, submit to your will.

Self-help gurus are an enduring feature of the American landscape, with roots in the First Great Awakening, prior to the nation's
founding.[33] Benjamin Franklin is the best-known proponent of pulling yourself up by your bootstraps,[34] but they have been an enduring feature of the landscape since its beginnings. The inspiration to

recreate your life through living boldly and becoming the master of your fate may be responsible for many of America's greatest cultural innovations. But there is a bubble in American egos, fostered by an ethic of self-inflation, and sold to us by personal development gurus, which destabilizes the economy and corrodes the culture. The president of vacuous vanity is but an unusually successful example of this far more common malady.

The self-help gurus of today are less likely to focus on inner transformation and more likely to tell us to "fake it 'til you make it." The credo is perhaps best exemplified by Timothy Ferriss's aptly titled blockbuster, *The 4-Hour Workweek*. There we are enjoined to outsource our own jobs to highly educated Indian personal assistants, for whom we pay but a fraction of our salaries, letting them do the hard work while we take the credit.[35] Ferris is a classic con artist, who brags about his deceptions and gains audience for his audacity. And perhaps his followers also play along because there is something fun about participating in something so degrading.

However, projecting an image of success need not be so unethical. It works because self-image is such a powerful motivator. By changing our self-perception, we can often transform ourselves in the eyes of others. We might begin incapable and unsuccessful, but this changes as we adapt to the new self-image, and others see us in a new light. Whether this works consistently is doubtful, but the real problems with this sort of boosterism are social and economic. When everyone projects an image of success, it sets in motion a competition for status in which the most deceptive reap the highest rewards. The result is a society of surfaces, in which overconfident shysters increasingly navigate a social hall-of-mirrors.[36] While inequality and corporatization have played their part in this strange death of reality, seldom do we give sufficient attention to the role of such cultivated self-deceptions.

Projecting an image of success does not scale very well. If everyone does it, we cannot tell who is successful and who is not—even the losers appear capable. And while new indicators of success and capability might be discovered, the indicators themselves will be quickly learned in an evolutionary competition in which everyone is out to deceive everyone else, increasing the difficulty of telling where people stand. In the confusion, many will be promoted to positions above their capacities.

Management thinkers call the idea that everyone is promoted to their own level of incompetence the Peter Principle.[37] Investors play their part in this universal overreach, over-investing in the inflated egos of entrepreneurs and their overconfident employees. And they deceive one another as well, emulating each other's overconfidence. Instead of inspiring individuals to work harder or smarter, we are taught to merely appear more productive. The appearance can be produced through a thousand subtle cues—feigned stress, hints at long hours, name-dropping, and the like. The result is a bubble economy bursting with confidence but resting on ephemera.[38] When an economic sector is massively overvalued, economists call it a bubble. Recent years have seen a string of bubbles in dot coms, housing, and finance, with some economists now saying we have shifted to a permanent bubble economy. This is partly because investors have moved from long-term investments in harder assets to short-term investments in liquid financial instruments, whose valuation is more difficult to determine.[39] Yet, part of the reason rests on the dissolution of agreed standards of truth: if nobody can agree on what makes something true, it is all the easier to get away with lies. And if it is easier to lie, small cults are free to create their own reality.

Yet, there is also a bubble in American egos, and the role of entrepreneurs is critical. If they can convince investors of their success, their impossible schemes will be financed by self-deceptive investors. The result is over-investment in all the wrong places. More failed businesses are started, more money is wasted, but everyone looks more successful—until it all comes crashing down. For as we have learned with the housing and financial crashes, wealth that rests on a cloud of illusions is a sort of inflation, which will sooner or later pop.

So long as it is just a few people inflating their egos in this way, they may grow in self-esteem, with few wider socioeconomic ramifications. Individuals capable of projecting success may even empower others to take control of their lives. Yet, the closer we get to universalization, the more this ability becomes a prerequisite to achieving anything. Projecting an image of success then becomes a sort of survival skill, like the elaborate graces of a feudal court; and worse still, we come to admire those whose smugness seems least touched by reality. And this is where the delusions of corporate culture coalesce in the new culture of fascism, in which the most dangerously deluded win because they are winning, and because they are winning create a false sense of confidence, which bolsters overconfidence in markets, and political overreach in followers, until everything comes crashing down.

When everyone learns to inflate their egos in this way, we lose the ability to make sense of the world and become alienated from the inside out. Deception becomes more common and acceptable, as social solidarity fragments. Businesses staffed by incompetents are overvalued, and the economy is destabilized. More worthless goods are sold in an effort to deceive a public confused by false signals. And we all pay the price by having to learn a new set of worthless social skills. The deceptive prosper, the honest lose out, and everywhere surfaces reign over depths. Meanwhile, it becomes easier to lose ourselves in delusional cults, and to ignore the threats that might otherwise pull us together.

Trump is the most egregious archetype of this new breed and a symbol of how far we have fallen. He built his business empire on a startling capacity to deceive others by projecting an image of success that was as empty as his pronouncements of grandeur. He built a political movement on lies, backed with neither the hard currency of facts nor logical arguments. He has succeeded through the sheer aplomb with which he is able to deceive others and the nonchalance with which he can shrug off his contradictions. The personality cult he has built is quintessentially American, its tenacity a measure of how well the country has been trained; and the movement he has built is its own self-enclosed epistemological bubble. It festers in a swamp of its incontinent excretions and is fueled by its sulfurous vapors, but sooner or later, it will pop, and reality will strike. It will implode because it rests on illusions, and it will burst because acting on illusions is dangerous, as fascist leaders before him learned the hard way.

OVERDEVELOPMENT AND ITS DISCONTENTS

*"I cannot help fearing that men may reach a point
where they look on every new theory as a danger,
every innovation as a toilsome trouble, every social
advance as a first step toward revolution, and that
they may absolutely refuse to move at all."*

ALEXIS DE TOCQUEVILLE,
Democracy in America[40]

America is a bit like a man with too much muscle. There are too many gadgets, too many brands, too many cars, and too many fields of knowledge. There is too much trash, too many people, too much information, and too many emissions. It is too much to know and too much to track, too much to tend to and too much to feel into. We suffer in other words from *overdevelopment*, a curious case of the complexity of development becoming too much to handle, and the things which once brought happiness increasingly appearing a burden.

The overdevelopment is unsustainable, and its unsustainability is a threat to the planet, but that is a different sort of problem. Over-development breeds a sense of anxiety and feelings of inadequacy. Since it is all too much, we experience the world as overwhelming; since we cannot keep up, we feel we are never enough. It is as if the world is too big and we want to hide away. And we all too often hole away in dangerous delusions and regressive ideologies, which in their inability to grapple with the complexity make the world appear even more threatening.[41]

The result is that it becomes ever harder to comprehend what makes complex phenomena like advanced democracies work. Since we do not understand all of the issues that matter, we tend to specialize, whether in the natural or social sciences, policy or economics—most of us who know a lot about something are specialists, so few can grasp where it is all going. This sense of being part of a big ship with no rudder makes us anxious. We are anxious because the world makes no sense, and it makes no sense because we see it in fragments. But of course, we see it in fragments because we are overwhelmed by our inability to get a handle on its entirety; and since we cannot get a handle on it, the experience is also alienating.[42]

The world is overwhelming and alienating, and as a result, all too many people feel they have no place in it. This makes us anxious, and the anxiety feeds the search for the next new thing. We run to social media, television and snacks, to feed the void.[43] The fact that so many of us are running after one thing or another just drives the complexity, for markets seeking to satiate our hunger just invent more gadgets and distractions, and quite a few genuine social improvements as well. In the process, they expand the domain of marketable commodities, alienating us still further, as markets come to encroach on once-sacred places and activities.[44] What once was a given is now subject to market forces, and everything solid melts into air.[45]

Now, development is usually a good thing. More options mean more resilience, more adaptability, and more freedom.[46] Development is not just good economically but socially, psychologically, and politically.[47] It is not easy to measure development, but it can be recognized in increasing levels of integrated complexity: more words, more information, more perspectives, more occupations, all intricately intermeshed, in a unified and dynamic whole. Developed individuals can see things from more perspectives and can thus better adapt themselves to a more complex world.[48] Developed states can integrate more viewpoints through democratic institutions, and thereby better serve their citizens.

The problem for the culture is that it can often appear as if the self is not developing in step with the wider socioeconomic system. There is in other words a *developmental split* between self and society. The self is weak and insecure, the society bold and multifaceted. The self is limited in its capacity to understand; the world is vast and variegated and impossibly complex. Of course, individuals can develop themselves in step with the world, deepening their intellects, widening their sphere of empathic concern, overcoming their psychological blockages. But the fact that many do so while many do not means that those who remain undeveloped experience themselves as failures, perpetually unprepared for life, like young adults who are always a step behind. And this just adds the anxieties of failure to those of confusion.

There is a developmental split between individuals and society, but there is also a developmental split between individuals within the society, with some welcoming the complexity, some retreating from it, and others waging war against it.[49] The split often shows up in the liberal-conservative divide, with less-developed conservatives being more uncomfortable with the increasing complexity of the world and more developed liberals sneering at them for their racism, sexism, and general ignorance. But there are quite a few liberals and leftists engaged in their own regressive projects as well, adding tribal undertones to this social bifurcation. Meanwhile, conservatives have traditionally focused on the relations closest at hand,[50] which all too often appear to be tearing apart with the social fabric.

Because Americans do not understand how it all fits together, the culture can often appear aesthetically incoherent. There are few monuments to make it cohere, few points of interest around which to organize perception. Clothes do not match cars; cars do not match buildings; buildings do not match one another. Things are typically so jumbled together that the attention must jump from one field of interest to another, like eyes unable to settle in a messy room. Attention bounces from sports we do not understand to reality shows that make no sense, from fascinating new games to incomprehensible new laws. This sense of aesthetic incoherence only adds to the anxiety of those who have failed to adapt.

Hitler and Mussolini both responded to cultures that were becoming in their own ways incoherent.[51] But whereas they responded with broadly aesthetic projects, which might bring everything into line through glorious symbols and extravagant rites, it can sometimes seem that Americans have found in Trump a mirror to their own incoherence. The normalization of confusion is essential to the new American fascism. While it may not look like that of early twentieth-century fascism, it is really only a variant on a common theme. It is only when a substantial portion of the population has lost the ability to make sense of the world that you can shamelessly lie about it without provoking a reaction; for if the truths we know do not make sense anymore, we lose the ability to distinguish truth from lies altogether.

It is all just too complex, and we long for a way to turn it all off.

Some of this complexity is the result of America being a diverse society, some the result of it being a new society, which still awkwardly hangs together. Whatever the reasons, Americans have met the wider worlds into which they have been thrust with personal and cultural contraction. Corporations have become more regimented and inflexible, politicians more petty and reactive, conservatives more fascist, liberals more tribal. Meanwhile, individuals seeking to get a handle on their lives have turned off their minds and made themselves simpler. But simple is no solution when everything around you is becoming ever more complex, for as you start to get a handle on your diminished expectations, the world around you becomes ever more incomprehensible. Meditation can tell you nothing of what is happening in the world; community projects do not scale up to global solutions. And in the effort to collapse the world into a smaller box, it all too often just implodes.

Enter the fascist who promises the greatest simplification of all. If America is too socially complex, we will get rid of the immigrants.

If it is too cosmopolitan, we will treat the rest of the world with disdain. If it is too morally complex, we will cast away compassion. If it is too conceptually complex, we will do away with truth. Never mind the fact that it is all an unworkable fantasy: the fascist is not actually interested in solutions but rather in temporary palliatives to soothe bottled-up anxieties.

The fascist answer to higher development is pathological regression. Whereas traditional and moderate conservatives seek to retrench the bureaucracy, the fascist takes a hatchet to it. Whereas traditional and moderate conservatives seek to limit the scope of moral commitments, focusing less on distant others and more on those closer to home,[52] the fascist rebels against morality altogether. It is in this disposition to development, which is not simply skeptical, nor even reactive, but rather stridently combative, that we can discern the nihilistic core of fascism.

Development brings with it greater adaptability, greater freedom, greater resilience, and a greater range of expressions that can make everything about it seem brighter and more beautiful. More developed human systems possess a greater range of adaptive capacities. Developed economies can better adjust to changing economic conditions; developed individuals can better weather the seasons of their lives. But there is always a risk that the end result of an ever-increasing complexity will be not greater integration and resilience but rather fragmentation, alienation, and incoherence; and it is precisely at those historical junctures where social and economic development have failed to make life better that the fascist leader seeks to ply his trade.

America has taken a pathological turn in its development. It is like an untuned instrument, played at the wrong time. Perhaps it was only a matter of time before a leader came along and mirrored its cacophony. If the message makes little sense, and the messenger himself bears a remarkable resemblance to an insane clown, masturbating to his own image in a funhouse mirror, perhaps it is merely a reflection of our own *pathological development*.

INEQUALITY AND THE REBIRTH OF RESSENTIMENT

*"Our minds are susceptible to the influence of
external voices, telling us what we require to be
satisfied, voices that may drown our the faint
sounds emitted from our souls, and distract us from
the careful, arduous task of accurately naming our
priorities."*

ALAIN DE BOTTON,
Status Anxiety[53]

There is something unnerving about the contrast between the
well-dressed businessman passing the homeless old lady on the
street without a glance. It is not simply that the woman possesses
nothing and the man so much. Nor is it merely a commentary on
the heartlessness of the businessman or the world in which we live.
Rather, the discomfort seems to lie in the inability of each to see into
the world of the other. It is this dissociation from one another and the
indifference it breeds that drives the callousness of all too many on
the right.

Most people understand why poverty is wrong, but few can say
much about what is wrong with economic inequality. This seems to
have something to do with the elusiveness of its psychosocial im-
pacts. When we bear witness to gross inequalities, we see ourselves
differently in relation to others. For in the simple act of witnessing
inequality, we come to see less the actual person we are observing
and more their position on the socioeconomic ladder.

When the old partier friend prospers, and his diligent but poorer counterpart slips into debt, it is difficult not to turn introspective. We wonder whether we got what we deserved and if it is all just a game of chance. Such speculations can suffuse our lives with a nagging sense of anxiety over the possibility that we too might someday sit at the bottom of the social scale. And it is just this fear that has driven many in the lower middle-class to seek solace in a movement promising to upend the social order. Many of them are poorer, many less educated, but many simply lack the ability to grasp the world in which they are living and thrive.

Inequality heightens the status anxieties of rich and poor alike, leading everyone to spend more time thinking about where they stand in relation to others. This decreases social trust and the willingness to sacrifice for others. It is not simply that capitalism pits us against one another in a struggle of each against all. Rather, the social inequalities that so often arise in unrestrained capitalist economies lead us to see ourselves as living at the expense of others. It is a stressful experience that has in recent decades transformed American society into a harsher place in which people are increasingly likely to exploit one another and praise others who do the same. The stresses of living in such a society tend to assault our bodies and minds alike.

The most unequal societies among the wealthier and middle-income countries tend to suffer from higher levels of mental illness and heart disease, obesity and depression, incarceration and domestic violence. Their murder rates and infant mortality are higher and their life expectancy lower. Epidemiologists Kate Pickett and Richard Wilkerson demonstrate how unequal societies tend to fare worse on just about every measure of social and psychological well-being in their masterwork, *The Spirit Level: Why Equality is Better for Everyone.*[54]

It can often feel as if the middle has dropped out of highly unequal societies, leaving everyone on the margins. Inequality acts as a great divider, with the increasing gulf between rich and poor exacerbating racial and regional divides as well. The unequal society is an incomprehensible world of differences, where everyone but the wealthiest and most socially skilled can come to feel misplaced.[55] In an interview for my book, *The Inner Climate: Global Warming from the Inside Out*, Pickett notes that the problem is only exacerbated by the inequality between rich and poor states to which we are increasingly exposed through immigration, social media, novels, and film.[56] The sense of displacement this engenders leads people to seek refuge, and many find it in ad hoc movements and ideologies like fascism. It is no accident that the most fascist governments in Europe lie in Eastern Europe, from which young immigrants routinely travel to work in the service industry of the vastly wealthier west.

Pankaj Mishra explores this experience of inequality and how we cope with it in perhaps the first classic of the new era, *The Age of Anger*.[57] Mishra views the rise of rightwing nationalism and fascism through the French concept of *ressentiment*, a jealous anger expressed by those at the bottom toward the system itself. Ressentiment generates its own value systems in order to justify unfavorable outcomes[58] and is a principal driver in the turn to social movements like fascism.[59]

Through adopting an entirely different scale of valuation, a person might subvert the social order and restore his dignity. Hence, the fascist flaunts his youth and vigor, the fundamentalist her moral purity, the terrorist her willingness to give her life, the communist his ability to descry the direction of history. Each seeks to reclaim their dignity through a grand metanarrative, upon which they stake their identity, and for which each is willing to give their life, resulting in a discharge of irrational violence, overflowing the bounds of all social constraints, like some uncorked flood bubbling over. Social movements built on ressentiment transmute their insecurities into aggression and project it outward.

The fascism this time thus walks in the grooves of many a modern movement.[60]

There are many kinds of equality. Legal equality assures access to the same laws and courts. Political equality assures access to the same voting rights. Equal opportunities provide the right to the same institutions. Equal access to opportunities provides the same quality of education and ability to apply for jobs.[61] But equal outcomes matter because it is here where we confront the stark contrasts between ourselves and others. If we cannot redress differences in outcome, we will continue to find ourselves assaulted not only by inequality itself but by all the irrational efforts to bypass its many indignities as well.

And this brings us back to the long-standing debate about what drove the initial support for Trump among the lower-middle classes in the first place. Some argue it was their economic grievances and that what they really voted for was a populist, but this fails to explain why they continued to stand by him as he chose a cabinet of billionaires and slashed taxes on the wealthy. Some argue it was their racism and sexism and that what they really voted for was someone who would allow them to express these sentiments openly, but as we have seen, there were far more pernicious reasons at work, most notably the nihilistic urge to tear it all down. Trump's racism and sexism might have galvanized his supporters, but something more was needed. By elevating the least virtuous person to the most powerful position in the world, they subverted the value system that placed them at the bottom, instantly transforming themselves into the new elite. And as they so often reported, suddenly, everything in their lives got better.

It is thus true in many ways that he was elected because of the inequality suffered by his core supporters. However, they were not seeking to redress their economic grievances but rather the anxieties that resulted from sitting at the bottom of the heap. The inequality caused them to feel marginalized, and this sense of marginalization led them to experience deep anxieties, which led in turn to addictive and destructive behaviors, roiling through their communities and wrecking their lives, as commonly happens when the socioeconomically insecure feel abandoned, with nowhere left to turn.[62]

It was this sense of marginalization to which they were reacting and not the inequality itself.

Trump promised to make them feel included, and he did so through building a movement that made them feel good about who they were because it told them the current order was based on the wrong set of values. The most important thing was not how much money or intelligence or empathy you possessed, but whether you were one of the chosen, who possessed the right ideology and were a member of the right movement. Trump's stupidity and incontinence made them feel better, because it suggested that the only difference between the people at the top and themselves was the random fortune of good old-fashioned luck.

The constant lies further worked to his advantage because they made members of his movement impervious to liberal criticism. Beating their marginalization required a drift into denial that could not be accomplished without first obliterating the difference between fact and fiction. Thus, they lined up behind someone who would invert the meaning of everything, thereby freeing them from the social realities they found so denigrating and oppressive. Trump was thereby able to subvert the social order. And if it took the Antichrist to make the first last and the last first, countless marginalized evangelicals were willing to treat him as the Second Coming.

The problem was that none of this came close to redressing the genuine economic grievances lying at the heart of these desires, and the succor he provided would only last as long as his own fleeting administration. But these were future concerns, of little interest to a movement immersed in the instantaneity of the eternal spectacle. Someday it would all come crashing down, but until that time, true believers would revel in the illusion of their invincibility, much like their leader, who built his order on ephemera as elusive as the fleeting life of a firefly, destined to fade into the oblivion from whence it came.

If there is a lesson to be learned for liberals, perhaps it is that inequality is likely to drive them to their own similar pathologies, as it did in the early twentieth-century for communists. The anxieties it generates are simply too great to bear. The desire to participate in an alternative hierarchy, which sets up its own system of values in order to subvert the dominant moral order, thereby satiating the unquenched desire for dignity, will persist until the inequality that drives the compulsion is finally redressed. In the meantime, social movements will arise and pass; and many will be dangerous; and many will be deluded; and while the fascism this time may be right-wing and populist, the fire next time may be leftwing and conspiratorial; or perhaps cultish and religious—anything that promises to alleviate the indignities of inequality, and turn the world upside down.

SECTION III

WHEN DEMOCRACY DEVOLVES INTO TYRANNY

"Tyranny is not a matter of minor theft and violence, but of wholesale plunder, sacred and profane, private or public. If you are caught committing such crimes in detail you are punished and disgraced; sacrilege, kidnapping, burglary, fraud, theft are the names we give to such petty forms of wrongdoing. But when a man succeeds in robbing the whole body of citizens and reducing them to slavery, they forget these ugly names and call him happy and fortunate, as do all others who hear of his unmitigated wrongdoing."

PLATO,
The Republic[1]

WHEN DEMOCRACY DEVOLVES INTO TYRANNY

*"It is ordained in the eternal constitution of things,
that men of intemperate minds cannot be free. Their
passions forge their fetters."*

EDMUND BURKE,
Reflections on the Revolution in France[2]

America was the first modern nation to become a democracy, but it may also be the first stable democracy to devolve into tyranny. It would be an astonishing progression, like a baroque concerto ending in atonal cacophony; but it would be rooted in a moral logic, foretold millennia ago, which has until this time proved to be inaccurate.

Plato suggests in his classic *The Republic* that tyranny is as much a state of mind as it is a political condition. Tyrants have bad tempers because they lack control over their own emotions, but they are also poorly tempered in the musical sense of being out of tune. Tyrants cannot control themselves because they lack discipline and have never gone through the arduous process of refining their thoughts and feelings. Hence, they grab at new ideas only to discard them again, like a monkey in an endless search for gratification. The tyrannical leader lurches from one program to the next, infusing disharmony into the nation itself.

Tyrants tend to be defined less by their powers and more by the way their power is wielded. Autocrats may have the freedom to rule by decree, but wise ones consult advisers and debate contingencies before taking action. Wise leaders proceed with caution because it is hard to build support and difficult to know what might go wrong until it is debated. But tyrants issue decrees on a whim and do their best to shut down debate.[3] It is a fitting picture of Roderigo Duterte in the Philippines and Jair Bolsonaro in Brazil, but also the current American president. Most presidents pick their first battles carefully and build consensus through debate. This strengthens support and their sense of gravitas. However, Trump fired off a multitude of controversial decrees in just his first few weeks in office; and he laid out virtually nothing for debate, as if congressional support did not matter, thereby setting the tone for a tyrannical presidency.

Plato believed that democracies are particularly prone to devolving into tyranny because they are vulnerable to takeover by demagogues, who appease the crowds in order to gain power. Demagogues may know what they are promising is not possible, but they play on the ignorance of the masses for political profit.[4] And since democracies are run by majority rule, and are thus prone to all the perennial hysterias of humanity, there is always the danger a demagogue will take power, and in never leaving transform a democracy into tyranny.[5]

It is a process playing out today in India and Brazil, Russia and Turkey, Venezuela and Hungary.

The tyrant begins as a popularly elected leader but soon insists on changing the constitution to remove limits on his time in office. He stacks the courts with cronies, undermines judicial impartiality, and shuts down the opposition press. He takes sole control of his party and shuts down dissent within it.[6] In the end, democratic institutions are transformed into an elaborate facade, fed to international watchdogs and an increasingly uninformed electorate. Elections can sometimes be used in these states to oust a tyrant from power, as in the case of Robert Mugabe of Zimbabwe. But in those that have progressed further along the path to tyranny like Russia, the best they offer is an opportunity to register dissent.[7]

Plato believed that governments pass through several stages, the last of which involves a devolution from democracy into tyranny. But it has been more common in the modern era for nations to *evolve* from tyranny to democracy, as did the Soviet Satellites of Eastern Europe. Development tends to proceed from the simple to the complex, from the less inclusive to the more inclusive, from the rigidly situated to the boundlessly resilient.[8] And compared with authoritarian governments, stable democracies are ragingly complex, wildly inclusive, and profoundly resilient. However, America has long been an exception, and many Americans sense their country slipping into tyranny. The feeling springs from the massive infusion of cash in political campaigns, the growth of familial dynasties, the rise of billionaire candidates, the normalization of political lies, the fracturing of the electorate, and the decline of reason.[9]

But the most salient sign of a slide into tyranny is the election of a leader who behaves like a tyrant.

It is this slide into tyranny that so many Americans fear from Trump, but it would arguably be the first time a stable and modern democracy in this way. However, the degeneration of institutions that we have witnessed has occurred in partial democracies, with checkered histories of dictatorship, weak legislatures, and corrupt ruling elites.[10] The American Constitution was deliberately crafted to prevent this kind of institutional degeneration. Its checks and balances make rule by executive decree next to impossible,[11] but the establishment of a democratic culture makes people less willing to go along with it as well.[12]

However, it is often said that a government is only as good as its people. And if a sufficient mass of people is more interested in their own agendas than their democratic institutions, the institutions may fall like a house of cards in the wind. More worrisome still is the intemperance of an electorate, unbounded by any notion of common citizenship and its accompanying duties.[13] When intemperate voters seek a president like themselves, what they are seeking is all too often a petty tyrant. A weakening of the collective will all too often precede the degeneration into dictatorship.

The world has gradually passed from one representative democracy in the late eighteenth century to a little less than ninety today. It has been a staggered path of development, with major waves of democratization being followed by a culling of the herd. The waves occurred after the First and Second World Wars, and then beginning in the early seventies.[14] However, according to Freedom House, the number of democracies worldwide has been on the decline for the past dozen years. And there has been a hollowing out of democratic institutions in more established democracies over this time as well.[15] Whether there will be yet another round of culling or a more ominous global collapse remains to be seen.

Democratic governance as we know it today hardly existed at the beginning of the twentieth century. Vast portions of the world were colonized, the United Nations was but a dream, and several dozen states that are household names today did not even exist. It would take a century of turmoil, including the First and Second World Wars, the decolonization of most of the planet, hundreds of social movements, and countless revolutions to drag us into the present in which about half the world's states are now reasonably democratic. This includes the vast majority of states in Europe, North America, and South America, as well as much of East and Southeast Asia.[16]

The transformation was largely silent, with most democratic transitions barely making the news. And yet, all these states have their founders and martyrs, social movements and constitutional conventions. Citizens sacrificed time and energy—and often their lives—so their children might live according to their lights, speak their minds, practice their faiths, choose their representatives, and shape their collective futures.

Democratic rights matter because the state sets the conditions for just about everything that happens in our lives. It lends shape to schools and structures the economy. It sets limits to parental authority and protects minorities. It regulates the behavior of people in power and determines institutional ground rules. Hence, if it is run by whoever possesses the power to seize it and use it to turn a profit, every social institution through which we pass will be rigged for their benefit, making our lives merely a means to attain their ends. This is what people the world over have struggled to upend for the last several generations.[17] This is what hundreds of thousands of Syrians gave their lives in vain to achieve.[18] And it is what led hundreds of thousands of Sudanese to overthrow a genocidal leader, and then take on the military that replaced his rule through nonviolent resistance alone.

However, the threats to democracy in the twenty-first century are legion. Social media and its accompanying epistemological bubbles have polarized many developed democracies, making it ever more difficult to pass vital legislation.[19] The turn from humanistic education and civic learning toward the maths and sciences needed to compete in a globalized economy has undermined the appreciation for democratic institutions that once sustained their support.[20] China has quietly sought to undermine the democracies of East and Southeast Asia while presenting a successful autocratic model of development that might serve as an alternative for developing countries in Southeast Asia, Central Asia, and Africa.[21] Meanwhile, the German Marshall Fund has identified Russian efforts to undermine democracy in twenty-five states, including several major democracies like the U.S., U.K., Germany, and France.[22]

The idea that the recent successes of democracy make its global triumph inevitable has now been put to rest. But it is far more worrisome to consider just how difficult it would be to replicate in this century the propitious conditions under which so many democracies arose in previous centuries. The path to modern democracy began with nobles reining in the power of absolute rulers they sought to place under constitutional rule. But the nobles went further in most of Europe and America, demanding that they be included in regular parliaments if they were to support the wars of their monarchs and consent to being taxed.[23] And it was precisely the absence of such representation that led American elites to boycott the British and eventually spark the Revolutionary War.

Over the generations, democratic institutions became more inclusive of women, the poor, and people of color. State institutions grew in size and proficiency, binding together stronger nations, shaped into a body by shared institutions and interests. A sense of national unity resulted from relatively stable levels of economic equality.[24] The sense of unity sprang from high growth rates leading to a sense of economic opportunity.[25] It was buoyed by mass civic education leading to a common sense of national purpose.[26] And it was dependent on large middle classes leading to big parties focused on compromise. It is difficult to imagine how a change in conditions might clip the wings of freedom once and for all, but endings are always difficult to imagine, not least the most inevitable ending of death. And the conditions of the twenty-first century do not look nearly so promising for democracy as those of the twentieth.

It is difficult to imagine how one man might sweep away the vast edifice of global democratic institutions, starting with its leading American light. For intemperance is as weakening as it is strengthening; and tyranny is as ineffectual as it is totalitarian. And yet, everything is falling into place like dominoes, and we need only look at the logic behind the momentum to see where it might lead if we do not vigorously defend American democratic institutions at all costs.

WHY CONSERVATIVES FEAR DEMOCRACY

*"The more powerful the class, the more it claims
not to exist."*

GUY DEBORD,
The Society of the Spectacle[27]

T he search for a smoking gun that might demonstrate how Trump coordinated with Putin to win the election has defined his presidency. But the real crime was committed in broad daylight when he openly asked Russia to hack Democratic Party emails. And when following the hacking and the blitz of fake news stories that contributed to his election, Trump tacitly rewarded Putin for it, the verdict of treason should have been complete. He rewarded Putin by attacking the intelligence agencies that revealed his interference in the election; by appointing the most pro-Russia team of advisors in American history; by undermining the sovereignty of Ukraine and threatening to end its military aid; and by threatening to pull out of Nato.

And while many Republicans initially supported an inquiry, few of his supporters cared as independent party voices were crushed.[28] In a short few years, we went from a fascist movement, to an authoritarian party, to an increasingly fascist state. And if the courts and military are further consolidated, we should expect a complete transition from democracy to fascist autocracy. It takes time to tear down a state and undermine its norms, after all; and a fascist state is all the more difficult to consolidate.

These days, almost nobody is openly opposed to democracy—not even Putin, who continues the charade of elections,[29] after exiling his rivals and assassinating the journalists of the remaining free press.[30] Nobody is openly opposed because most everyone recognizes its superiority. Democracy is a superior form of government because it breaks the stranglehold of elites, who use the state to siphon off wealth.[31] The ultimate theft has long been that of the state itself, for as Plato noted, the law is a window through which everything can be stolen. From this standpoint, oligarchy is simply the legalized bribery of state representatives, monarchy the inheritance of stolen social goods. In the absence of democratic constraints, the state may be necessary to keep the peace, yet it is a Faustian bargain in which the balance of benefits is seldom certain.

All this makes conservatives seeking to preserve the status quo uncomfortable, for the status quo is seldom just, and the holders of power are rarely innocent.

But democracy is not just about preventing the state from abusing its power, or "shackling leviathan," in the words of Daren Acemoglu and James Robinson.[32] It is essential to human development,[33] for it encourages citizens to think for themselves and speak their minds. The democratic state need not fear self-actualized individuals but rather gains from their abilities. Hence, democratic states often educate for civic participation,[34] and they tend to provide more education, often extending deep into postgraduate studies. Whereas in autocracies everyone is out to protect their own, democratic participation inspires citizens to think of themselves as in it together, aligning their interests with those of the collective, broadening their morals to include the nation.[35]

Democracies are in this way morally expansive,[36] and the development they foster tends to extend far beyond national borders.

Citizens of the most stable and long standing democracies have widened the ethical sphere to include the rights of animals and refugees, future generations and unborn fetuses.[37] The most stable democracies have pioneered the extension of universal rights and humanitarian aid internationally.[38] And it was precisely this sort of ethical extensionism that Plato found most absurd.[39] But in caricaturing moral development, he merely demonstrated his moral limits. Democratic systems foster the psychosocial and moral development of their citizens because, in being led by the citizens themselves, democracies serve the people. And perhaps the greatest service that can be rendered unto a person is the fostering of their fullest potential.

Democracies foster social development through channeling conflict into reasoned debate.[40] Whereas things tend to get done by force in autocracies, democracies get things done by compromise and convincing fence sitters. This requires crafting arguments and communicating them to others; and it is through arguments that national challenges are tackled. Building ports and highways, eradicating disease and educating the poor, are accomplished first and foremost by convincing people they are worth achieving. While wealthier states are more likely to become democratic,[41] stable democracies are more likely to sustain economic growth.[42] It is a virtuous circle in which democracy generates prosperity and vice versa. Political leaders are more likely to act in the national interest when they must answer to the whole nation; and they are more likely to make the government function better for everyone when their jobs are at stake in regular elections. However, this is unlikely to happen if it is mainly the wealthy who put them in office.

If all this sounds idealistic to American ears, it is because its democratic institutions are falling apart. And the fault lies mostly with Republicans, who are virtually unanimous in their support for the unregulated bribery of campaign funds. If politicians rely on big donors to stay in office, they will be indebted to them and often return the favor: you cannot make laws for *everyone* when you are most beholden to *someone*.[43] And if every politician now depends on much the same set of oligarchs, it is only Republicans who refuse to enact the reforms needed to break their hold on power.

This is all a bit ironic because Republicans like to brag about American democratic institutions. They like to argue that Islam is inferior because democratic institutions rarely exist in Muslim states—even though the most populous country in the world today that has not undermined its democratic institutions is arguably the Muslim state of Indonesia. Republicans like to argue that democracy is a Western form of government that makes us superior—despite its absence in most of the West through most of modern history, and in spite of their own antipathy to Europe.

Even if Republicans believe their policies will bring economic benefits, they are tailor-made to increase inequality. But democracy is dependent on equality, for citizens cease to identify with one another without it, and this leaves them open to autocratic power grabs. Meanwhile, wealth finds a way to usurp power, and the greater the divide, the easier it is for the wealthy to carve up the electorate.[44] Democracy on the other hand makes citizens equal in the eyes of the law and gives them equal voting rights. Legal equality means equal opportunities for work and schooling. And when everyone is given the same chances, living conditions tend to even out as well.

It is no accident that the most equal countries—Sweden, Denmark, Germany, Norway, and Finland, for example—get the highest marks on Transparency International's Corruption Perception Index:[45] democratic institutions tend to root out corruption and support greater equality. Nor is it a coincidence that these nations tend to have the highest taxes and the largest state sectors: people are more likely to care for one another in equal societies and are thus willing to spend the money on it. Nor that they tend to be the happiest countries in the world:[46] equal societies tend to foster greater happiness as well.[47]

The most equal states are now the most democratic, the wealthiest, and the happiest—but the most unlike the Republican ideal—and this is where Republicans start to get uncomfortable. The problem with democracy is that while it tends to improve the quality of life for everyone, it also diminishes the status of elites. And like conservatives in most times and places, it is primarily the interests of elites that Republicans have come to serve.

Republicans talk a lot about freedom, but they fail to grasp its essence. The philosopher Phillip Petit defines freedom in accord with the Ancient Roman conception as the absence of domination.[48] The domination might come in the form of corporations limiting the options of consumers, employers abusing the rights of workers, husbands threatening the freedom of wives, or landlords coercing tenants into paying extra fees. But whatever form it assumes, over and over again, Republicans tend to favor it. Democratic institutions free citizens from domination by protecting them from arbitrary abuses of power. This sets the conditions for everyone to live according to their lights, to speak their minds, and to freely associate. However, the benefits of freedom are accompanied by a burden: democracy forces people to embrace a freedom all too many would rather slough off. People want their children to be born into stable democracies because democracies work for the people.[49] But democracy does not work when people want to throw off the burden of freedom.[50] In an age of proliferating choices and no fixed roles, it should be no surprise that conservatives the world over have turned to fascism.

Conservatives fear democracy because democracy sets them free.

WHAT HAPPENS IF AMERICA PULLS THE BLANKET

*"... would-be totalitarian leaders usually start
their careers by boasting of their past crimes and
carefully outlining their future ones."*

HANNAH ARENDT,
The Origins of Totalitarianism[51]

A lone man now surpasses climate change, overpopulation, nuclear war, and food security as the single greatest threat to human civilization, for America lies right in the middle of them all, and
if America pulls the blanket, everything on the table falls. Redressing
the great challenges of the twenty-first century requires a functioning
global order;[52] but there can be no such order when its most powerful
state is ruled by a leader as erratic and unpredictable as Trump, and
this makes him more dangerous than any other challenge on the table.

The current global order has been governed for decades through
a loose and overlapping network of organizations and agreements
overseen by mostly developed democracies. It includes accords ban-
ning chemical and biological weapons, laws of the seas and climate
treaties; a constellation of alliances, and a set of shared norms, which
regulate the behavior of states, where international law is lacking.[53]
But the election of Trump and the rise of authoritarian regimes in
Europe have drawn this order into question, because they simply see
no need for it.

It is a largely dysfunctional order, and it does not get much done, but it routinely objects to human rights abuses, sanctions authoritarian regimes, promotes democratic governance, contains environmental threats, and provides peacekeeping where states have all but collapsed. The institutions at the heart of this order mostly had their start in the closing days of the Second World War. They were started to prevent another great war, and they made possible the most peaceful and prosperous era in human history.[54] It was an era in which democracy came to reign in almost half the world's states,[55] and the mass-murder of war began to be contained.[56]

But it is an order that is now melting before our very eyes.[57] It can be credited with much of the democratization that occurred in the late twentieth-century.[58] When poor states collapsed and descended into civil war, major democracies commonly initiated peacekeeping missions, culminating in constitutional conventions and elections. These efforts ended civil wars, built states, and generated several stable democracies,[59] and quite a few broken ones as well.[60] Retreating colonial powers even mirrored this process in many cases, as in the British retreat from India and Ghana. The same international institutions incentivized democratization with international recognition, administrative advisors, peacekeepers, and humanitarian aid.[61] Sometimes they supported democratization because their powerful backers believed in it, but democracies also rarely if ever go to war together; hence, they were more likely to prove reliable allies and better trading partners. And yet, democratization was often the only way to bring warring parties to the table.[62]

It was this vision of a peaceful and prosperous world, comprised of largely democratic states, bound together by a commonly shared international order, which inspired so many liberal internationalists,[63] who built and sustained a world order that is now quickly passing into oblivion. In retrospect, it was a utopian vision, all too often honored in the breach; democratization was supported selectively, when it did not threaten critical alliances, and every now and then a fledgling democracy would be sacrificed to political expediency, most blatantly

Iran in 1953, Guatemala in 1954, and Chile in 1973.[64] But perhaps the most astounding thing is that big, often imperial states ever supported democratization at all.

By the late twentieth-century, it had become possible to imagine a peaceful and poverty-free world[65] in which authoritarian regimes might eventually disappear.[66] The vision was pursued by centrist scholars at the Council on Foreign Relations and wealthy elites in Davos, Switzerland, left-leaning humanitarians at Human Rights Watch and neoconservatives like Francis Fukuyama. Virtually nobody was talking about a global government, but it seemed everyone supported this loose framework of overlapping institutions.

If it was an incomplete order, it was also necessary; but it is now strained to the breaking point; and if it passes, the world will be beset by a multitude of unforeseen challenges.

The biggest worry may lie in the fate of the American nuclear umbrella. Trump has argued that America should not defend allies in Eastern Europe and East Asia, leaving dozens of countries vulnerable to a newly aggressive Russia and China. But if Hungary and Poland can no longer rely on American support, they can be expected to look elsewhere. If Japan cannot rely on American support, they can be expected to go nuclear, for they possess the capacity to do so rapidly. Threatened states like Latvia, Lithuania, and Estonia will do what it takes to preserve their freedom, and this must already be leading to discussions about the trade-offs of going nuclear. Perhaps the biggest danger lies in the breakup of Nato and the European Union. Rightwing authoritarian and fascist parties have now taken power in several states in Central Europe,[67] and any change in American commitments can strengthen their hand, along with that of Putin, with whom they tend to be friendly. The end result may be that the nuclear genie is once and for all let out of the bottle. It is all the more likely given the countless signals that have now been sent to autocrats that they will no longer be held accountable for their actions.

Just as the first waves of fascism in the early twentieth century were characterized by genocide, a seldom noted dimension of the fascism this time has been the normalization of crimes against humanity. Shortly after Trump was elected, the Burmese military began razing hundreds of Rohingya villages to the ground, terrorizing their residents with gang rape[68] and brutal child murders.[69] In the end, they ethnically cleansed over half a million Muslims. At the time, Obama was gradually beginning to withdraw support for Saudi Arabia in their war against Yemen's Houthi rebels, due to their war crimes and blockade of ports, which were beginning to starve millions.[70] But Trump stepped up arms sales and logistical support to Saudi Arabia,[71] with the result being eighteen million people slipping into the brink of starvation. The U.N. warned in 2018 that the hunger engulfing the country could degenerate into the world's worst famine in a century,[72] but not much has changed as this book goes to print. China was beginning its own cultural genocide of Muslim Uyghurs as Obama was leaving office, but since Trump began his first term, roughly a million have been detained in concentration camps, where half a million children have been separated from their parents and sent away for "re-education."[73] Since being elected in Brazil, Jair Bolsonaro has meanwhile unleashed a war against Amazon's indigenous people that many have dubbed genocidal.[74] Narendra Modi is building concentration camps for two million Muslims he has made stateless in Assam,[75] while placing millions more under months of house arrest in Kashmir.[76] And Israel has shot tens of thousands of demonstrators in Gaza.[77]

Crimes against humanity that might previously have been adopted as the cause celebré of a generation are now barely noticed, for there are just too many with which to keep up. Meanwhile, the violence has bred a sense of insecurity and chaos. Now it is every "nation for itself," in the words of Ian Bremmer,[78] with the predictable result of a global nuclear arms race,[79] bringing to power still more authoritarians and sidelining humanitarians. International treaties are being broken; climate agreements are falling apart. Failed states are proliferating, with each more dangerous than the next; and as they grow, so also does the number of refugees, which has been reaching record highs now for several years running,[80] empowering rightwing movements the world over.

The isolationism driving these threats may appear to have little if anything to do with fascism, but the retreat is premised on an inability to cope with a vast and overwhelming world, which the fascist experiences as an alien threat to be defeated at all costs. It is premised on a rollback of moral commitments, driving a virulent xenophobia, indifferent to the suffering of others, and unwilling to do anything about it. As the world becomes more threatening, immigrants flood in from broken states, and people turn to rightwing nationalists and fascists, who promise to take care of it all, but can't because they lack both the skills and solutions. Hate thus becomes a substitute for problem solving. Meanwhile, participation in hateful movements becomes a substitute for real human community. It is much like the thirties, when the election of Hitler sent a shock wave through Europe, leading to the militarization of the continent.[81] America is exporting its own fascist sentiments to an increasingly frightened world, through the insecurity fostered by its erratic and impulsive leader—only the fascism this time is possessed of nuclear weapons.

When the most powerful man in the world is a tyrant, with little concern for anyone but himself, we should expect a tyrannical global order. When the world's most powerful man lacks the ability to control himself, we should expect an anarchic and dangerous order. But when the world's most powerful man cares for little but himself and flaunts his indifference with reckless abandon, we should prepare ourselves a shelter far from the madding crowd. Whether the world can survive such a shake-up, amid so many global challenges on which it is already losing ground, remains to be seen. Make no mistake, the world itself is in a race against Trump, and the prize is its preservation.

WHEN THE FASCIST DRUM BEATS

TO NUCLEAR BLASTS

"The real problem of humanity is the following: we have paleolithic emotions; medieval institutions; and god-like technology."

EDWARD O. WILSON

The use of force involves a cascade of hormonal and biochemical reactions that blunt horizons and obscure reason. The reactions ripple through the psyche, transforming the world into a minefield of objects, which must be manipulated at all costs. Attention becomes spatially and temporally contracted, blinded to the wider ramifications of any single action. And everything becomes a threat, as the heart throbs to primordial rhythms all too often ending in war.

Making war is a form of bonding through which whole societies share in these reactions. The world historian William H. McNeill notes in his definitive *Keeping Together in Time: Dance and Drill in Human History* that rhythmic and coordinated muscular movements, shared by large groups of people, lie at the heart of human cooperation. Humans have labored together in fields and threshing houses, celebrations and performances, for millennia.[82]

These experiences eased the pressures of conformity and the burdens of responsibility, which threatened to burst the cords that bound human society together. They lightened the workload and brought often strained communities together in celebration on regular occasions. But collective rites have been stripped from our lives, leaving us to seek them elsewhere;[83] vicariously, in athletic and musical performances; dangerously, in drug-induced highs and risky experiences; and where a fractured social body languishes in discord, all too often in war.

Twentieth-century fascists orchestrated military spectacles and collective rites, which infused the march to war with euphoria. The experience fulfilled itself in an orgy of killing that ended in the ashes of Auschwitz, and it is unlikely to be repeated amid the blooming buzzing confusion of the information age. The fascism this time is too slovenly and disheveled. It masks its dangers in entertainment and dissembles its aggression behind an easy deniability. But when leaders lash out with stunning aggression, their followers' hearts will beat in unison.

The danger this time is that an impulsive Trump will unleash the same primal impulses as Hitler, with the drumbeats this time pounding to the rhythm of nuclear blasts. If ever he has his finger on the button, we can only hope to blunt his impulses with an array of constraints that bring him back to reason. But where most leaders are checked on multiple fronts, Trump's impulses reign free. Consecrated by followers and transmuted into virtues, they lie in wait to spring into action, unleashing their furies on a hapless and vulnerable world. It is a danger inherent to autocracies the world over, but it is all the more dangerous when the leader in question possesses the arms needed to destroy it. Hence, the need for multiple cushioning constraints.

There are four primary ways in which leaders tend to be constrained in their ability to make war. The first level of constraint happens within leaders themselves. They feel anxious and uncomfortable going to war. The anxiety can stem from empathy for its victims or fear of its outcomes. Leaders might be cautious with the contingencies or uncomfortable with what they do not know. This is normal when considering mass murder, but Trump will have none of it.[84] The second level of constraint is social. Leaders are constrained by advisors who present conflicting positions, stifling the drive to blow it all up; by the trouble of getting things done, which means selling it to the public with a coherent plan; and by friends and family whose anxieties make them think twice; but Trump lacks these constraints as well. The third level of constraint is legal. Leaders must present their cases to cabinets, legislatures, and international bodies.[85] The debate can get heated in democracies, but prejudice and adrenaline must take a back seat to reason, as leaders make their case for fighting. This slows the slide to war and bogs it down in moral reflections. Stable democracies virtually never go to war with one another: reasoning through blowing each other up usually helps them settle their differences.[86] But Trump ignores legal constraints, because he does not understand them or believe in the rule of law. The fourth level of constraint is environmental and includes geopolitical relationships, strategic calculuses, and the terrain of adversaries. These factors can be bypassed by American technological and military might, but they slow the rush to war by demanding careful study. And yet, the stable genius just goes with his gut.

Together these constraints constitute a sort of rudimentary moral fabric that initially allowed vast numbers of primates to live together in harmony, where impulsive expression might otherwise tear them apart.[87] But they are also the result of democracies setting a higher bar for war-making. They are institutional and sentimental, bringing neighbors into concord and harmonizing foes. Empathy and understanding, friendliness and tolerance, decency and dignity, all conspire to make us allies in pursuit of the common good.[88] In this sense, the constraints are simply part of human nature, as it is played out in the social cooperation of any decently functioning society.[89] The problem with the fascism this time is that it suppresses and denies this inherently political nature, insisting instead that individuals go it alone. And it goes still further, plunging downward in a forced regression to the patriarchy of the primal horde in which the strong rule and everyone else is forced to fall in line.

The greatest danger for the world today may be that Trump becomes a wartime president, with all the freedom from constraint implied therein. For only in war can his tyrannical tendencies reign free. And it is only through surrendering these constraints that he can gain the support to carry out his agenda. The rush to war is addictive after all, and it is all the more so when even your enemies praise you for it.

WHY TRUMP COULD PROVE
MORE DANGEROUS THAN HITLER

"Enlightened statesmen will not always be at the helm."

JAMES MADISON,
The Federalist Papers[90]

Most people would be hard-pressed to name a single leader of a major democracy in the past two centuries who is so narcissistic, so corrupt, so inarticulate, or so dishonest as Trump. But none have been all these things at once, and there is arguably only a single case of a more hateful and vengeful demagogue, with such mendacious and erratic tendencies, heading a major democratic state in the past two centuries, and the democratic system by which he came to power did not last for long.

Reasonable people do not take comparisons with Hitler lightly. His murder of six million Jews—and two million more Roma, communists, homosexuals, and disabled people—was just a portion of his crimes against humanity, which included among other things a plan to starve thirty million Slavs in Eastern Europe.[91] His hatred was murderous and intense, and he routinely whipped himself into a frenzy in speeches. Hence, the idea that the erratic buffoon we are so fond of mocking might prove as dangerous can seem a stretch. But whereas Hitler possessed the most powerful military in the world, that which Trump commands is better financed than the next eight most powerful militaries combined,[92] and he possesses enough nuclear weapons to destroy the world many times over. If for no other reason, Trump could prove more dangerous than Hitler simply because he possesses greater firepower.

Yet, it is also easy to forget that most Germans in the thirties did not believe Hitler would take the country to war.[93] Hitler actually kept the peace for six years before launching a mostly quiet invasion of Czechoslovakia. And it was several years before he backed his first military campaign, siding with Franco against the Spanish Revolution in 1936. Meanwhile, Trump has already stepped up arms sales and logistical support to Saudi Arabia in their blockade of Yemen, which has taken eighteen million people to the brink of starvation. And he has already bombed two major cities to rubble in the fight against Isis, Raqqa in Syria[94] and Mosul in Iraq.[95] And before North and South Korea came together for peace talks, he had taken America to the brink of what might have easily slid into a nuclear war with its most inscrutable adversary, as he later did with America's most dangerous in Iran.

The idea that this kind of brinkmanship can be sustained without catastrophic consequences is foolhardy; the idea that it is more peaceful than Hitler is ahistorical.

The world got a whole lot more dangerous when Trump took office not simply because of what he might do but because of what he might not do as well. America has long served as the guarantor of global stability. This has meant participating in a multitude of global institutions, which can galvanize action on everything from terrorism to trade. But it has also meant punishing states that threaten the peace and mobilizing coalitions to preserve the global order.

It is no accident that the list of adversaries with which America has recently gone to war is a rogue's gallery of the world's most reprehensible forces: Saddam Hussein, Slobodan Milosevic, Muammar Gaddafi, the Taliban, and Isis. The military interventions have often been ill-considered and punishingly stupid. They have often sprung from an ill-deserved sense of self-righteousness. They have often been partial, selective, distractive, and irresponsible. But dictators intent on ravaging their own populations have had to contend with the possibility that it might become a pretext to remove them from power. And this has surely disincentivized land grabs and genocide.

America itself has been a sort of global leviathan, which has kept the peace among all others, reserving the right to war-making to itself alone.[96] But Trump has no interest in preserving the global order and is more apt to praise the most oppressive dictators. This has sent would-be war criminals a signal that crimes against humanity will go unpunished, and the results have been predictable. Burma has carried out a genocide against its Rohingya minority. Saudi Arabia has stepped up its forced starvation of Yemen. China is carrying out a cultural genocide in Xinjiang. Brazil seems poised to do the same with indigenous peoples in the Amazon. Assad and Putin have intensified the slaughter of Syrian rebels and their civilian charges in Idlib. And Israel has taken to shooting thousands upon thousands of Palestinian demonstrators, many of whom have been children, while beginning to annex the West Bank.[97]

Any state with a score to settle against some restless minority knows that if it acts fast, it is likely to get a free pass—and given the chaos, just might go unnoticed. So, if Israel has been waiting to commit genocide in Gaza, now is the time to do it. If Filipino president Rodrigo Duterte wants to carry out a genocide against communities where there is heavy drug use, the leader of the free world who has praised his work can be expected to have his back. If Bolsonaro wants to kill off the remaining indigenous people of the Amazon and turn it into farmland, there may be no one to stop him from burning it down, and with it the future of human civilization.

Much as was the case with the fascism last time, it is in this unleashing of genocide, where the inversion of moral order comes turning around to crush everything in its path, that is the greatest threat. However, American liberals do not seem much concerned with whether Trump will participate in the forced starvation of millions in Yemen. Nor do they seem much concerned that genocide has been exploding under his watch, nor that the geopolitical order is falling apart, and could lead to countless wars in power vacuums around the world. Rather, the big question on everybody's mind seems to be how far he will go in the forced expulsion of undocumented immigrants, for this could quickly degenerate into an ethnic cleansing on American home soil.

Refugees are now so densely packed in their cells that they are standing on toilets in order to breathe, according to an internal report of the Department of Homeland Security. They often cannot move in their cells, whose maximum capacities were exceeded seven times over when they were recently inspected. Hence, many are not bathing for weeks at a time. Dozens have now died in Immigration and Customs Enforcement custody since the beginning of this administration,[98] including at least seven children.[99] Meanwhile, close to a couple hundred have been sexually molested by their jailers, and thousands more by other children, demonstrating an utter disregard for their safety, according to Health and Human Services.[100] Administration officials have argued unsuccessfully in court that they are under no obligation to provide children with toothpaste, shampoo, bedding, and flu vaccines.[101] But a quarter of circuit court judges have now been appointed by the Trump administration,[102] and the administration has shown no compunctions about flouting the law.

If Trump remains in office for a second term, conditions are likely to degenerate, as the system itself grows in extent, at which point the language of "concentration camps" will cease to be controversial. The American Heritage Dictionary defines concentration camps as "camps where persons are confined, usually without hearings and typically under harsh conditions, often as a result of their membership in a group the government has identified as dangerous or undesirable."[103] While they are typically associated with the Holocaust, they have also been used, among other places, in the Boer War and the Bosnian Genocide, in the Xinjiang province of China today, and it is increasingly clear under the Trump administration in twenty-first century America.[104]

They are the inevitable result of basing a political movement on the dehumanization of immigrants and refugees, using their imprisonment to deter their arrival, detaining more people than can be processed humanely, privatizing the facilities that provide their food and shelter, and attacking the press which is exposing the crime. As was the case in Nazi Germany, the camps are in short the inevitable result of fascism; and the logical result of continuing this state of affairs is that it will only get worse. Stress and overcrowding will intensify the trauma and incidence of disease. Detaining more people will intensify the overcrowding and dehumanization. It will stress the guards, whose tendency to dehumanize detainees intensifies; and it will deaden the consciences of its supporters, who drift deeper in denial.

Already, these camps constitute one of the worst abuses of a civilian population, carried out on home soil, by the federal government, in American history. Their conditions are far more inhumane than the internment camps of Japanese-Americans in WWII. And they could soon rival the ethnic cleansings on the Trail of Tears, which were carried out under a president who Trump compares himself to favorably. The Indian Removals were carried out over the course of a generation, killing several thousand of the 16,000 Native Americans ethnically cleansed from their homelands, mostly due to inadequate provisions. But the concentration camps are new, and conditions in them could easily degenerate, as they ultimately process millions more immigrants and refugees, under a shambolic administration, where cruelty proliferates, and abuses of power are so pervasive that critics can't keep up.

The problem is that if the administration wants to deport undocumented immigrants at a faster rate, they will either need to ship them away without trial, leading countless citizens to be swept up in the deportations, or else they will need to shelter them as they await trial.

But this will mean more makeshift camps, which will only decline in resources as they grow in inmates. Either way, it could quickly start to look like a classic ethnic cleansing, and this means not only the degradation of its victims but also the brutalization of its perpetrators. Crimes against humanity are always crimes against the victims who must bear the brunt of the cruelty and the perpetrators who carry it out alike.

America may possess stronger institutions than those of the Third Reich, but they are fast eroding as the chaos of this administration spreads. As time passes, Trump appointees will increasingly dominate the military, the courts, and the bureaucracy. Thus, if he is re-elected, we should prepare for an increasingly brutal government. And if the camps keep filling up, while provisions stay slim; and if the famine in Yemen begins killing hundreds of thousands, or perhaps even millions; and Trump draws closer to the authoritarians he praises, who are carrying out their own crimes against humanity; it is not inconceivable he would start to resemble Hitler in the eyes of the world.

It may be inconceivable in the present, but so also was the Second World War and the Holocaust to ordinary Germans in the thirties.[105]

WHAT IF TRUMP'S HOLOCAUST IS ALREADY
HAPPENING?

*"In order to escape accountability for his crimes,
the perpetrator does everything in his power to
promote forgetting."*

JUDITH HERMAN,
Trauma and Recovery[106]

Imagine how you would respond to the news that eight million people were starving as a direct result of American actions and that the situation could get worse, affecting another ten million, leaving a substantial portion to die. Numerous commentators have compared Trump to Hitler, yet none have suggested he might actually commit a genocide of Holocaust proportions. But what if he were already carrying it out, and we were watching it unfold right before our eyes, and yet, somehow, mysteriously, we did not notice a thing?

Ordinary Germans living under the Third Reich knew Jews were being shipped away and not returning. Soldiers were writing home about "the Holocaust of bullets" in Ukraine, where Jews and Slavs were being shot by the thousands and thrown into pits.[107] The theft of Jewish wealth was largely fueling the German economy,[108] and enough soldiers worked in the concentration camps for word to get out. Yet, most tended to ignore the topic or explain it away altogether.[109] And given the way people participating in mass extermination tend to explain it away,[110] we should not expect ourselves to behave much differently.

Most people have no idea how they would respond if their government carried out such a holocaust. And yet, the United Nations reports that eighteen million Yemenis are, at the time of this writing, on the brink of famine.[111] The famine can be linked to chronic food shortages in a water-scarce country[112] and the fighting more generally. Houthi rebels are also besieging some cities and starving them into surrender. But the single greatest cause is the Saudi blockade of ports, which is starving the country, with the help of British and American arms and logistical support.[113] And yet, even as American involvement intensifies, Americans themselves have little to say about the matter. There are too few articles, too few protests, and too little concern.

To get a grasp of the magnitude of suffering, imagine a city of children the size of Paris that is starving to death. Miles and miles of streets, laid out in every direction, as far as the eye can see, littered with children struggling to breathe. Neighborhoods plagued by cholera, skyscrapers of toddlers on life support, and millions upon millions of adults, struggling to make it out of the barren suburbs alive. According to Save the Children, at least 85,000 kids have already died of hunger,[114] with an additional 1.8 million starving. These alone would fill a city the size of Paris. But the eighteen million on the brink of famine could fill a combined Rome, Berlin, Boston, Atlanta, Madrid, Seattle, and San Francisco.

Saudi airstrikes have targeted hospitals, wedding parties,[115] aid warehouses,[116] and infrastructure, like bridges and ports, critical to food distribution.[117] Yemen is a largely rural country, where most people live in isolated villages, and it imports 90 percent of its staple foods. Hence, the closure of ports is life-threatening to a substantial portion of its inhabitants.[118] And it is beginning to show in the countless photos of emaciated children, whose starved bodies are reminiscent of the Ethiopian famine of the eighties.

And yet, the famine is being ignored, much like the Ukrainian Holodomor of the early thirties, in which Soviet officials forced hungry peasants to hand over their last stores of grain—tearing apart their houses to search it out—as the dead and dying littered the countryside. In the end, roughly three million Ukrainians died of hunger, as thousands resorted to cannibalism just to survive. Meanwhile, the Western press corps, which regularly read about the famine in Moscow, where they were stationed, failed to report w it, lest their press credentials be taken away. They even undermined the one brave Irish journalist, who traveled the countryside to get the story.[119]

It is common for people to ignore the warning that millions might die in a famine, only to be shocked when, after a few years or so, they start to die off. It is not simply that we cannot imagine it happening; we are also so horrified by the thought of it that we ignore the threat completely.[120] There is something surreal and unimaginable about such a total collapse of everything we count on to survive. But each and every American is now at risk of becoming like those Germans who denied the Holocaust, even as it was happening before their eyes.

Many would argue America is just one of many countries in the Saudi-led coalition attacking Yemen and that Trump did not start the war, but rather picked up where Obama left off. Yet, whereas the Obama administration initially supported the Saudis in their effort to reinstall the internationally recognized Hadi administration, with full U.N. support, following the seizure of power by Houthi rebels, by the time he left office, Obama was curtailing arms sales and threatening to downgrade the American-Saudi alliance.[121] Moreover, since that time, Democrats have been almost united to a person on ending arms sales to Saudi Arabia. Meanwhile, Trump pulled closer to the Saudis upon entering office. He stepped up arms sales and bragged about how much money it would make American weapons suppliers. American logistical support also increased, thereby intensifying American complicity.[122]

In the end, it is possible that several million Yemeni civilians will die as the famine enters its fifth or sixth year. While this differs from the Holocaust in that Yemen is distant and the intention behind driving so many millions to the brink of starvation is murkier, history may not judge it all that differently if the famine persists—or if the coronavirus, which is raging in Yemen as this book goes to print, takes its toll on a weakened population, whose medical infrastructure has been obliterated. The Great Leap Forward, which unintentionally killed 30—45 million Chinese under Chairman Mao, who forced peasants to smelt down their agricultural implements in backyard furnaces, is routinely referred to as a genocide, after all.[123] And it is much the same with the Bengali Famine, in which Winston Churchill diverted food from Bengal to British troops stationed elsewhere in the Second World War.[124] If the intent is not to kill off a substantial portion of the Yemeni population, the effect may be just the same; and i. If it looks like genocide and smells like genocide, and future generations will refer to it as such, we should call it genocide now so that, in recognizing its consequences, it does not get worse.

Hitler had not come close to this level of destruction until he had been in office for over half a decade. But for Trump, it is a matter of course, yet another outrage amid a constant barrage of scandals. The Holocaust was lost in the noise of so many other aggressions of the Nazis, but in the end, it was the chorus that would condemn them for eternity. If you think it cannot happen here, then you may be more like those Germans who could not face the Holocaust than you might like to think.

THIS LOVE AFFAIR WITH DICTATORS HAS GOT TO END

"Once the philosophical foundation of democracy has collapsed, the statement that dictatorship is bad is rationally valid only for those who are not its beneficiaries..."

MAX HORKHEIMER,
Eclipse of Reason[1]

THIS LOVE AFFAIR WITH DICTATORS
HAS GOT TO END

*"Fascism is a manic attack by the body politic
against itself, in the interests of its own salvation."*

BRIAN MASSUMI,
A User's Guide to Capitalism and Schizophrenia[2]

A couple of weeks after Trump visibly shoved aside Montenegrin President, Dusčo Marković, at a Nato conference,[3] Russian agents tried to get rid of him altogether. Just before a scheduled vote on joining Nato, a Serbian cabal staged a failed coup and assassination attempt against Marković, for which two Russian agents would later be prosecuted in absentia.[4] Soon thereafter, Montenegro's parliament voted unanimously to join Nato, with Russian allied Serbs boycotting the vote.[5]

Whether Trump's shove was just another attack of narcissism or part of a more concerted attack on Nato itself is debatable. But Trump would later go on to note that it made no sense for Nato to come to the defense of a tiny country like Montenegro, which most people could not even locate on a map.[6] Yet, if Russia attempts another coup in Montenegro and Nato does nothing, it will empower them to do the same in the tiny Baltic states of Latvia, Lithuania, and Estonia, where prosperous democracies arose after the fall of the Soviet Union.

There are consequences to Trump's praise for dictators like Putin and Kim Jong Un, the most salient being that it sends them a signal they can do what they please; and what all too many dictators want is to take over weak and defenseless democracies like Montenegro.

It is all reminiscent of cold war politics, but this time the American president is not working against but rather with his autocratic counterparts in Moscow. And the American allies under threat are not semi-liberal authoritarians in obscure places but rather electoral democracies, where citizens have become accustomed to speaking their minds and enjoying the fruits of freedom—and they are often located in the heart of Europe. The Baltic states are members of the European Union, so attacking them without consequence would render Nato moot. But if Nato falls, the E.U. fall might as well. For in the absence of a common means of defense, many will side with the most powerful state in the region, which is altogether hostile to a united Europe. And while an attack on a European Union member state may seem unlikely, it already happened when Russia carried out the world's first cyber-war, which targeted Estonia in 2007. It was the first of many Russian attacks on sovereign democracies, with the attacks striking ever closer to home until they hit at the heart of American sovereignty itself.[7]

But what woke American liberals like a shot in the night had been happening elsewhere for almost a decade. Following the attack on Estonia, Putin launched a war in the former Soviet state of Georgia, which had since turned democratic, where he carved out a small Russian enclave in 2009. Undeterred, he sent masked troops into the Crimea in 2014, where a minuscule Russian-allied party passed an illegal and flawed referendum breaking away from the increasingly democratic Ukraine.[8] Shortly thereafter, Putin sent troops into Russian-speaking parts of Ukraine, where identities were divided between the two states, in a bid to further break up and destabilize Ukraine.[9]

But he went further still, with a now familiar pattern of abuse. Bots, trolls, dummy sites, and fake news stories fueled the British campaign to leave Europe in 2016, which Russian oligarchs helped fund. The pattern was then replicated in America, France, and Germany, where Russia-funded rightwing nationalists shared the same goal of breaking up an increasingly fragile alliance of democracies.[10]

Many on the left argue that American electoral interference was deserved, because America has done the same to other states, but Montenegro and Ukraine suffered the same fate without doing anything of the sort. Meanwhile, the idea that Americans deserved it, when many opposed their state's worst abuses of power, is an unjust form of collective punishment. As previously before, the U.S. helped overthrow democratically-elected governments in Iran in 1953, Guatemala in 1954, and Chile in 1973. But its election interference usually involved an effort to preserve democratic institutions through keeping antidemocratic parties out of power. American interference in other states since the end of the cold war has mostly been against brutal autocracies, like Saddam Hussein, the Taliban, Milosevic, and Qaddafi, after his U.N. team warned he would commit genocide against protesters.[11]

America maintains closer relationships with democracies and usually supports democratization,[12] for democratic alliances tend to be more peaceful and prosperous. Many political scientists argue no two stable democracies have ever gone to war with one another in the modern era, and this is largely because of the sentimental identification the citizens of such states feel for one another. The attachments are fostered through higher levels of travel and trade, but also shared norms and values. Political leaders share these same affinities, leading to massive strains in alliances with autocrats.[13]

However, America did not possess the luxury of forging alliances on shared values until the end of the cold war. At that time, the world saw a renaissance in democratization. According to Larry Diamond, perhaps the world's foremost expert on democratization, no less than forty democracies arose between 1990 and 1994, as Russian support for autocrats dried up. With barely a shot fired, America and its European partners aided in the democratization of several dozen states through diplomatic pressure, financial incentives, administrative support, peacekeeping operations, and preferential access to international institutions.[14] It was a largely silent revolution, but as Soviet power evaporated, America was transformed into the sole global hegemon—and to the mind of many, a threat to world peace. This perception was only reinforced when the administration of George W. Bush tried to build democracy at the barrel of a gun in Iraq, thereby sullying the very notion of democratization itself. Many of the democracies built in the nineties began to falter around this same time as well.[15]

Building democracies takes hard work and requires an institutional culture that was often lacking in these states.[16] Hence, they were soon beset by corruption, as citizens lost faith in democracy itself. Democratic freedoms can be a burden that many seek to throw off,[17] all the more so when globalization in a complex world increases the challenges involved in thinking for oneself.[18] Hence, demagogues soon arose to "drain the swamp,"[19] in one nation after another, when what they were really promising was an end to freedom.

Trump has now praised a number of these dictators. He has told Duterte of the Philippines that he is doing a great job. Yet, Duterte has compared himself to Hitler, saying he would be happy to slaughter his country's "three million drug users."[20] He has praised Saddam's efficient killing of terrorists, though most of the citizens he slaughtered were not terrorists but rather the minority Kurds whom he gassed.[21] He celebrated Xi Xinping's maneuver to make himself president for life in China, saying he thought it was a great move, despite Xi's effort to revive Mao's cult of personality. And of course, his flattery of Putin has been endless, while his attacks on virtually every major democratic ally have been withering.

But if America and the international institutions it helped build played a significant role in the rise of a democratic world era, the withdrawal of American support will mean many simply collapse.[22] Smaller democracies will perceive themselves as increasingly vulnerable; hence, movements will arise to ally with more powerful states like Russia and China, which will favor dictators over electorates, as recently witnessed in Hong Kong and Taiwan. The same thing will happen as well on a regional scale, as we have already seen in the Middle East with Saudi Arabia and Iran. Newer democracies will see the incentives America used to bring stability to their institutions dry up and disappear. And international organizations, once dominated by democracies, which incentivized human rights and fair elections, will be weakened in favor of those dominated by autocrats.[23]

In the end, Trump's tenure in office could spell the end to as many democracies as were built in the early nineties, and the deaths they die may be just as quiet as their births. A more likely result is that most states will simply see a weakening of their democratic institutions. Real people suffer when democracies die: just consider the fate of America itself. But the fate of countless democracies is now intimately tied to the fate of American democracy. For when American support dries up, all too many smaller democracies, like Montenegro and Estonia, will be left vulnerable to the whims of greater powers. Trump's praise for dictators is simply an announcement that they can now do what they please, and what all too many of them want is to expand their influence abroad.

MUSLIMS ARE THE NEW JEWS

"A specter is haunting Europe—the specter of Communism. All the powers of old Europe have entered into a holy alliance to exorcise this specter; Pope and Czar, Metternich and Guizot, French radicals and German police spies."

KARL MARX,
The Communist Manifesto[24]

A rightwing nationalist was recently elected president in Adolf Hitler's birthplace of Austria. Upon being elected, he joined a block of rightwing authoritarians and fascists from Poland and Hungary, the Czech Republic and Slovakia. Their commitments to democracy are rapidly deteriorating.[25] They are opposed to immigration, and they are intensely Islamophobic. The European Union will somehow have to accommodate their views, as it requires a consensus of member states to vote them out, and they are loath to turn on each other. But the last time Europeans started electing rightwing nationalists and fascists,[26] the continent was engulfed in war, and the minority at issue was largely killed off.

Muslims have come to occupy much the same social niche previously occupied by Jews. Europeans worry that they are taking over, that they cannot fit in, that they are the agents of cultural decay, and that they will remain a perpetual enemy.[27] It is eerily similar to their view of the Jews—just before six million were murdered in the Holocaust.

Author and therapist Arnold Mindell suggests communities seek out individuals to take on "ghost roles," which routinely arise in groups. Depending on their unconscious needs, groups might look for enforcers or provocateurs, scapegoats or heroes—whatever it takes to round out their identities. If a role remains unfilled, groups will imagine a substitute to fill it; if a substitute cannot be found, they will draw another member of the group into playing it. Thus, a family accustomed to an abusive and authoritarian father may push the eldest son into the role after the father leaves; a nation accustomed to blaming a minority for its problems may find another to blame after the exodus of the first. While the substitute may be a poor fit, it matters little to the group, who reduce it in their minds to the role they need it to play.[28]

There are few Jews in Europe now, but the cultures that expelled them remain. While most countries in Europe are now more globalized and multicultural, they still struggle to assimilate minorities.[29] They still possess much the same national pride, the same attitudes of cultural superiority, and the same political rallying points. And from the Czech Republic to France, rightwing nationalists and fascists are organizing to keep Muslims out.[30]

The fascism last time may have focused on Jews, but the fascism this time is obsessed with Muslims, and it is much the same in China, India, Israel, and America.

Most European cultures are tight-knit and highly democratic. They possess a strong sense of belonging, which makes it easier to maintain generous social programs. But this means immigrants pose a costly threat not only to a right that fears their otherness but also to a left that fears for its social programs. Immigrants threaten social solidarity and with it the welfare protections resulting therefrom.[31] It is a deadly concoction that can fast become explosive. But much of the challenge lies in a cultural sense of superiority directed at minorities. While it is common to hear American liberals and leftists bemoan their historical memories of genocide and slavery, French and German travelers to the states typically forget their more recent and brutal perpetration of genocide and imperialism when judging Americans. It is as if their own most dangerous tendencies have not sunk in.

European societies were quite diverse prior to the Second World War, consisting of a multitude of national and ethnic minorities.[32] But the minorities of which they consisted tended to be Christian and white, and they usually came from nearby locations.[33] Hence, Eastern European states like Czechoslovakia may have consisted of Czechs, Slovaks, and Germans, which each spoke different languages, but they shared a root religion and generations of cohabitation. It was different with the Jews and Roma, who were all too often racially, culturally, religiously, and linguistically different. And as these nations democratized and became more unified, all too many opted to get rid of the alien others.

Jews were just one percent of Germany before the Holocaust, and Muslims are just about two percent of the European population today. Their numbers are minuscule, but the racism against smaller minorities tends to be less about assimilation and more about their sense of difference. Isis terrorist attacks are probably the most immediate cause of the hatred and fear of Muslims. At first glance, this would appear to make Islamophobia different from Antisemitism. Yet, the Nazis were also animated by a fear of the dangers posed by Jews, who stood at the leadership of communist movements in Russia, Hungary, and, most importantly, Germany. The threat of communist takeover was real, and while carrying memories of the genocide they had so recently perpetrated in Namibia,[34] Germans were also quite familiar with the genocide communists had just inflicted on Ukraine.[35]

The hatred and fear of Muslims is also driven by the refugee crisis, spurred by conflict and state failure across the Middle East and Africa.[36] While this might also seem unique, it parallels the modernization process that drove Jews from the ghettos, where they had been confined for centuries. Suddenly, a long-hidden minority came out of the woodwork and made itself felt. People tend to retreat into smaller worlds in times of great change and to close themselves off from the alien other.[37] The response is all the more pronounced when the greater part of the change lies in the intermixing of peoples. Vast economic disruptions are then blamed on an ethnic scapegoat, and collective fantasies of revenge are used to mobilize the masses. The end result is all too often a retrogressive fascism, which mobilizes alienated masses around populist messages of national regeneration. And just as the attacks last time focused on Jews but were soon extended to other marginalized groups, the attacks this time initially focused on Muslims but were increasingly directed at Jews.

Islam and Judaism are both kissing cousins to Christianity. While Christianity reveres the founding figures of Judaism, Islam venerates both Jewish and Christian prophets. Adam and Moses, Noah and Jacob, each play a role in all three faiths, as does the same God of Abraham.[38]

This deep historical entanglement highlights their parallels and the significance of the Holocaust. The Holocaust represented to many a fundamental rupture that ended the innocence of humanity. It was said that God had failed humanity, and nothing would be the same again. Of course, genocide had been happening for ages and it did not stop.[39] And yet, if the Holocaust represented so great a rupture, Europe might find redemption in the unconditional support for a Jewish state.[40] Jews had been wiped clean from Europe, but they shared a millennium-old dream of returning to Jerusalem. However, their triumphant return to Israel culminated in the ethnic cleansing of roughly 700,000 Palestinians,[41] mirroring their own displacement by the Romans two millennia earlier. It was a process that transformed them from victim to perpetrator in a matter of months.

The wandering Jew had finally found a home but in the process transformed the Palestinians into the homeless new Jews.

It was the first of countless displacements across the New Middle East, which would culminate in the backlash of secular dictators against the Arab Spring and the implosion of Syria.[42] Soon refugees would be flooding into Europe,[43] and Europe would react with much the same repulsion as it did to the Jews.[44] But Jews are now more integrated, and their powerful backers and lobbies[45] have been pioneers in Islamophobia,[46] while goading leaders to engage in a war of civilizations so vague as to virtually guarantee its endless perpetuation. Israel has funded genocidal campaigns against Muslims in Bosnia[47] and Burma,[48] and it has become a close ally of an openly fascist India,[49] whose Hindu Nationalist government recently transformed two million Muslims in a single state alone into stateless refugees, while placing millions of Muslims under months of house arrest in the Muslim state of Kashmir. Meanwhile, the Germans and French are willing to forgive the new state of Israel seemingly every injustice in an effort to expunge a guilt of which they all too seldom speak.

And somehow, amid the contingencies of history and the countless moral and strategic errors of Muslim authoritarians and Islamists alike, a role reversal so complete has occurred through which not just the Palestinians, but Muslims of every race and ethnicity, have become the new Jews. Now they wander from country to country in search of a home, carrying with them only their education and the will to persist.[50] In America and Canada, they are emulating Jews in their academic and professional paths to success. But in Europe they have become the new underclass, and in China they are targeted for cultural genocide. The role reversal is astonishing, and while the roles themselves are simply products of the imagination, examining their transmutations over time can provide a lens through which Europeans might glimpse their cultural shadow and the dangers haunting their horizons.

Muslims and Jews alike have always been many things besides

the religions into which they have been born. Scientists and street sweepers, fathers and friends, liberals and authoritarians: their values and commitments are as wide-ranging as the human experience itself, and the religions into which they have been born are often the least of their concerns. But fascists want to reduce us all to the accidents of our birth, and in the process place everyone in straitjackets so confining as to threaten implosion. It is a sort of European suicide belt that now appears ready to explode.

Hence, we would do well to remember, amid complaints of Christians streaming out of the Middle East, and Muslims "invading" Europe, that the only European genocide since the Second World War was actually perpetrated against Muslims in Bosnia, and another might have been perpetrated against Muslims in Kosovo as well but for a timely military intervention. Make no mistake, there is a specter haunting Europe; but it is a specter whose ghastly presence is as insubstantial as the thicket of prejudices upon which it rests.

TOTALITARIANISM IS THE NEW AUTOCRACY

*"To be governed is to be watched, inspected, spied
upon, directed, law-driven, numbered, regulated,
enrolled, indoctrinated, preached at, controlled,
checked, estimated, valued, censured, commanded,
by creatures who have neither the right nor the
wisdom nor the virtue to do so."*

PIERRE-JOSEPH PROUDHON,
General Idea of the Revolution in the Nineteenth Century[51]

China has now laid the groundwork for a totalitarianism more thorough than any the world has yet to see. Ubiquitous video cameras now track Chinese citizens. Facial recognition technology allows police to pull up personal information in an instant. Google glasses allow police to do it while walking the streets. And social credit scores attached to each and every citizen allow them to instantly recognize dissidents, deviants, criminals, minorities, and slackers.[52]

The full regime of technologies has only been implemented in the vast Xinjiang province,[53] where minority Uyghurs were recently itching for autonomy, but are currently suffering a cultural genocide that appears aimed to wipe away any trace of their history. However, if the government wants to, it can now invade the privacy of every citizen to a previously unimaginable degree. Every curiosity you look up, every article you read, every purchase you make, every network you join can be integrated into your social credit score and identified instantly. Police can scan a crowd for low scores in real time; government officials can plumb the depths of your soul.

Meanwhile, a previously unimaginable level of thought control is fast being made accessible for every middle-income autocracy that chooses to use it. Visit the wrong website and your social credit score declines, look up the wrong book and it drops further, mention the wrong phrases on social media and it sinks so low that alarms go off in the camera rooms when your face flashes on the screen. The opportunities this presents for behavioral modification are simply astonishing, as the exploration of every forbidden idea or acquaintance can be made part of a social credit score, whose every drop causes another shock in the hearts of the lowly ranked.

While we can only guess at the ultimate uses to which these tools will be put, China's president, Xi Xinping, has recently removed every possible successor from the Central Committee from which successors are typically drawn, setting himself up for lifetime rule. He has enshrined his thought in the constitution and rehabilitated the memory of Mao, whose status had been downgraded in the party for killing millions in the Cultural Revolution in order to maintain his rule.[54] And Xi has ousted a multitude of challengers under the guise of an anti-corruption campaign, which is far from complete. Over the remaining decades of his life, he will be able to refine these tools if he so chooses, and add new ones to the mix, thereby consolidating his power and stunting the social development of a fifth of the world's population. As this book goes to press, it looks like Hong Kong is next on the agenda.

The only question remaining is if he cares to go so far and whether the Chinese will resist.

Yet, whether or not China goes so far, they have developed the tools needed to implement a security regime more totalitarian than even that of the East German Stasi, at a fraction of the effort and far lower cost, for any autocrat who chooses to go that far. Russians and Turks, Poles and Hungarians, could soon find themselves entering a vise from which they never escape. For once such a security regime is implemented, resistance can be shut down in ways not previously imagined, while independent thinking is gradually snuffed out. Rising middle classes, nurturing democratic aspirations, which might have been expected to achieve democracy, may soon find their aspirations quashed amid a tightening authoritarian grip.

If the implementation of these systems is not met with heavy resistance, they could easily become as normalized as internal intelligence agencies. Israeli Defense Forces could use the technologies to scan the social credit scores of Palestinians whenever they pass through checkpoints, instantly targeting anyone who has ever attended a demonstration, signed a petition, or joined a social media group protesting the occupation. Putin could use them to implement a new series of work camps, where he places dissidents, deviants, drug users, and homosexuals.

The danger is less that democracy will be wiped from the face of the earth and more that once it disappears in any given state, it will be far more difficult to restore. This is particularly worrisome, because democratic transitions seldom occur all in one go. Rather, they tend to take root over the course of generations. And they evolve through a dialectic of democratic and autocratic rule: new institutions are established only to become corrupted, new norms take root only to fall away.[55] However, the new totalitarian tools may create a ratchet effect, whereby every step backward holds, while progress forward is stopped in its tracks. Yet, the greatest danger may be that of conformity.

Authoritarian regimes will almost certainly use these tools to administer an endless series of gentle nudges to make their societies more conformist, for conformity is the lifeblood of authoritarianism. Freedom from tyranny always depends on freethinkers, who are difficult to manipulate.[56] Freethinkers can imagine how things might be done better and therefore do not like to be told what to do, especially when things are being done poorly in order to benefit elites who have stolen their futures. Since dictators depend on people doing what they say, this makes the people who might not do what they say a threat. Hence, autocrats try to contain the ideas of freethinkers, sometimes through censorship, sometimes worse. But doing so alienates other constituencies needed to rule while exacting a hefty managerial price.

It is easier to rule in a traditional culture, which censors itself from the ground up. Traditionalists need conventions to bring order to their lives and leaders who can tell them what to do. Traditional authorities maintain order through the family, the church, the police, and other social institutions. They ostracize eccentrics, reward obedience, and educate for conformity. Since traditional institutions are structured hierarchically, autocrats need only win the allegiance of the people at the top to secure their rule. This usually requires a good bit of compromise and deal-making with traditional elites, and there is always a chance the authorities will turn on them in a crisis, so these compromises usually exercise some check on autocratic power.

However, fascists, as we have seen, try to bypass the old order altogether by setting up their own alternative bases of power. Doing so usually takes great charisma and a propitious set of social circumstances involving substantial anomie and alienation.[57] And it is for this reason that fascists are rarely able to hold power for long.[58] However, the right algorithms might now allow dictators to cut out the traditionalist middlemen, thereby freeing them from conventional constraints. They might also be able to free themselves from the costs associated with harsher authoritarian rule. Punishing algorithms are easier to manage and less likely to provoke a reaction than the blunter tools of censorship and imprisonment. They are also less likely to be noticed, for their jolts can be dispersed, exacting a price on every threatening move, thereby raising the bar on dissent, until it is starved out altogether. This may explain why the Chinese have been so slow to resist an ever more authoritarian state, in spite of their rising levels of wealth and consumer freedom. If China has been the exception to wealthier states democratizing, it may owe as much to careful thought control as the unique features of its culture.

Market mechanisms use similar nudges to incentivize conformity. Hard work and thrift, friendliness and delayed gratification, are all rewarded with greater earnings.[59] But qualities like these are incentivized from the ground up, through the laws of supply and demand. Either business managers want them in their employees, or else consumers want them in the businesses they frequent. However frivolous, inane, and unequal, markets give the people what they want; totalitarian control gives the rulers what they want. Sometimes it is greater wealth, sometimes greater power, but seldom fulfilling their subject's wishes, especially when they constitute a threat.[60] Still, the power of autocrats has always been limited: even the Nazis had to contend with numerous bases of power, with which they often compromised.[61]

The new totalitarianism may be able to bypass traditional bases of power altogether, though. Hence, it may prove the most thoroughgoing totalitarianism yet. However, it is not as if the proponents of freedom will not have their own sets of technologies as well. For every sword, there is a shield; for every more powerful sword, a stronger suit of armor. And it is up to the next generation to develop the shields that might protect us from the fascism this time.

IF DEMOCRACY IS TO SURVIVE
THE TWENTY-FIRST CENTURY

"Those who have ever valued liberty for its own
sake believed that to be free to choose, and not to
be chosen for, is an inalienable ingredient in what
makes human beings human."

ISAIAH BERLIN,
Four Essays on Liberty[62]

The greatest crisis confronting humanity today is arguably the rapid degeneration of democratic institutions in every major region of the world.[63] It is a greater crisis than climate change because, without the ability to influence political outcomes, climate advocates will be mostly powerless to impact energy and transportation policy. It is a greater crisis than inequality, because autocratic states tend to be structured to siphon resources from ordinary people to ruling elites.[64] It is a greater crisis than any other to which we might respond, because our very capacity to collectively respond to crises is premised on the ability to shape social and political outcomes, and this cannot be accomplished without the aid of democratic institutions. Thus, if you care about climate change and inequality, or any number of other progressive concerns, you would do well to focus first and foremost on saving democracy.

If democracy goes, we should expect to live in more unequal and environmentally degraded societies, but also increasingly authoritarian and patriarchal societies, for personal freedom is rare where it threatens the power of ruling elites.[65] Thus, if we cannot stem the degeneration of democratic institutions, we should expect gains in liberal priorities like gay and transgender rights to be reversed, and the liberation of women from subordinate roles the world over to be undermined. But this is nothing compared with the freedom of thought and expression that will likely be curtailed for everyone—for there is no greater threat to autocrats than the freedom of thought. They will shut down the schools, the press, public gatherings, artistic productions, even scientific research to make sure it does not affect their rule. If democracy goes, we may all find ourselves leading more claustrophobic and oppressive lives.

The freedom and security that comes with democratization is now under threat in every major region of the world by a poisonous cocktail of conditions that are only likely to increase over the course of this century.

First, if automation continues to replace middle-income jobs, then developed states will become increasingly unequal. But the most democratic states have usually been the most equal—for a strong middle class means large numbers of people with enough of a stake in the system to demand a say in their futures.[66] When the middle class decreases in size, poor people tend to become marginalized, and the wealthy seize power.[67] And while the poor can always win back power by banding together under charismatic leaders, the populist heroes of today tend to become the autocratic demagogues of tomorrow.[68] This is at least what Aristotle observed two-and-a-half millennium ago, and it does not look much different today.[69] Either way, democratic participation is likely in many ways to degenerate.

Second, if globalization continues to increase, and humanity carries on enlarging its store of information, citizens will need to become increasingly conversant on an ever-widening array of issues. But as the burdens of citizenship increase, people will tend to focus on the few issues they can grasp while ignoring the rest. The result is that they will either talk past one another or else increasingly defer to expert opinion—much as we see today. Either way, democratic participation is likely in many ways to weaken.

Third, if multiculturalism continues to increase, democracies will experience more conflict and less trust. Multicultural democracies may be stimulating and innovative, but they often fall apart when one group tries to shut the other out of power.[70] More commonly, they are paralyzed by disagreement and plagued with corruption due to the mistrust of the ethnic other. The lack of trust makes people unwilling to sacrifice for their fellow citizens; thus, multicultural democracies tend to have weak social safety nets as well.[71] Yet, virtually every state in the world today is now faced with either shutting out substantial portions of its inhabitants or else becoming increasingly multicultural. Either way, democratic participation is likely in many ways to become fragmented.

Finally, if population continues to increase, as is expected up to at least the next century, the voices of citizens will be increasingly drowned out by their ever more numerous compatriots. Consider the case of the United States and Denmark. Since there are roughly 300 million Americans and seven million Danes, this means each Danish vote for their head of state is over forty times more effective than their American counterparts. It is much the same for other small states like Belgium and Switzerland; democracy is more difficult to achieve in larger states because each citizen possesses a relatively smaller stake in the system. They are less likely to speak with their representatives and make the national news when they do get involved. And it is worse when we look to global institutions like the United Nations, which represents the will not of millions but rather billions of people. If globalization continues to link every major issue to every other, and the global population continues to grow, people will increasingly experience themselves as the subjects of global institutions over which they have little control—even if we can somehow manage to democratize their governance.

The political scientist Robert Dahl first highlighted these challenges to democratic governance in his 1998 masterwork, *On De-*

mocracy, where he suggested that it would be hard to turn back the clock on democratic governance, but that its quality would probably degenerate over the course of the next century.[72] Few states are considered legitimate today if they are not democratic, and yet the number of democracies has been in decline for over a decade. Democratic institutions are deteriorating even in core democratic states like America and Britain.[73] Rightwing authoritarianism is growing in every region of the world,[74] and many newer democracies like Hungary and the Philippines increasingly appear fascist. People increasingly feel shut out of their polities and so find themselves ever more ready to tear it all down. Desperate for solutions and ignorant of the issues, they yearn for a dictator who can ease their consciences by removing their burden of freedom.[75] The danger is not so much we will not be able to maintain our democracies, but rather that we will not want to—and that is a challenge for which the more psychologically and spiritually adept might provide some answers.

My first book, *Convergence: The Globalization of Mind*, highlights the challenges involved in thinking about something so vast as a world. The sheer quantity of information and issues that must be studied to make sense of the world is overwhelming. The vast depths of suffering that must be confronted to feel for its inhabitants is mind-boggling. The countless things for which we must take responsibility is burdensome. But human beings have always confronted such challenges whenever they have advanced to a higher level of social complexity, and most of the time, they have beaten the odds. They have beaten the odds with visionary solutions to their greatest challenges, but also by simply muddling through.[76]

The latest wave of fascist leaders may be removed from office and the movements they built scattered in the face of defeat, but the conditions that brought them to power will remain. The fascism now plaguing the world has its origin in forces confronted by every single individual and nation the world over. They are the same forces overwhelming our hearts and dizzying our minds, and they will not let up until we develop the capacity to withstand their assaults. But many of the same forces that helped bring rightwing nationalists and fascists to power in the first place can be used to remove them as well.

If we want to preserve democracy, we are going to have to meet the challenges of the new millennium within ourselves and our social movements. We are going to have to become more comfortable living in a vast and overwhelmingly complex world. We are going to have to know more and hold more in our hearts. And we are somehow going to have to learn to love it. Anything else, and we will find ourselves losing the things we love the most.

THE FASCISM MOMENT WILL END:
THE ONLY QUESTION IS WHEN

"The strategic adversary is fascism... the fascism in us all, in our heads and in our everyday behavior, the fascism that causes us to love power, to desire the very thing that dominates and exploits us."

MICHEL FOUCAULT

It is quite possible the new global fascism will end in a nuclear winter that kills most life on the planet—but it is not probable. Three vast historical forces will likely sweep away the rightwing nationalist and fascist movements that have arisen in Europe and America, Russia and China, India and Brazil. The only question is whether they will do so in time.

The first force is demographic. The younger generations have taken to the streets in recent years from Brazil to Egypt, Iran to Russia, demanding democratic rights and an end to corruption.[77] They will soon begin taking power, and when they do, they will bring with them a penchant for innovation and an embrace of freedom. They are more cosmopolitan, open-minded, and diverse than previous generations. They are concerned with inequality; they often identify themselves as socialists. And they are arguably more level headed and sane.[78] Hence, we may now be witnessing the last dying gasp of the tribal nationalistic id: if demography is truly destiny, it is only a matter of time.

The second force is that of social media. New communication mediums are always explosive.[79] The printing press brought about the Protestant Reformation in the sixteenth century. Radio brought about fascist propaganda in the early twentieth-century.[80] Now social media seems to be bringing about a wave of rightwing demagogues in the twenty-first century. But like so many communication mediums of the past, social media will likely be tamed.[81] The bullying will be contained, the politics will become more mature. And the people who so recently used it to manipulate the masses will find themselves once again marginalized. This will happen because social norms usually emerge to contain social disruption, if only they are given time.[82] And when they fail to, social systems tend to collapse. This doesn't necessarily mean we will like the look of "the civilizing process."[83] It could result in greater corporate hegemony or a wider curtailment of free speech rights, so the question of whether the chaos is contained from the top-down or the bottom-up will be central to the long fight for freedom. But absent total systemic collapse, the disruption will almost certainly be contained. In the meantime, since social media is not inherently rightwing but rather anti-elite, the rightwing nationalists and fascists who have so recently taken power will soon find themselves subsumed by the very forces that brought them to power.

The third force is that of globalization. While globalization has caused much of the nationalist backlash,[84] it can also undermine it as well. The forces of globalization are far more powerful than those of the backlash. Trade will continue to overflow the highest tariff barriers, because advances in transportation and communication make it easier for services and goods to cross borders. Immigrants and refugees will bypass the walls that are erected in their paths, because developed states with low birth rates will need their labor and services. Technological advances will continue to increase the flow of information, the pace of travel, the ease of shipping, and the transfer of financial assets.[85] They will continue to make it easier to set up international organizations and to forge global communities.[86] And they will continue challenging us to think more globally about everything from climate change to nuclear proliferation.

And it is just this global thinking which will lead us to widen our moral imaginations and grapple with the multiple planetary risks we must now confront.[87] In a globalized world, power accrues to those who can think globally, if only because those who cannot are a danger to us all. And sooner or later, in an age of rapid information flows, the truth of the matter will become clear: if you cannot see the forces over which you are governing, you will fall victim to them and fail. None of these forces are necessarily liberal or good, but all of them may be put to good use. It is only a matter of time until most of them take effect, but given the hazards that might occur in a world of nationalists with little concern for the other, they may not do so in time.

Most of the forces that have carried rightwing nationalists and fascists to power will continue undermining democracy over the next century. Globalization will leave us more distant from real centers of power. Information overload will leave us struggling to make sense of what is happening in our polities. Automation will leave us more economically divided. Immigration will leave our cultures more disrupted.[88] Preserving the liberal democratic institutions into which most of us have been born will thereby require hard work, and we will need to contain these threats through active engagement and visionary solutions. But the same forces that bring leaders like Bolsonaro and Netanyahu to power can also be used to undermine their rule. Doing so will require a global movement, built on these forces, that will knock down fascist governments from Washington to Moscow. Just the recognition that we are all in it together, and that there are sweeping historical forces that will sooner or later blow away now triumphant nationalists, will put the wind in the sails we need to keep moving forward.

Marxists used to have a word to describe the condition of poor people who were brought together in a single body in factories but could not recognize their common cause. They were knit together through the same productive processes that transformed them into appendages on assembly lines. They were tied together through the same poverty, which forced them to live cramped together in fetid conditions. They were brought together through the same forces of capitalism that pitted them against one another in the competitive economy. And they were united by the same class interests, which made them natural allies in political struggles they might win if only they would recognize their shared interests.[89]

Marxists called the condition "false consciousness," because their consciousness denied the conditions of their existence.[90] And it seems we might attribute a similar false consciousness to the various movements for freedom and democracy in the world today. We are brought together by the same generational transition that pits millennials against baby boomers. We are brought together by the same social media that are being used to undermine democracy, the same forces of globalization that lead us to compete against each other, and the same planetary struggles that threaten us all. Everything, in short, points to a global democracy movement, capable of building a just and sustainable future. Yet, over and over again, we find national movements going at it alone.

Then, as now, the solution is much the same: if you want to defeat the forces that have pitted you against those with whom you might otherwise live in harmony, the first step involves recognizing your common humanity. The next involves organizing yourselves into a global movement in support of your common interests. The final involves hammering out an agenda more appealing than the fear and hardship promised by your adversaries. The only difference between then and now is that this time when we band together, we will be doing so in support of the same democratic institutions into which most of us have been raised and working to resolve challenges that threaten us all. The new global fascism will end, the only question is when.

BENEATH THE ARCHES OF GREAT DEMOCRATIC
CATHEDRAL

*"Beginning to reason is like stepping onto an
escalator that leads upward and out of sight. Once
we take the first step, the distance to be traveled
is independent of our will and we cannot know in
advance where we shall end."*

PETER SINGER,
The Expanding Circle[91]

The balance of constitutional powers is a bit like the flying but-
tresses of a grand cathedral, where the opposing forces of rival
political parties and branches of government, weighed against each
other with equalizing force, open a void in which ideas might be
formed and public opinion debated. But while it is a cathedral built
of opposing bodies, it is a space of communion through which a more
perfect union might be forged. It is much the same with democratic
deliberation: in coming together to debate the future, we define the
issues that matter and affirm the values that most move our hearts.
Democratic debate generates norms, develops laws, inspires mutual
understanding, and brings legitimacy to social and political institutions.[92]

And yet, America today is beginning to look like too many cathe-
drals of Europe, whose widening fissures foretell a coming collapse.

Democratic societies have always been places of vigorous debate. Ancient Athens was an incubator of great philosophers and playwrights, because they could express themselves freely. This meant philosophers like Socrates and playwrights like Euripides often challenged the status quo. Freedom of speech and assembly made the public sphere a marketplace of ideas, where philosophers conversed, and philosophical debate spurred political upheaval. Since free individuals tend to arrive at their own idiosyncratic values, all too many of which are doomed as failed experiments,[93] democracy may be the perennial incubator of not only good ideas but discontent as well.

Yet, for all their strife, democracies tend to arrive at an astonishing degree of consensus.[94]

The social theorist, Herbert Marcuse, excoriated liberal societies for this conformity in a sixties classic, *One-Dimensional Man*. He argued that advertising and the media of advanced industrial societies create false needs, resulting in one-dimensional personas, divorced from the things that matter most, and entrained to a life of work and consumption.[95] The idea would become a cornerstone of sixties protest, which enriched thinking on consumer capitalism, environmentalism, and personal development. But Marcuse ignored a deeper consensus arrived at through reason and debate: when everyone has access to the same information and can talk about it freely, some ideas die and others thrive, as reason moderates and society arbitrates. Meanwhile, the best ideas tend to be grounded in reality, for it is easier to form winning coalitions around commonly accessible notions of reality.

The liberal center has long held around commonsense rationality backed by science: informed individuals reason through what they know and confirm it with science. We think through the need for a higher minimum wage and then listen to the economists, reason through the debate on genetic engineering with an eye toward science. Since everyone has access to the same set of tools, they tend to arrive at a similar set of beliefs. As Walter Cronkite used to say at the end of his newscasts, "that's the way it is."

However, as scientific studies multiply and scientific disciplines become increasingly specialized, commonsense rationality parts ways with science, which tends to yield increasingly counter-intuitive results. The sheer volume of information and perspectives makes it virtually impossible for any one person to canvass the facts that matter. And anyways, science has placed it all under dispute, so individuals trying to make sense of the world are left without reference points. The center no longer holds, and the political consensus implodes.

It is a curious thing to watch the fracturing of a republic. Perhaps the most poignant product of it is the pervasive sense of mistrust. Epidemiologists Kate Pickett and Richard Wilkenson demonstrate how unequal societies are more mistrustful. As more and more people feel marginalized, mistrust for government, the media, and fellow citizens grows.[96] Meanwhile, the mistrust suffuses debate until reason, and with it reality itself, is no longer trusted.

As the volume of information overflows, and everyone swims for their own epistemological islands, conspiracy theorists make waves with ever more outlandish fabrications. The world appears to them a frightening place, where anything can happen. Political leaders appear pathological and irrational, contradictory and deranged. The conspiracy theorists have no idea what is going on and lurch from far left to far right in search of answers. Yet, their efforts falter because their conception of the world is fragmentary. And since the world they construct is fundamentally illogical, truth itself begins to unravel.

The conservative statesman and philosopher, Edmund Burke, once complained of the representatives of a leftist faction as having acquired their understanding of politics through assembling fragments of news stories.[97] While newspapers can tell you what is happening in the world, they seldom have the space to explain it in depth. Hence, Burke considered such knowledge prone to undermining the kind of social and political norms that take centuries to build and a lifetime to comprehend. For in the failure to comprehend the meaning of long-standing institutions, they are all too often forsaken, and in the process destroyed. But the fragments of leaked documents and scattered memes, through which conspiracy theorists construct their sense of reality, represents more a state of epistemological collapse.

Epistemology is concerned with how we know what we know, and it is often said the far-right lives in its own epistemological bubble. It is not simply that they have their own news sources and commentaries, through which they make sense of events, as analyzed early on by Cass Sunstein.[98] Rather, as the psychologist Jonathan Haidt suggests, they have different personality styles.[99] And as the cognitive scientist and linguist George Lakoff notes, they have different frameworks through which they assimilate information.[100] And while liberals and progressives may be right that the conspiracy theorists are anti-science and irrational, liberals and progressives have their own news sources and commentaries, crafted to appeal to their own personality styles, contextualized within their own moral frameworks.

The problem is that in a fragmentary social universe, leaked documents and conspiracy theories masquerade as primitive talismans invested with the aura of magic. Pre-scientific views are often magical—for where science is lacking, the world is harder to understand. And that may be fine for a Jungian psychoanalyst, whose commerce is in the world of dreams. But when the world of politics begins to appear as little grounded as a dream, political dreamers tend to experience the world as a nightmarish house of mirrors. Hence, the need for the solid shore of empirical facts.

It is all reminiscent of the fundamentalist response to the march of science. The historian of religion Karen Armstrong notes that fundamentalism is not some ancient interpretation of scripture. Rather, it is a reaction to the undermining of it by science. As science knocked the legs out from under religion with a more coherent worldview, religious activists sought to turn religion into a science. However, scripture is inherently metaphorical, and the idea of God has always been amorphous. Meanwhile, the fundamentalist reaction was scriptural pseudo-science, which dispensed with the best of science and religion alike.[101]

My partner who is an Oxford doctorate in clinical psychology suggests the conspiracies work in much the same way, providing a justification for the inability to cope with a complex and often overwhelming world. Conspiracy theories provide a reason why we can't make sense of the world: we are being fooled—and if only we could find out who is fooling us, the world would come into focus and start to make sense. In this sense, the conspiracies reflect our lack of influence and control, and the anxiety is the greater for the boundlessness of possible viewpoints.

The philosopher Charles Taylor takes the conversation a bit deeper, noting that late modernization consists of a proliferation of ways of knowing and being. Different groups gather in their own communities, consume their own information, formulate their own perspectives, and craft their own identities. While social media may exacerbate their epistemological bubbles, the communities preceded social media by decades. And far from producing Marcuse's "one-dimensional man," the fact that evangelical Christians and Buddhists, hipsters and hippies, yuppies and bikers, all traffic in their own unique consumer goods, and generate their own narratives of what it means to be human, suggests that the problem is actually that of expressive diversity.[102]

Alisdair MacIntyre wrote of how the bottom had dropped out of the very concept of public virtue as far back as the eighties, but postmodern society is also a Babel of competing voices.[103] If ever there were neutral arbiters of truth, we have lost the capacity to identify, much less agree upon, who they are. Yet, if we cannot know what is true, there is no basis for common action. Politics is thereby transmuted into a battlefield wherein the winner is determined by who can yell the loudest, measured in dollars raised. Leaders like Bolsonaro and Modo are simply expressions of this far deeper challenge. But if the world can appear increasingly incoherent, it need not be, and John Dewey suggested as far back as the thirties of the last century that the answer may lie in a renewed spirit of democracy.[104]

Democracy is not simply a process for adjudicating political disputes but a way of being. It requires that we work out our fates with others by listening to their needs and incorporating them into our own; that we recognize their equality and compromise when our interests conflict. Democracy challenges us to develop working models of what is happening in the minds of others in order to enact our visions of the good life. And in so doing, it reconstructs both a shared understanding of the world and a working model of public virtue.[105] Through our engagement, it can make us more tolerant and fair-minded, adaptive and resilient, to the actual conditions of the societies in which we are embedded. It might tell us something about what it means to be human. And it is ultimately essential to the enactment of our highest visions, which would be doomed to failure if not for its capacity to bring us together in shaping our future.

Democracy is integral to the process of reconstructing national identities, which have been so battered by inequality and globalization. It is also essential to generating the kind of programmatic responses that might soften their worst blows. However, since democratic participation encourages a responsiveness to the world as it is, it might also facilitate the development of more global identities,[106] for the forces we are up against are increasingly global.

SECTION V

UNLEASHING THE SPIRIT OF DEMOCRACY

"Stories about what a nation has been and should try to be are not attempts at accurate representation but rather attempts to forge a moral identity."

RICHARD RORTY,
Achieving Our Country[1]

UNLEASHING THE SPIRIT OF DEMOCRACY

"Our national character is still in the making."

RICHARD RORTY,
Achieving Our Country[2]

S ome cultures are imbued with a spirit of imperial grandeur, which once lost leaves their inhabitants clinging to the past and protecting their heritage. Some drift like a lazy river, exhibiting a purposelessness matched only by the personal stagnation of their members. Yet, some create their essence through sheer force of will, which must be rediscovered and rejuvenated with each passing generation. While every culture is malleable, each can be said to possess its own animating essence, which Georges Wilhelm Hegel dubbed its spirit;[3] and the American spirit could be said to lie in its historically unprecedented sense of mission, which has so recently been perverted.

Ever since Puritans sought in the early seventeenth-century to build "a city on a hill," on the stony coast of what would soon be christened New England, Americans have seen themselves as possessed of a mission. The mission has usually been cast in moral terms, and while it has typically been construed as secular, its earliest instantiations were more often than not religious. Over the centuries, the exact nature of the mission has assumed numerous guises, from freedom to dignity to moral renewal. But democracy has always coursed through its veins and found a way into its thrumming heartbeat. However imperfect they may have been, America's greatest achievement has probably always lain in its democratic institutions.

America was the first modern democracy to take root in such a vast territory, and at several historical junctures, it spread its institutions to the peoples of the world. Following its war of independence, at the close of the two world wars, at the curtain call of empires, and the fall of the Berlin Wall, American leaders pressed authoritarian cultures to adopt democratic institutions. Most of its own state governments and countless town councils were democratic prior to its founding. These protected Americans from the rapacity of elites and the corruption of petty officials; and they imbued their culture with a spirit of freedom so absolute that Americans often reject even their own protection from abuse.

The democratic spirit meant Americans often did for themselves what no government existed to do for them. Alexis de Tocqueville suggested in the first half of the nineteenth century that "there is scarcely an undertaking so small that Americans do not unite for it." Contrasting Americans with the British and French, he noted that "Americans use associations to give fêtes, to found seminaries, to build inns, to raise churches, to distribute books, to send missionaries to the antipodes; in this manner they create hospitals, prisons, schools."[4]

All of this enterprising activity lent to the character of the culture a bustling sense of activity. America began as a nation of pioneers, so everything had to be built from scratch. There was no ancient infrastructure of roads and canals, no hospitals, no schools, no prisons, no village councils. Far from it, wherever settlers opened new lands to cultivation, there were no laws and scarcely any semblance of order, except for that of the Native Americans, who were fought off, hemmed in, pressed back, and ultimately cleansed from the land. This lent to an otherwise democratic culture a lawless shadow of violence, which periodically exploded on the national scene, and perpetually vexed its foreign policy, whose democratic mission was all too often perverted by imperial pride.[5]

Its history of slavery, like an early childhood disease, crippled it from the start, and it infused into it a countervailing spirit of hierarchy, which periodically broke into open conflict with its better angels of democratic innocence. At their best, Americans strove to make right in one generation what they had failed to accomplish in the last, building in the process a progressive tradition of civic renewal. At their worst, they appeared like priestly pedophiles, preaching morals they could not master, and in the process perverting their own development. And it was all on display in their unique brand of capitalism.

America's hyper-competitive business culture and its more innovative start-up culture are heavily indebted to this tangled legacy of exploitation. Entrepreneurs are prone to fetishizing technology, yet innovation plays only a small part in business success. Rather, it is in the tweaking of designs, the arrangement of distribution, the facilitation of sales, the organization of management, and the structuring of firms where business success usually lies.[6] Americans excelled at these micro-innovations in no small part because of their institution-building legacy, but they also excelled at the teamwork needed to carry out collective enterprises.

The spirit of innovation ran deeper still. Americans invented jazz, blues, country, and rock n' roll; baseball, football, and basketball; and for all practical purposes, the quintessentially American art of film. If it is a cultural legacy consisting largely of kitsch, it is a testament to the creative genius of freedom unleashed. In many ways, America reinvented the world, which made it easier for their culture to take it over; and the ability to do so sprang from the unrestrained expression, which has lately degenerated into fascism. At the dawn of the twenty-first century, the spirit of cooperation so essential to democracy was transmuted into its opposite by a reckless and individualistic capitalism, which would assemble people only to tear them apart.

Conservatives would come to worship markets as the engine of American progress, which brought economic development and, through its accoutrements, freedom of expression, and all the comforts of the good life. They would contrast this "free market innovation machine"[7] with the dead hand of government. Yet, in so doing, they would overlook the institutional origins of city councils and government bureaus, which also required real people to come together to get things done. From its inception, government arose from the ground up; and when it started to become so unwieldy that some would find in it a threat to their freedom, the source of their anxiety could be found in civic institutions, sprung from the minds of citizens. Civil rights legislation was adopted in the sixties because African-Americans built the National Association for the Advancement of Colored People; workplace safety and health protections were adopted in the seventies because of a string of consumer organizations, inspired by the work of Ralph Nader, an ardent advocate of civic renewal. The welfare state itself sprang from concerned citizens, struggling to improve their government, and through its institutions their national life.

Thus, American nationalists have been waging a war on their own most vital institutions. The same spirit of institutional innovation that built the first schools and hospitals was also applied to the passage of legislation, which embodied the will of the people and lent shape to their ideals. In this way, the array of bureaus comprising the federal government constitute the essence of the American heritage: they are the only institutions built by all Americans, both those who are living and those long gone. It was only the lawless shadow of the nation that was rearing its head when reactionaries began to reject the order it represented in its entirety. Still, the bucking of traditional orders has long served as a source of creative tension, spurring citizens to recreate their nation when all seemed lost.

Its manners and mores emerged from a confluence of cultures, making their way on the margins of civilization. The divisions between Euro-Americans, African-Americans, and Native Americans were perhaps the starkest; but it is often forgotten that British,

French, Irish, German, Italian, and Jewish immigrants seldom got along so well as we might imagine. Nor were relations easy between later Chinese, Mexican, Puerto Rican, and Cuban arrivals.[8] In this way, America is both a land of promise and an endless series of contestations, and its national spirit is, among other things, liberal, expansive, innovative, and expressive.

The profusion of identities, each with its own language and manners, subdivided by region and class, meant that harmony would require compromise. But where some compromise through a rigid code of morals, and others authoritarian conformity, Americans compromised through the pulsing rhythms of give-and-take. The dazzling diversity, and its extemporaneous essence, was perhaps best articulated in the improvisations of jazz and the poetry of Whitman, who absorbed its burgeoning contradictions, sat with its dying soldiers, worked with its sweating laborers, inhaled its vast multitudes, and euphorically, voraciously, and always lovingly, made of his own heart an offering both humble and sublime.[9]

It was a vision of equality, exalted for the lofty ambitions of an impossible people. But the perpetual pullulations of American social life were more prosaically mediated by democratic institutions. Without democracy, the whole cultural edifice would have fractured into a thousand irreconcilable differences, and splintered into incoherence; but with it, somehow, the center managed to hold. Democracy provided the institutional architecture needed for each generation to create itself anew. Perhaps more so than any other, American culture is the result of this artifice, which must set to work each generation, reforming the national character, while propping up its democratic institutions. In this way, the American character remains as unformed as its manners.

As long ago as 1890, Frederick Jackson Turner was able to declare the closing of the American frontier.[10] However, Americans continued moving westward. The Mamas and the Papas were going to San Francisco with flowers in their hair in 1967; the Village People were urging gay men to go west in 1979. The California encountered in my travels in the nineties was a whirl of diversity and a smorgasbord of spiritual cults and communities, who were pushing into the outer reaches of consciousness itself. It is this spirit of reaching, searching, exploring, and creating that has allowed Americans to continually recreate themselves and renew their national life. And it might once more allow them to take up the mantle of global leadership, in pointing the way to a more cosmopolitan global culture, and in casting off the fascist menace. Yet, fascism rejects this spirit of innovation, contracting in conformity, casting out aliens, venting complaints, and evading responsibility. It is a surly rejection of the teeming multitudes and the democratic vistas extolled by the poetry of Whitman.

Cultures like minds are a terrible thing to waste, for they contain within them the wisdom of generations. Like ancient trees, gnarled with age, and twisted by the weight of their branches, they carry the scars that lend them their identities. American liberals and leftists are but leaves on the branches of a single tree, containing within themselves the moralism of Puritans, the pacifism of Quakers, the hypocrisies of Jefferson, the loftiness of King, and the murderousness of Jackson. They are the same hopeful failures who made their way from Europe, the same hapless victims shipped from Africa. And it is up to progressives, who have all too often abandoned their culture, and with it the vision needed to restore the country, to create the nation anew and discover in themselves a more tolerant and inclusive culture, which might contribute to a more democratic and cooperative world.[11]

FOCUSING ON THE PRESERVATION OF FREEDOM

*"The United States are destined either to surmount
the gorgeous history of feudalism or else prove the
most tremendous failure of time."*

WALT WHITMAN,
Democratic Vistas[12]

The Democratic Party is a bit like the proverbial man searching for the glasses on his own nose. For decades, it has been trying to forge a winning platform that would unite the center with the progressive left and energize the base without alienating the middle. Where it has succeeded, America has benefitted, with incremental programs in stair-step fashion; where it has failed, hopes and dreams have been deferred through yet another round of Republican budget cuts. Where it has succeeded, divides have been bridged with magical hopes and unfulfillable promises; where it has failed, charismatic presidents made us believe, then dashed our hopes on the shores of political reality.

Nobody has yet found a better way to square the circle that would unite the center with the left to once more win. So, the center-left inflates what it can achieve, while the progressive-left exaggerates how much it can do better. It is a common challenge for liberal parties the world over, which stand and fall with the success of the system itself, and often struggle to articulate why democratic institutions matter. In France, we have seen the center-left Emmanuel Macron savaged by the far-left; in the United Kingdom, it was the far-left Jeremy Corbyn, who was pummeled by the center-left, which virtually guaranteed his loss to the rightwing nationalist, Boris Johnson. But as a conservative British friend recently noted, the most distinctive feature of the Democratic Party agenda is now hiding right there in their own name, and it can provide the basis of a winning platform that might unite not just left and center but America itself: Democrats believe in democracy. They believe that elections should not be bought by the highest bidder; that politicians should not have to answer to plutocrats; that everyone deserves the right to vote; that each vote should be counted equally; and that no one is above the law.

Democrats believe in democracy, because it frees them from domination in their homes, their schools, their jobs, and the market. They believe every person deserves respect and thus oppose discrimination in all its forms. They believe this respect is integral to democratic institutions, for it infuses participation into the social sphere. Democrats believe in democracy, because it liberates women, protects children, and invigorates the economy with the spirit of innovation. Democrats believe that when people are included in the decisions that most shape their lives, they are more likely to live well and thrive—and when individuals thrive, we are all better off. Democrats believe in democracy, because without it there is no real environmentalism. Corporations game the system to increase their profits, and propagate lies to preserve the status quo. Climate change is treated as a political football, and future generations are removed from debate. And we know this because it shows up in their records and the way they speak. Democrats believe in democracy, but it is seldom noticed and rarely discussed, for until recently, Americans have taken democracy for granted. They assumed their institutions would outlast them and their leaders would respect the constitution. Now all of that is gone. The greatest threat to the nation today is not this or that party program but rather the end of democracy itself. Democrats should capitalize on the fact that they are in both name and deed the only major democratic party left. But to make this claim, they will need to do some house cleaning.

When the party fails to live up to these standards, people who might otherwise support it not only feel betrayed but ready to throw away their votes in protest. They are offended that party elites might choose their presidential candidates, that wealthy donors might dictate their platforms, and that their votes do not really matter. So, if Democrats are to win, they need to listen to the disenfranchised left and make it clear they do not want to be reliant on wealthy donors. Democrats generally support campaign finance reform, and do not like to spend their time fundraising from wealthy donors—and it was the conservative controlled Supreme Court that opened the floodgates to big money, after all.

Former President Bill Clinton once said, "Democrats want to fall in love; Republicans just fall in line." Liberals tend to believe their leaders should represent not only their values but their aspirations; conservatives believe that hierarchy is inevitable and necessary to get things done.[13] It is a difference rooted deep in the liberal faith in human nature, which holds that people can manage their own affairs and can do so better when granted the freedom to decide their fates,[14] and the conservative distrust of democratic participation,[15] which is rooted in the belief that everyone is out for themselves and themselves alone.[16]

Republicans oppose campaign finance reform laws, arguing money is speech, and the wealthy have the right to dominate debates. They oppose lobbying reform, arguing that everyone deserves access to political leaders, with the wealthiest individuals and corporations by implication deserving the most. They drive the process of gerrymandering districts to win majorities where they lack majority support. They refuse to approve Democratic court appointees and then pack the courts when it is their turn to govern. They undermine faith in elections by lying about vote-rigging; undermine faith in the press by making up stories about fake news; exclude voters by disenfranchising ever-larger blocks. They have betrayed American democratic institutions to an autocratic and genocidal rival: Trump himself called on Russia to intervene in the presidential election, asking them to hack Clinton's emails, and top advisors repeatedly lied under oath about their Russian connections. These facts are now long past dispute.[17] Whether or not there was a quid pro quo deal with Putin is beside the point, for Trump had no qualms with inviting Russia to subvert American elections—and the rest of the party was willing to play along. There is an expression for this betrayal of the country, recognized by military leaders the world over: they call it treason, and the punishment is typically death. Republicans, on the other hand, call it fake news and muster their courage to stand it down with lies.

Conservatives must engage in full-time indoctrination to keep their troops in line. Their messages are repeated endlessly on conservatives talks shows, strengthened by a stultifying conformity, reinforced by a punishing obstinacy. And when they fail to fall in line, they are simply cast out. The language is visceral, combative, emotive, and blunt. It draws distinctions in black and white, pits insiders against outsiders, and paints the opposition as unreasonable, immoral, and stupid. Dismissive of science and resistant to dialogue, its boundaries are circumscribed, its immunity to reason near complete: Republican propaganda is unreasonable, undemocratic, and in its rejection of free expression, utterly un-American.

The lines would break like a poorly trained militia before a modern well-equipped army if the party were ever to mount a full-on attack on this betrayal of democratic commitments. It is a line of attack that might be mounted from across the political spectrum, drawing on a long national history of democratic ideals. It would be the most principled campaign in generations, because it would involve a fight to preserve the most vital institutions, and to protect against the most dangerous administration, through the adoption of a platform that just might sweep the country. Meanwhile, Democrats need to meet the plutocracy head-on.

Perhaps the most exciting proposal was set forth by two constitutional scholars, Bruce Ackerman and Ian Ayres, in their book *Voting with Dollars*,[18] which was later adopted by Andrew Yang. In it, they argue that the Supreme Court has made it clear campaign spending is a form of speech, which for the most part must remain free of regulation. However, they are more open to publicly funded campaigns but do not trust the government to spend the money fairly. Hence, they argue that we should provide public money to individuals to spend as they please on campaigns. They set the figure at $100 per voter for each election cycle, provided in the form of credits on a card, which can be spent only on campaigns and advocacy groups, arguing this money would cancel out the ill effects of private money. The total would come out to something like 5–$10 billion a year, depending on how many people make use of it, and would quickly be recouped in all the boondoggles that never happen. There is no need for a constitutional convention, no need to control the Supreme Court, just the need to focus on the right legislation—and in one fell swoop, we might be able to knock out the latest instantiation of the plutocracy, once and for all. And since the model can be replicated by democracies the world over, it has the promise to revive democratic institutions everywhere.

UNIFYING LIBERALS, SOCIALISTS, AND
COSMOPOLITANS

"For in politics, as in religion, it is equally absurd
to aim at making proselytes by fire and sword."

ALEXANDER HAMILTON,
The Federalist Papers[19]

D emocracy must now be defended on three simultaneous fronts.
It needs to be defended from rightwing nationalists and fascists
and their threat to undermine basic democratic rights, and this requires a liberal response. It needs to be defended from the breakup
of the democratic-led world order and the threat to end international support for democratization, and this calls for a cosmopolitan response. And it needs to be defended from inequality and its threat of
oligarchy, and this demands a socialist response.

Liberals value the spirit of tolerance critical to liberal democratic
institutions, articulated in the early modern period by John Locke.[20]
They believe in the power of reason and the capacity of each and
every human being to develop it; and they believe its free pursuit
will result in social progress and human flourishing, perhaps best
expressed in John Stuart Mill's, *On Liberty,* at the height of British
industrialism.[21] Hence, they seek to protect its expression through
liberal rights like freedom of speech, association, and religion. These
rights are tied to a more ancient notion of liberalism associated with
a broad-minded spirit of generosity, outlined in Aristotle's *Nicoma-*

chean Ethics.[22] Liberalism has long been associated with the tolerance of human fallibility,[23] as well as a respect for the many paths to the good life, commonly associated with a range of values.[24] But this tolerance tends to extend to different lifestyles, cultures, habits, and religions.[25] Hence, more contemporary expressions of liberalism, associated with the effort to eradicate racism, sexism, and other forms of discrimination, are part of a much older tradition.

Cosmopolitans see themselves as citizens of the world and therefore value the international institutions that facilitate global cooperation.[26] And while cosmopolitanism is an ancient school of moral thought, focusing on personal autonomy and duties to humanity,[27] there is a more popular sense of the expression as well. When most people speak of cosmopolitans, they imply individuals without roots.[28] They are generally well traveled and tied to an emergent global elite, whose embrace of free trade is associated with the bursting of national bonds. Commonly referred to as neoliberals, the economic policies they advocate have brought growth to the developing world and inequality to the developed.[29] In the process, they have come to be seen by many as a new elite, which embraces multiculturalism and more liberal social values, but which is oblivious to the harms of inequality.[30] However, the "rootless cosmopolitans" of today are often like the rootless Jewish cosmopolitans of the nineteenth and twentieth-centuries, refugees fleeing persecution and immigrants in search of a better life. And while the popular and philosophical conceptions of cosmopolitanism are typically at odds in their politics, they are united in their globalism. Cosmopolitans of every hue recognize we are living in one world and increasingly interconnected.

Socialists value social and economic justice, and they see themselves as the protectors of the downtrodden. They believe that social protections, and a strong social safety net, can provide everyone the opportunity to live with dignity and self-respect; and they believe social engineering can dramatically improve the human condition. Moreover, they believe that liberal democratic institutions need to be protected first and foremost from the corruptions of oligarchy, which they associate with the new cosmopolitan elites. Contemporary socialists are skeptical of democracy without equality and liberalism without dignity. Nevertheless, their visions are dependent upon strong liberal institutions and inclusive social values.

While the values of these groups differ, they are not necessarily incompatible; but they all too often appear to be, and the groups they mobilize are all too often at odds. Liberals and globalists might recognize the threats to democracy posed by rightwing nationalism and the attack on the global order, but they are far more skeptical of the socialist policies that would bring about greater equality. Socialists might recognize the threats to democracy posed by oligarchy and rightwing nationalists, but they are far more skeptical of the global institutions that have done so much to promote it.[31] And the personality styles of the individuals drawn to these groups often put them at odds as well.[32]

However, saving democracy will require liberals, socialists, and cosmopolitans to come together in defense of the democratic institutions that are integral to each of their visions of the good society, much as the popular front coalitions did in the thirties, when they banded together to fight fascism.[33] They will need to come together, because the numbers matter for winning elections, and we lack the time to settle on a plan upon which we can all agree. And they will need to recognize themselves as engaged in a common struggle because they share more in common than the forces they oppose, and the stakes are too great to waste their chances fighting among themselves.

It is all reminiscent of the non-aggression pact between Chiang Kai Shek and Mao Zedong in the Second World War. Reasoning that neither could defeat the Japanese alone and that their failure to join forces would mean they both lose, nationalists and communists set aside their differences, living to fight each other another day. And if it can be accomplished in such a deadly contest, these more peaceful coalitions in the present should have little trouble—yet troubles remain.

A major challenge lies in building solidarity between neoliberals and their socialist foes. The coalition is threatened on the right by neoliberals defecting to rightwing nationalists who promise to protect their assets. But it is also threatened on the left by socialists defecting to rightwing nationalists who promise to rebuild their social programs, particularly in continental Europe.[34] Older European socialists are also defecting to the right out of a fear of multiculturalism, as they did in Labour's heartland in the Northern U.K., when Jeremy Corbyn lost to Boris Johnson. But the real problem is less defection to the right and more a sort of aimless attack on the liberal center, which is fueled with ressentiment.

The dangers of a socialist attack on the center can be witnessed in France, where a coalition of liberals, socialists, and cosmopolitans brought Emmanuel Macron to power and then quickly fell out themselves. However, the coalition was better managed in Canada, where the progressive disillusionment with Justin Trudeau resulted in the rise of the more leftwing New Democratic Party, which formed a coalition with his Liberal Party. The end result was that Trudeau's government remained intact while being pulled to the left. Something similar seems to be at work in the Democratic Party in the United States, where a powerful democratic socialist has continually pulled more centrist candidates to the left.

Holding these sorts of coalitions together is often treated as a technical matter of good organizing. But it is just as much a matter of temperance on the part of its members. Maintaining these kinds of coalitions requires patience and perspective, tolerance and compromise. But it also requires vigorous and visionary leadership. The members of the coalition need to be able to recognize the limits of what they can achieve, and they need to work together in good faith. Moreover, they need to recognize the limits of their own ideological positions and open themselves to what they might learn from their partners. And they need to think a lot harder about how to synthesize their goals and harmonize their values. If the divisions at the top are to be minimized, people at the bottom will need to remember what they are up against. None of our goals will be accomplished under an autocrat, and we are going to need all the help we can get to save democracy. In the words of Benjamin Franklin, "We must all hang together or, most assuredly, we shall all hang separately."

The challenge lies in building a spirited movement that sets forth a program that can win over the center, reinvigorate liberal democratic ideals, and rein in inequality and the plutocracy that sustains it. Sometimes this will require postponing our most progressive ideals, which cannot be implemented without preserving liberal democratic institutions. Yet, sometimes it will mean inspiring people to work toward a more just and sustainable future.

The Women's March provides an inspiring model. It was bold and beautiful, vigorous and sane. It found a place for everyone, affirmed the highest liberal values, and eschewed violence. It was easy to imagine it sweeping the country when things really got bad, and it looked like the start of a winning campaign. The Black Lives Matter protests against police brutality, while far less orderly, had a similar impact when they first got underway. Perhaps it was because control of the streets plays a far more powerful role in the national imagination than most people tend to believe, or maybe it was a bandwagon effect, wherein the pent-up energies of the nation just sought an outlet, and many would join whichever movement promised to express their rage; but in both cases, Trump's favorability ratings tanked. And yet, protests against inequality and systemic corruption, which have recently brought down autocrats across the world, could be even more impactful, and they would build on the work of others in countless countries across the world, helping the process to build a more global movement.

Fascist administrations will crumble like houses of sand in the wind if we can succeed in simply channeling the opposition to their programs in such vigorous and positive directions. Sometimes this will mean taking to the streets, sometimes building electoral coalitions, sometimes working pragmatically, sometimes aspiring to our highest ideals. But in every case, it will mean inspiring action, building movements, seizing the narrative, and riding the wave to victory.

GETTING UP OFF THE MAT AND WINNING

"The greatness of America lies not in being more enlightened than any other nation, but rather in her ability to repair her faults."

ALEXIS DE TOCQUEVILLE,
Democracy in America[35]

Perhaps the most ill-conceived scheme in the history of cinema was Rocky Balboa's plan to take repeated blows to the head until his opponent wore himself out with all the punching and could no longer put up a fight. But it often seems that liberals have been taking their cues from Rocky, staying their hand as they were beaten into oblivion. Rightwing bullies mastered the art of insulting liberals and deceptively framing issues in their favor. Every time liberals called out their lies, members of their own party would chastise them for incivility. Some of the reason lay in the fact that both parties shared the same corporate donors, whose campaign funds came at the price of passivity; some in the competition for uninformed swing voters, who did not respond well to a fighting liberalism.

Yet, much of the reason lay in a belief that politics was a dirty business, and establishment politics all the more so. Liberals were withdrawing from politics, because political participation had all too often become anathema to their vision of the good life. The withdrawal could be witnessed in spiritual literature and the opinion pages of the *New York Times*. The liberal quest for justice took a back seat to a more expansive quest for fulfillment. Hence, it should have surprised no one that Democrats would find themselves like Rocky, bruised and beaten and struggling to get up off the mat. For when good people withdraw from politics, power is forfeited to the avaricious and greedy, who do everything they can to keep it.

Now, as this book is going to press, Republicans control the presidency, the senate, and the courts, and they have given every indication it is a fight to the finish. They are happy to steal Supreme Court seats and elections, disenfranchise minorities, and rig electoral maps, because it is the only way to keep winning elections without majority support. And they have to maintain power if they are to protect the privileges of their donors, which are enshrined in corporate law and tax policies, in the freedom to pollute and abuse employees.

Republicans are an increasingly fascist party that distracts attention from their unpopular agenda by stoking hatred for the marginalized and weak. Trump is quite pleased with himself in declaring the only good Democrat a dead Democrat,[36] applying a genocidal slogan once unleashed on Native Americans to half the population. And over and over again, he has shown himself more than willing to send armed protesters, who have often killed, to battle with his liberal and leftist opponents. And while liberals and the left have begun to put up a fight, few have articulated a vision of civic participation that would allow them to sustain it past the coming elections. How we got here and what we need to do about it may be the most pressing questions.

Somehow, the fighting creed of liberalism, which oppressed masses once mustered to protect them from the powerful, was transformed over the course of a few generations into the milquetoast manners of neoliberal elites. It was a long journey that is usually told in terms of changing demographics and political influence, but it is also the story of how political complacency emerged out of spiritual escapism. Somehow, it was believed, civility would always win, so the more you stepped back to refine yourself, the greater your influence would be. It was a form of magical thinking with the faintest thread of reasoning to back it up. Yet, the roots of the escapism ran deeper than the hero's journey all too many liberals imagined themselves to be on.[37]

Spiritual escapism was normalized by spiritual teachers and self-help gurus who counseled a turn within. The idea was that if individuals transformed themselves, institutions would follow. And while they may have believed in voting, they also tended to suggest that advocacy would degenerate into anger, and out of anger, little change would come. It was a spiritual counterpart to an identity politics that also sought answers in introspection and a neoliberalism that deferred political decision-making to market forces. Wherever you looked, liberals were on the retreat, perpetually collecting themselves for fights from which they never ceased to shy away. The victims of injustice were probably the greatest losers in this flight from anger, but escapism has a way of marginalizing us all.

At the end of his book on the moral sentiments, the philosopher David Hume noted that doing good makes us happier in almost every instance—except that of fighting for justice. Work for justice can leave us hated, for the victims of injustice tend to be distant while the people inflicting it are near. It can thus frustrate friends and family while alienating us from the powerful, who hold the keys to worldly success. And because the victims of injustice are often poor and marginalized, work for justice is rarely well rewarded.[38] As a result, it is often stressful and leaves us riddled with anger.

Anger tends to be a self-defeating emotion. The spirit it musters is seldom channeled usefully while the fuel it burns is all too often our most vital energy. If indulged in personally, it can drain us of energy, while collectively, it can become dangerously violent. And what can be said of anger applies doubly to its near cousin hate.[39] Hence, it is little surprise that smart people tend to treat it as either something to be feared or suppressed, and smarter people still try to work it out of their systems.

But whether we like it or not, anger usually accompanies the confrontation of injustice. We feel angry when bullies gloat over the humiliations they inflict and when rapists mock their victims. The anger energizes us and prepares us for a fight, and it appears to have primal roots. Numerous studies have shown that mammals get angry when they witness injustices and are often willing to sacrifice their own good just to spite a bully.[40] But if anger is integral to confronting injustice, justice itself is all too often a casualty in the battle against it. In the words of Cicero, "Extreme justice is injustice."[41]

This presents us with something of a paradox. Anger is by its nature an uncivil emotion, which makes us prone to violence. But it is also so integral to the fight against injustice that we run the risk of encouraging it when we try to do away with our frustrations. Every time we conclude that reasoning is futile with a rightwing bully, we are assenting to their domination, with all its accompanying hate. And the net effect of millions of encounters like these has been to hand them the country, and with it, our norms restraining the expression of hate. Fascists dominate because they want to, and we let them, and this not only encourages their anger and aggression but infuriates their victims as well. In this way, the flight from anger has only intensified it, while polarizing the society.

But liberals embraced their passivity, along with a hedonism that sought to overcome the moral burden of responsibility through listening to their hearts. We were continually counseled we would benefit society by doing what felt good, if only we were attuned enough to what truly felt good deep inside; and that less developed people would follow, if only we led by example. But conservatives seldom followed, and as liberals withdrew from the public sphere, the right filled the void with an ever-increasing contempt for the very institutions liberals took for granted.

Yet, conservatives were also withdrawing into religion and the family, and a faith in authority[42] that would have stunned past generations. However, conservatives were not nearly so successful as liberals in getting it together in their own lives.[43] And as their more conservative values failed to prepare them for life in a post-industrial economy, and as their focus on the family left them looking callous and brutal when it came to everyone else, they projected their failures onto liberals and minorities. And the liberal withdrawal into spiritual perfectionism only fueled their rage, for it appeared bizarre and threatened their smaller worlds.

But as conservatives attacked, liberals withdrew further, which only encouraged them to attack more fiercely. It was a vicious circle that ultimately ended in vicious conservatives electing the most vicious president in history. And while liberals tended to get the healthy lives they sought, they also got a society shaped by authoritarians and oligarchs. And there was no escaping an increasingly punishing market, which at any moment could throw you on the street, and an authoritarian culture that brutalized the meek.

And it has all come to a head in the upcoming election. If liberals cannot get up off the mat and win, Republicans might dismantle the few remaining checks and balances that would allow them to be taken out of power in the future. But liberals cannot win if they refuse to fight, because in the words of Winston Churchill, "You cannot reason with a tiger, when your head is in its mouth." And having taken a few too many to the chin, perhaps we would do well to look to Rocky for inspiration. Whereas Democrats have been playing nice, Rocky was actually mustering the spirit of the downtrodden by theatrically demonstrating the arrogance of power. And while it may have made for bad boxing, it is an excellent electoral strategy, for everyone loves it when an underdog starts punching back. It is time for liberals to get up off the mat and win, and in winning to find a sense of purpose that is greater than our own petty personal struggles.

NAMING THE DRAGON AND SLAYING IT

"If names are not correct, one cannot speak smoothly and reasonably, and if one cannot speak smoothly and reasonably, affairs cannot be managed successfully. If affairs cannot be managed successfully, rites and music will not be conducted. If rites and music are not conducted, punishments will not be suitable. And if punishments are not suitable, the common people will not know what to do."

CONFUCIUS IN THE ZHU XI[44]

Perhaps the greatest mistake that was made in halting the rise of rightwing extremism was failing to call it by its true names. When confronted by orgies of hate and the praise of dictators, we called it "populism" instead of the more obvious fascism.[45] When confronted by a candidate calling on a foreign power to hack his rival, we labeled it "disloyalty" instead of the more salient treason.

We pretended things were not so bad in order to get on with our lives, but the more salient language also sounded extreme. Liberals worried about losing the center, but they were also shying away from a fight. So, journalistic standards of fairness and political norms of propriety conspired to flood us with a vacuous stream of euphemisms. We called lies "misstatements of fact," concentration camps "holding facilities," and the starvation of millions in Yemen "war crimes," instead of the more descriptive genocide.

In the process, we minimized the horrors and downplayed the

threats. The result was an endless sense of astonishment and a queasy feeling of alienation. We were surprised because we had been telling ourselves things were not so bad, alienated because we had been living a lie. And at times, the veil we drew was so thick we were simply blinded. How else to explain the virtual silence over a president bragging about making billions in arms sales to a Saudi regime that was deliberately using them to starve millions of children?

The process started many years ago when liberals began cultivating a smug sense of self-satisfaction in the face of rightwing hate. No need to debate them on social media, because "haters gonna hate;" no need to worry about the movement claiming your black president is a foreign-born Muslim, for no one will take them seriously. We convinced ourselves that anger could not bring about change, so the haters were wasting their breath, and our indignation and resistance were therefore intemperate.

So, when they stole the Supreme Court in their unprecedented refusal to even grant Merrick Garland a hearing, we simply let it go. And we did the same when they filibustered legislation, gerrymandered districts, and talked of assassinating our leaders. We let it go because we had convinced ourselves that reason and truth always win over anger and lies; and we let it go because we told ourselves things weren't so bad. Still, the problem was not simply that we were not calling things by their true names, for even when we did the language we used tended to inspire inaction. A "deliberate misstatement of facts" is the exact same thing as a lie, but lies are universally condemned as immoral. And "hate speech" might be the same as racial incitement, but incitement is cause for alarm and punishable by law. And when the words are set in a moral framework, calling things by their true names not only inspires action but is an action in itself, like the boy who disrobes the emperor by saying he is wearing no clothes.

The linguistic philosopher J.L. Austin identified a strange species of what he called *performative statements*, which are highly relevant in this regard. Making a vow or committing to marriage cannot be verified as true or false, for instance; rather, the declarations themselves are actions.[46] Austin limited this class of statements to those with clear consequences, but it can also be applied more broadly, as in the case of the congresswoman calling for impeachment. For in calling for impeachment, she is both making a statement and initiating a process. Speaking truth to power is no mere intellectual exercise, but it is all the more powerful when implicit in the truth speaking is this call to act and do what's right.

This sort of thing tends to make liberals uncomfortable. The linguist George Lakoff suggests that liberals tend to speak the language of the enlightenment, laying out the facts in neutral terms; but conservatives speak the language of marketing, moving listeners to act. Liberals tend to believe that in speaking objectively, they can initiate a debate in which reason will win. They muster their facts and studies, expecting to win over neutral swing voters. Yet, it is seldom like that in real life, where words always tell an emotional story that guides our next moves.[47]

Consider what it means to describe Trump as a tyrant. Everyone knows how tyrants behave and the damage they can do, because we have seen what happens when they head up nations and families. Tyrants try to control others but are not in control of themselves. As a result, their projects tend to end in disaster. Hence, by calling Trump a tyrant, we are not just describing his character but pointing the way to what needs to be done. It is much the same when we call him a bully. Everyone knows how bullies behave, because most of us have been bullied. We know they play dirty and make things up, and they tend to be weak inside and fall apart when stood up to. This is because their strength is based on an illusion. Hence, in labeling Trump a bully, we are not just describing him but implying what to do. And what can be said of tyrants and bullies might also be said of liars and cheats.

So, when congress finally spoke with one voice and declared the actions of Trump illegal, immoral, and unacceptable, and called for his impeachment, because it is the right thing to do, something shifted in the spirit of the nation. Suddenly, we were speaking the truth and acting accordingly, and this unified not just the resistance, but something deeper in the heart of the nation. Yet, there is so much further to go in casting out the fear that leads us to temper the language with which we seek to describe his abuses.

Karl Marx once wrote that "philosophers merely interpret the world; the point is to change it."[48] Changing the world requires that our interpretations lead to action. The language we use needs to be accurate, but it should also tell a story about what needs to be done. And it should remind us of who we are and what matters most. This is not to suggest that we should not remain open to reason, but we need to reason not just about what is true, but also what matters and what is to be done.

The tyrant and bully labels describe Trump accurately, but they also suggest a course of action. Labeling him a fascist, who is putting kids in concentration camps, while starving millions more in Yemen, tells a story about the devastation to which his administration is heading. If the labels are not right, the narrative will not make sense; if the narrative doesn't make sense, the inspiration to action will fail to materialize; if the inspiration to action fails to materialize, the cause will be lost, and ruin will ensue. Therefore, it is essential that we craft our language carefully and call these things by their true names.

TAKING THE STRUGGLE FOR FREEDOM GLOBAL

*"The spirit of democracy cannot be imposed from
without. It has to come from within."*

MAHATMA GANDHI

A couple of years back, thousands of fascists from the English Defense League marched through London, attacking and injuring
police in defense of a leader who was recently invited by Republicans
to speak before Congress. They are an anti-Muslim hate group, and
members often give the Nazi salute.[49] However, their former leader for whom they were demonstrating is popular with the American
Israel lobby, and the country whose interests they promote,[50] where
he recently toured and posed for photos with the military. Racists
from across the world have begun to unite, and as a pioneer in the
Islamophobic propaganda that fascists use to mobilize the masses,
and as the leading human rights abuser among developed democracies, Israel often finds itself at the heart of these alliances. But fascist
rage has traditionally been directed at Jews, many of whom are quite
uncomfortable with the strange new bedfellows whom their more
conservative brethren have befriended.

Consider Viktor Orban of Hungary. He is good friends with
the Prime Minister of Israel, with which he has brought his country closer. But he just ran an intensely Antisemitic campaign focused
on George Soros opening borders to Muslim refugees, in which he
counseled against "mixing colors."[51] It is much the same with what

may now be Israel's closest ally in Europe, Poland. After passing a law making it illegal to discuss the nation's role in the Holocaust, its leaders praised 60,000 white nationalists, who marched through their capital, chanting anti-Muslim and anti-Jewish slogans.[52]

But perhaps the most stunning tie has been its relationship with the Trump administration. In spite of building the premier white nationalist publication, his former strategist Steve Bannon is an ardent supporter of Israel, who describes himself as a "Christian Zionist." And conservative American Jews refuse to abandon the president because of his support for Israel, despite his rhetoric helping spur the most deadly attack against Jews in American history.

But while Israeli ties to neofascists may be alarming, they highlight the way shared hate trumps shared identities in contemporary fascist movements. British fascists may hate Poles, but they are happy to work with them when they chant about killing Muslims. Western fascists may hate communists, but they are happy to work with a former KGB chief, who has rehabilitated Stalin, while trying to bring down America and its European Union allies.[53]

And yet, the alliances among fascist fringe parties and racist states are a small part of a more malignant threat: rightwing nationalists or fascists head almost every territorially large and highly populous state, and most share an affinity for one another. It is an astonishing reversal of a world order that recently championed democracy for its role in promoting peace and prosperity. Now the institutions through which it was promoted are crumbling, along with the alliances sustaining them, and the world's most fascist states are joining together.[54]

Alliances between rightwing nationalist and fascist states are much like those between movements. They begin with leaders like Putin and Trump, Netanyahu and Bolsonaro, Johnson and Orban, expressing mutual admiration. They are reinforced with shared state visits and attacks on democratic allies, like Justin Trudeau and Angela Merkel, who are increasingly shut out of discussions. And they end in formal changes to the geopolitical order, spurred by new alliances, built by autocrats with shared affinities.

Alliances are forged in the heart and formalized in treaties.[55] They consist of a mysterious concoction of shared sentiments, cultural affinities, historical ties, trade agreements, and military pacts, and they are always up for question. Hence, fascist leaders need only highlight their shared affections and cultural similarities to pull closer together; but they can also just ignore old alliances and forge a new set. Like all things human, alliances are constantly changing.

The danger is that we might find ourselves living under a fascist world order, which incentivizes autocracy not democracy, nationalism not globalism, and competition not cooperation. Putin now stands at the center of it, contributing to fascist parties across Europe; hacking elections that might weaken the alliance; and sponsoring invasions of possible rivals.[56] China has created many of the same incentives in its sphere of influence, and Saudi Arabia and Iran are doing much the same in their own.

And this time, there is no anti-fascist alliance among powerful states to stop it.

However, a global movement for democracy is emerging as well, which is strikingly relevant to Americans, who find themselves in a limbo between tyranny and freedom, wherein we helplessly watch our democratic institutions hollowed out while life goes on as before. It is an alienating experience, because friends and family are perpetrating the institutional attacks; and it is an infuriating experience because they revel in their power and the bluntness of their attacks. But it is also a disorienting experience, because it all seems so nihilistic, irrational, nonsensical, and insane.

And so we find ourselves sharing in the experiences of people living under more oppressive tyrannies: the astonishment and bewilderment, alienation and exhaustion, guardedness and shutdown, that results from living under arbitrary and self-interested rule.[57] It is a twist of fate that has made us the allies of Palestinians fighting occupation, Hong Kongese struggling against totalitarianism, and the very refugees who are the scapegoats of fascist animus the world over, whether Assad in Syria or the Taliban in Afghanistan. And somehow, the alienation from fellow citizens and family is being transmuted into a far richer and more global solidarity through which we might find social and political redemption. It can dampen our alienation while making us stronger; provide new models while showing the meaning of sacrifice. The protesters in Sudan and Hong Kong, Palestine and Algeria, are ready to die for their freedom; and they are showing that nonviolence can work, even in the face of a genocidal power.

Consider the overthrow of Sudan's Omar Al-Bashir. Bashir held power for three decades and oversaw one of the world's most deadly conflicts in South Sudan, which killed two million and displaced another four million. He is wanted by the International Criminal Court for genocide in Darfur. And yet, protesters removed him from power, following a series of skillfully orchestrated nonviolent demonstrations. Never let it be said again that you cannot remove a genocidal leader from power through nonviolent protest. But the military took over after his fall and, armed by the Saudis and Emiratis, who are in turn armed by the Americans and British, began raping and killing protesters. And while the ultimate outcome remains unclear as this book goes to press, they removed the military from power as well.

Movements like these should inspire the resistance to bolder action everywhere.

And in the face of Israeli smears against progressives, and Russian assaults on elections, the fight against fascism must be global if it is to succeed. It must be global, because if it isn't, it will be swamped by trolls, who unite across borders, sabotaging journalists and elections alike. And it must be global, because tyrants are more restrained when the whole world is watching. A global movement can publicize the abuses of autocrats, where there is no free press, and isolate them internationally; it can share tactics and strategies and assure asylum to its persecuted leaders.

A global movement would be united in its struggle for democracy, its condemnation of corruption, and its opposition to racism and sexism. Racism is much the same in Burma and Britain, Hungary and Poland, India and China. Whereas twentieth-century fascism focused its fury on Jews, twenty-first-century fascism projects it onto Muslims. As the racism boils over, it then applies its animus to any marginalized group that stands out. And since Islamophobia is present among liberals and conservatives alike, a global movement would highlight the need to examine our own prejudices. It is much the same with the sexism from which fascists draw so much strength and the anti-black racism that divides societies like America and Brazil.

A wider movement might remind us that the desire for freedom is universal; that while the rhetoric may vary, the aspiration is primordial. And the argument is more powerful when it reaches these psychic depths. A global movement might inspire us when dictators are toppled in isolated backwaters. It might remind us we are not alone if we are defeated in one place; for freedom can never be snuffed out, because it is part of the human inheritance. Such a movement might undermine nationalism and build the kind of momentum that defeated British colonialism and Soviet totalitarianism alike.

The struggle against tyranny is much the same as that against climate change: either we unite across borders or civilization will melt away like a glacier in the sun. And there is no better time than the present, when the forces uniting us are so visceral, to build a global civil society that might take it on. In uniting in a global movement for freedom, we stake our claims as citizens of the world and build the networks needed to win the future.

Embracing global citizenship also reminds the world that nationalism is small-minded. Freedom is an open window through which we might step into a wider and more beautiful world. Its air is more inspiring when accompanied by billions of allies, and its vistas are wider when they compass the planet. The solidarity of a global movement may not compensate for the relationships lost closer to home, and it may not be a sufficient condition for winning the battle against tyranny. But it opens horizons where most are shutting down; it may be a necessity for keeping the spirit of freedom alive.

Meanwhile, the number of leaders willing to challenge the fascist excesses is few and far between, because when they do, they are punished for it. A global movement can protect the ones who stick their necks out and honor them with awards. It can transform them into heroes and assail their attackers with reason and passion and numbers. But to preserve our freedoms, we will have to fight for them, like the subjects of an autocracy, who mobilize to resist in order to survive. We are going to have to reach out to people in far and away places fighting for the same freedom. We are going to have to stand shoulder-to-shoulder on social media, as we debate with trolls over the value of democracy and human rights, and articulate the principles for which we stand. This will mean forming friendships across borders, which nourish and enrich us through the shared struggle for freedom. The brave doctors and youths of Sudan, and the Palestinians taking bullets on the border of Gaza, are now leading the world in the fight for freedom. And they are counting on us to stand in solidarity, and to remember that the fight for freedom is global, and that democracies stand or fall together. The whole world may not be watching, but we should be, and we should be linking their plight to our own.

This time the struggle against fascism will have to come from below, and it will have to be global.

GENERATING THE NEXT MORAL REVOLUTION

*"The intellectual was rejected and persecuted
at the precise moment when the facts became
incontrovertible, when it was forbidden to say that
the emperor had no clothes."*

MICHAEL FOUCAULT

Political correctness was always a dubious way of framing the effort to banish racism and sexism from the public sphere. The expression was popularized by Rush Limbaugh in the nineties and quickly became a catch-all for the effort to expand our moral horizons. It helped conservatives dismiss concern for brutalized battery hens with a wave of the hand—you are just being politically correct. It made a mockery of efforts to rein in bullying—you are just being retarded. Commentators mocked liberals for the shallow and arbitrary nature of their new codes, and the criticisms rang so true that liberals themselves often shared in the frustration. There was a grain of truth to the criticism. Liberals who were skeptical of gay marriage but a decade and a half before it became a national issue were somehow treating its opponents as pariahs; liberals who had not given a thought to transgender bathroom preferences but a few months prior to it breaking into national debate were somehow offended by those who could not care less.

The post-industrial era saw a massive expansion of moral concerns. As lower needs were increasingly satisfied, we turned to self-actualization; as we became sensitive to our own needs, we sensitized ourselves to others.[58] Suddenly, evangelicals were worried about the rights of fetuses, environmentalists about other species, and economists about ending world hunger.[59] And everywhere people experienced moral burdens they could neither comprehend nor appreciate. But new moral codes can appear arbitrary and senseless. The problem is not simply the pressure to extend the moral sphere: ethicists have always pressed us to take on more responsibilities. Rather, moral reasoning challenges us to generate moral principles that can be neutrally applied, and in thinking through their contradictions, the scope of our moral concerns is extended.[60] It is simply not possible to assert the anodyne claim that it is wrong to make someone suffer for your pleasure, for instance, without coming head-to-head with the suffering inherent to meat-eating.

The problem was that the late twentieth century brought us face-to-face with so many contradictions at once.[61] Greater numbers of people were pressed together in cities, raising the question of what we owed to strangers.[62] More cultures were coming into closer contact, raising questions about what respect they deserved.[63] Ecology and the earth sciences were demonstrating a more intimate relationship between animals and humans, begging the question of what rights they possessed.[64] Ethology was demonstrating that mammals and birds enjoy a richer emotional and social life than previously thought possible,[65] pressing us to protect their habitats. And climate scientists were telling us just about everything we do today will have ramifications deeper in the future than previously imagined, burdening us with commitments to unborn generations.[66]

The result was a revolution in ethics, of which most people remained hopelessly unaware.

Many on the left seemed to think that each new ethical challenge should be immediately taken up and that the failure to do so constituted an unforgivable moral lapse. But it was not simply a problem of the left, for conservatives did the same with fetuses, without giving much thought to the needs and aspirations of women, and the social impact of bringing a generation of unwanted children into the world. As a new breed of neoconservatives began to note, it was a moment of upheaval in which received values were being questioned across a range of subcultures with far too little reflection.[67]

Ethical extensionism was far from the most obvious solution to the tensions of the times. In fact, it was so far from obvious that liberals themselves often adopted a live and let live approach, counseling tolerance at all costs. As conflicting moral claims were pressed upon them, they declared a pox on both houses, espousing a moral relativity as contradictory as it was self-defeating. For the idea that people shouldn't exhort others to adopt their moral positions is itself a moral position that is being exhorted because it is believed to be better.[68] Contradictions like these tied liberals up in knots.

Hence, when conservatives dismissed the liberal tendency to express offense over minor episodes of political incorrectness, they found a ready audience among liberals who had themselves also been smacked down by overzealous moralists. In this way, everyone piled on against political correctness, but the real problem lay not so much with the extension of empathy and ethics, nor the conservatives who found it so offensive. Rather, it lay in the failure to explain why we had suddenly become transfixed by the rights of animals and fetuses, ecosystems and transexuals. Explaining why we had suddenly taken on so many new categories of moral concern might have laid the groundwork for a deeper moral transformation—but the issues were politicized instead.

The response was symptomatic of a deeper failure of moral reasoning. Liberals opted to condemn racism and sexism instead of spending more time explaining why it is wrong to make judgments about the accidents of birth, and conservatives condemned abortion instead of talking about the consciousness of fetuses, at least in part because they lacked the ability. Of course, there were exceptions, especially among academics and public intellectuals; but there was a noticeable decline in public reason among citizens at large.[69] We got activism instead of reason, politics instead of morality, because the cultivation of the moral imagination had ceased when education in the humanities ended.[70] And we got two separate codes associated with liberal and conservative morality and a nation divided against itself because we failed to think hard enough about the moral foundations of the rapidly changing world in which we had so recently been immersed.

But the moral degeneration implicit to fascism may soon provide another chance at laying a deeper moral foundation. Nobody before Trump thought it was acceptable to brag about the sexual violation of women or mock disabled people. No one found it acceptable to brag about their penises in public or threaten violence from the stage. No one found it acceptable to make genocidal comments about the political opposition like "the only good Democrat's a dead Democrat." And far from representing a triumph over political correctness, his victory actually highlighted the moral underpinnings of a commonly shared culture. When conservatives vowed not to vote for him, they were not being politically correct but rather morally decent. However dissimilar their politics may be from those of anti-racists, they are bound together in moral decency. And the alignment hints at the way a wider moral scope might transform the very notion of decency. What that looks like remains to be seen, but it would likely include some sort of respect for the sanctity of life and a more empathetic and dignified conversational ethic. And it would likely include some of the public norms whose undermining began with the sixties counterculture and culminated in Trump.

If the left and right come together to forge a new set of norms at the close of this fascist moment, they will simply be repeating the cycle of the fascism last time. Following the close of the Second World War, Europe was rebuilt by Christian democrats of the center and right working hand in glove with social democrats of the left. And far from simply rebuilding, together they took up the extension in ethics that had begun at the close of the First World War.[71] A time will likely emerge when we begin again to extend the range of moral concerns, and we would all do well when it arrives to find the patience to invite conservatives along for the ride.

REINVENTING THE ENLIGHTENMENT

"You need a new Enlightenment that tells you what reason is all about."

GEORGE LAKOFF, *quoted in,*
The Inner Climate: Global Warming from the Inside Out[72]

There is something sublime about gazing on the heavenly kingdom of clouds outside your window. The vast white mountains billow and roll, stretched wide before the reaches of the imagination. Inside there is a roaring, outside the refracting sun, splendorous gold and tinged with violet, as you make your way across the white-steppe of the planet. For thousands of years now, the sky has remained the terrain of the gods. We have imagined their omniscience, bowed down before their omnipotence, reasoned if we were pure enough, we might ascend to their heights. For the realm of the gods has, most of all, been thought a place of purity and serenity.

The linguist and cognitive scientist, George Lakoff, argues that morality is metaphorical. When we speak of being morally *upright*, we are speaking about an experience of being wakeful and alert, detached from work, and above everyday squabbles, as if standing tall with shoulders wide. The *high-minded* are alert and *above* the fray; people with *low* characters lie around in sloth, rolling in their own filth. *Open* minds are like wide windows through which new ideas might enter; *closed* minds are like locked doors through which nothing new passes.[73] These metaphors are formed early in life, according to Lakoff, through repeated experiences, accessible to everyone, lending them an appearance of universality—and they show up everywhere.

The European Enlightenment of the eighteenth century unknowingly used these sorts of metaphors to frame an ideal of reason. *Enlightenment Reason* sprang from the minds of Voltaire, Diderot, Jefferson, Montesquieu, Smith, Hume, Kant, and other lesser luminaries, and it imagined that through reason, we might arrive at universal ideals. Enlightenment philosophers believed in human progress and perfectibility, and they set the tone for modern life through the twentieth century. The democratic principles of Enlightenment philosophers tend to be logical and constructed like edifices, brick upon brick of reasons reaching toward the sky. We can see them at work in the *United Nations Charter* and *Declaration of Human Rights*, whose promise remains unfulfilled but whose ideals *lift us upward*. Humanity may not yet have *scaled these heights*, but still, they *press us forward*.

Metaphors show up everywhere in this conceptualization: it is *the great march of reason, pushing us onward and upward, progressing toward some higher end of history*. Enlightenment Reason pressed the peoples of Europe and the Americas to apply their ethical commitments consistently.[74] Thus, we find the extension of democratic rights from rich white men to the poor, from women to people of color. And perhaps we are seeing the faint echoes of this march of reason in marriage equality, transgender, and animal rights.

Yet, this same distance from day-to-day affairs has a murderous side as well. The God of the Hebrew Bible not only looked down upon wars and pestilence with equanimity but also commanded the Jews, in no less than five places, to commit genocide—killing every man, woman, child, and living thing. God is imagined through the Medieval Christian, St. Bernard of Clairvaux, to command the orgy of violence and cannibalism that was the Crusades.[75] The God of high places was everywhere complacently murderous, however much this may be written out of the religious doctrine handed down through the ages. And the high-minded Enlightenment was, let us not forget, a time of empire as well. The British would stand aloof, arguing over the benefits of free trade, in the 1840s, as two million Irish starved, and look away in the 1940s, as Bengalis starved. High-minded reason all too often masked the brutal incarceration of the diseased and elderly, indigent and criminal, mentally disturbed and physically disabled.[76] The dangerous skies of today, overcrowded by greenhouse gases, were no less so in the past.

And it is for just such moral failures that the left has tended to excoriate imperial reason. Postmodernists deconstructed it, feminists undermined it, conservatives abandoned it, and Wikileaks exposed it. In the aftermath of this regicide, we tend to hear in the soaring rhetoric of a president Obama less the inspiration of progress and more a cause for cynicism; and it is perhaps for this reason that the late twentieth century saw the dissolution of the old left and the rise of a cynical new spectatorial left.[77] For far beneath the heavenly kingdom of universal reason, outside the hallowed halls of the philosopher-king, war and genocide, corruption and ecocide, as if in some perennial myth of the eternal return, roll in upon us like some black tide of filth.

Following the fall of the Soviet satellites in 1989, Francis Fukuyama speculated that perhaps we had reached the end of history to which humanity had for so long aspired. For while autocracies might lag behind near the rear, and closed economies might limp along, the great train of humanity was moving in a clear direction. And while some countries, like Denmark and Sweden, might lead the way, nobody doubted that democracy was superior to autocracy and that some form of market economy was vastly more conducive to prosperity.[78]

But history is a tangled path with no clear direction. Development can be defined as an increase in integrated complexity, and it happens because the universe remembers, and humanity all the more so. And in remembering, we accumulate information, insights, capabilities, and strategies.[79] Human systems tend to grow in complexity, because they retain the memory of past experiences, and in so doing, increase their resilience.[80] But development is never guaranteed. It can take on a life of its own in runaway development. It can dissociate itself from what came before in alienated development. It can fragment in uneven development. It can become unstable and pathological, imponderably complex and prone to regression, overly burdensome and ultimately unsustainable.

Now history is breaking upon us again.

The global consciousness that so recently appeared an inevitable byproduct of globalization has increasingly come to appear utopian; and the global consensus needed to solve the great challenges of the twenty-first century, like climate change and nuclear proliferation, is coming undone amid a renewed brutality in political discourse and military battle. Inundated by complexity and swamped with information, all too many have retreated inside themselves, along with the phantasms of fascist propaganda. For in the end, we lacked the norms to guide our institutions, and found ourselves plunging down the ladder of development.

And perhaps Fukuyama was right that the greatest threat to his thesis was the perversions implicit to ressentiment, which have shaped the current era.[81]

And yet, we remain embedded in all the same institutions and symbols of an incipient global civilization. When we go online or enter the calm of an airport, when we speak about climate change or read the international news, we experience an incipient global culture, which remains in place amid these more recent convulsions. And it will continue to remain whether or not the global order falls, and isolationism overcomes our more magnanimous natures. Enlightenment Reason may have concealed a brutal imperial shadow, and its progressive logic may have proved a myth, but its deconstruction seems to have only made it more resilient.

Enlightenment values have flourished amid what should probably be dubbed *the great regression*, not simply in the private recesses of the socially advanced, but increasingly in the public sphere.[82] The battle against sexism and racism has been taken deeper within, even as it struggles without. The climate and animal rights movements go from strength to strength, even as the challenges they confront intensify. In perhaps the greatest irony of all, the rightwing nationalists have been forced to carry out their fight for the future of civilization, not in the places of their birth but rather globally. And the demographics of destiny mean that every one of their number that is buried will be replaced by another who was born and raised in a multicultural and global age.

If reason is to triumph, it will need to overcome the great dualities of nature and culture, mind and body, self and other, us and them. It will need to widen the criteria of moral inclusion to encompass animals, the disabled, and the whole of humanity, as Martha Nussbaum suggests in *Frontiers of Justice*.[83] It will need to recognize its own metaphorical structure, as is pressed by George Lakoff in his body of works on the matter.[84] It will need to embrace a wider system of thinking, as is suggested by Peter Singer, and a more ecological thinking, as pressed by Frances Moore Lappé.[85] It will need to be more global, as suggested in my work, *Convergence: The Globalization of Mind*.[86] And it will need to recognize its extraordinary achievements in peace, prosperity, and humanity, perhaps best articulated by Steven Pinker,[87] but taken on by countless others as well.[88]

The shape of a more expansive reason may be difficult to predict; the feel of a more inclusive reason may still be elusive, but the possibility of a more humane and meaningful reason is sustained by the circumstances thrusting us together. The fascism this time is not the bold vision of youth but rather the last gasp of a drowning way of life. The fascist moment will end: the only question is when—and how much it will damage in the meantime.

AFTERWARD

THE FASCIST MOMENT AND
THE FATE OF THE EARTH

*"If the experience of the Third Reich teaches us
anything, it is that a love of great music, great art,
and great literature does not provide people with
any kind of moral or political immunization against
violence, atrocity, or subservience to dictatorship."*

RICHARD J. EVANS,
The Coming of the Third Reich[1]

In the waning days of the twentieth century, a strange spasm of pessimism washed over my generation. Amid a strong economy and a global renaissance in democratization, we became overwhelmed with worries for the fate of the earth. The same globalization bringing greater prosperity and freedom was also revealing global environmental challenges for which few solutions were in sight. And the fears we felt were but a harbinger of a crisis that is fast breaking upon us.

There is a tendency to treat climate change as a proxy for a multitude of interlocking challenges like despeciation, desertification, rainforest destruction, and the death of the oceans. But there are actually several major, more human issues that tend to be overlooked as well, like world hunger, state failure, overpopulation, and nuclear proliferation. Together, they constitute a monstrous conundrum: humanity possesses neither the institutions nor the resources needed to grapple with a storehouse of troubles only a handful of people even recognize, leaving us to solve global problems at a local level; and yet, acting locally tends to inspire small-scale thinking—when what we really need is global thinking and action.

Few have given much attention to the psychological impact of looking upon a world of troubles for which there appear no solutions, with the consequence of inaction being the fate of the earth. But it is almost certainly greater than we have hitherto imagined. Environmentalists facing these threats often go through years of despair, while those who carry on are often plagued by an angst that never really passes. Meanwhile, the denial of these threats can only be maintained at the psychological cost of shutting down access to the wider world. This means turning against the scientific tools that might provide the solutions to the biggest conundrums, while shrinking into our own smaller universes, whose conditions might be more easily controlled. It is all a matter of how we manage our despair.

A peculiar set of pathologies arise in the face of impossible challenges. Organizations fall out among themselves, nations look for enemies abroad, and all too many simply drift into their own reality. Few reconcile themselves to failure while still maintaining a clear-eyed view, but taking on a world of troubles for which no solutions are in plain sight requires it.

If people tend to shrink into pathological behaviors when confronting impossible challenges, then we need to worry about another global crisis that has gone almost completely unnoticed, and that is our internal reactions to these external threats. What happens when humanity looks upon the world and stammers over challenges for which it can imagine no solutions; what changes in the structure of human societies when they gaze into the future and find only the faint outlines of the apocalypse?

Stretch your mind as you may, the world will always remain too vast to compass. But it is simply inconceivable that a globally interconnected humanity might live sustainably on a planet of which it can barely conceive. Somehow, we are tasked with wrapping our hearts and minds around a world that will never fail to leave us overwhelmed. Hence, it is little surprise that as everything about the world presses us closer together, the multitude retreat into the smaller worlds of fascism, fundamentalism, nationalism, and romanticism.

The ultimate genocide has always been that which might be waged against the human race itself. Its potential outbreak has long been present in the prospect of nuclear annihilation, but it is increasingly dormant in the possibility of catastrophic climate change as well. And the last people you want in power in such an existential crisis are those capable of casually committing genocide.[2] Not only will they carelessly set in motion catastrophic events, but they will distract us from them by unleashing repeated cycles of lesser crises, like little fires breaking out on the outskirts of a great conflagration.

And yet, the genocidal tendencies of the new rightwing nationalists are everywhere staring us in the face. Putin has leveled cities in both Chechnya and Syria. Duterte compares himself to Hitler. Trump is starving millions of children in Yemen. And most dangerous of all, Bolsonaro is threatening a genocide of native peoples in the Amazon in a drive to exploit it, which might release the final dose of emissions that would doom us all. Hence, the climate advocates are right to focus on the threat these leaders pose to all life on earth; but their link to crimes against humanity in the present is critical, and few are making it.

Trump's most horrific crimes are now hiding in Yemen. For it is in the swollen bellies and protruding heads of starving children where the mask slips, and he assumes his identity as another Hitler. And it is in the casual profiteering, which sustains the war, that the real evils of unrestrained capitalism appear most crudely. But the real danger is that the same genocidal tendencies, which formerly contributed to the extermination of this or that group, might be turned against humanity itself. While the impulse to exterminate sometimes arises out of a fear of being exterminated, it all too often springs from far less conscious and more nihilistic impulses.

And it is just these impulses, which pervade the fascism this time, that should be most worrisome.

What is needed now more than ever is the security to step back and take in the planet at a sweep and to peer generations into the future. But everything is conspiring to drive our attention into the black hole of an eternal present, inching us closer to oblivion. Humanity is now in an existential crisis over the fate of the earth, wherein the failure to act could spell the end of civilization as we know it.

We run from what we cannot understand, but if civilization is to survive, we must find a way to understand it. It is a central paradox of the age, and the failure to solve it may spell our demise. But in the end, it may not be our inability to solve these knotty conundrums that sinks us, but rather the way we react to our own shortfalls. For what at first seems impossible all too often turns out to be easy: we simply could not see a way forward until we dug a little deeper. But when we give up before we get started, escaping into a world of make-believe rather than facing reality, everything tends to fall apart.

There are countless causes for the new rightwing authoritarianism. Still, our inability to face these massive global challenges—for which economic globalization and rising rates of immigration are all too often a scapegoat—may be the most overlooked. The real problem is not living with people different from ourselves, or the financial insecurity wrought by global capital flows, though these may add to the burden of life in a complex world. Rather, it is our inability to make sense of the world itself when our very survival depends on it.

Most every adult these days can conceive of the world as a whole, and many of us even identify with it more than we do with the nations of our birth. But few are capable of thinking about global challenges like climate change with the same kind of comprehensive balance that we apply to more national problems, say, the national debt or health care. There are just too many variables, contributing to too many ill effects, spread across too many places, affecting too many people. Thus, when we think about climate change, it tends to appear far too big to grasp; and in our failure to make sense of it, we come to treat it as an apocalyptic force over which we can exert no influence. It is the same with many global challenges, and all of them put together are all the more overwhelming.

If we are to live well in a globalized world, then we must learn to think globally. Otherwise, we will find ourselves continually confronted by problems we cannot understand, and the world itself will seem an incomprehensible mystery with which we cannot cope. The retreat in the smaller world of fascist nationalism is merely a symptom of this bigger problem of living in a global civilization in which the greatest challenges we face are playing out on a far more vast and interrelated field.

And yet, rumors of the apocalypse, to paraphrase Mark Twain, have been greatly exaggerated. Every few years or so, someone somewhere sets a date for the end of the world, and every few years or so, that day comes and goes like every other. Nevertheless, there is a growing sense of alarm among the most educated and prescient that human civilization may finally be unraveling.

The world is probably in worse shape today than at any time since the Second World War. There are arguably more groups engaged in genocide, more states collapsing, and more democracies degenerating than there have been in generations. Meanwhile, the world is confronting a planetary plague that has collapsed the global economy. And it is all made worse by the fact that the international organizations whose work for peace and human rights we so recently took for granted have been crippled by a rising tide of rightwing nationalism and fascism, which pits each nation against the rest in a Darwinian struggle that might easily spiral into a third and final world war.

It is quite possible we have reached the high watermark of a growing fascist tide, and everything will start to look better tomorrow. But it is also possible we are witnessing the perfect storm to which human civilization itself might finally succumb, for the twenty-first century was always going to be difficult, given the twin challenges of climate change and the prospect of feeding more than ten billion people. Now with the coming to power of rightwing nationalists and fascists in each of the world's biggest states, except Muslim Indonesia, things just got harder.

Humanity has long been dogged by the idea that human civilization might simply unravel,[3] but we stammer at the thought of what that might mean. The idea is a bit like death itself. There could be nothing more predictable than that life would end in death, and yet few of us can imagine its appearance until it arrives at our doorstep and takes us unaware. Still, human civilization is so much bigger than ourselves, and the idea of its collapse so abstract, that talk of what it means quickly takes us into the realm of myth, where grand metanarratives might better summarize where we have come from than where we are going.

It is an understandable response to want to summarize something so vast as the world in which you live, but little is so dangerous as this drift into fantasy in a moment of crisis.

Everything human is prone to collapse, so the idea that human civilization itself might simply fall apart is merely a consequence of its nature. But few can face this brutal logic—and those who can tend to be so mesmerized by its implications as to become incapable of thinking much else. And it is this sense of being transfixed by our imminent demise where our thinking about the end times can truly become pathological. The worry that human civilization will collapse is common in times of great change, when social bonds have come undone and it is difficult to tell what will set things right. At such times, we tend to experience ourselves either as the puppets of some great conspiracy or else the playthings of fate.

And everywhere, we find the oscillating extremes of frenetic activity and passive acquiescence.

Nothing is more common at such times than to retreat into smaller worlds. Either we long for escape into a romantic past when everything was simpler, and people relied on the land for sustenance, or else project ourselves forward into some fantasized utopia where the real world evaporates amid the march of technological progress. Each aspiration offers the same result: an escape from present-day challenges through the illusion of some timeless desideratum. But where eco-romantics and techno-optimists look to their respective pasts and futures, fascists generate myths of an eternal present, dissolving the messiness of the real world in a welter of lies.

Fascists rely on the kind of big lies propagated by Vladimir Putin and Donald Trump, for they shield them from complexity and the unraveling of the world. But if fascism is an effort to escape the complexity of the present, its power lies in its apparent realism. The fascist imagines himself facing hard realities, trimming the fat, muscling up for a fight. But it is an illusion based on a set of lies so poorly fitted to reality that the fascist fails at every turn. In place of the real world, the fascist creates a fantasy and retreats into the herd, whose myths and lies send them hurtling toward a precipice. Witness the United States today, which at the time this book goes to press is experiencing its worst pandemic since 1918, its worst economic depression since 1933, its worst civil unrest since 1968, and its worst leadership in its long and colorful history.

And yet, all too many leftists are also embroiled in romantic delusions and absurd conspiracies, reactive hatreds and support for genocidal dictators, like Putin and Assad. Both the pathological left and the fascist right are responding to a real world over which they feel themselves possessing little control. But whereas the right tends to organize around the protection of the status quo, the left is united around a vision of justice and social progress, which might reweave the fabric of a tattered civilization.

The left believes the world can be made better and that everyone can live in dignity if only we could enact the right laws and build the right institutions. And while the history of the left is riddled with the wreckage of genocidal dystopias, like Stalinist Russia and Pol Pot's Cambodia, liberals and leftists have also built the most successful states in history in Scandinavia and Northern Europe. And they have continually pressed America to be better and to include more.

The question that remains, then, is how the left might regain its footing and move forward while the world itself is falling apart. The momentum is probably to be found less in policy and more in the right attitude and ethos. In the words of philosopher Richard Rorty, the left needs to achieve "the promise of our country"—and this requires that it develop a positive vision of where we are going and how it might be achieved.[4]

Almost everyone is overwhelmed by the world today, and almost everyone seems to be retreating into smaller worlds. Hence, the challenge lies in overcoming our pathological responses to collapse and taking up the call to action with unity and a sense of purpose. The world might be won by whichever side can face the crisis with equanimity and a positive vision of the future. It will require renouncing lazy reactions and tired old formulas; and we will have to think hard about the kinds of compromises needed to join hands across racial, ethnic, religious, national, and ideological bounds.

And if halting the regression to fascism requires that we think more broadly and feel more deeply for a wider range of beings, then there is a intersection between our internal and external freedom. For defeating fascism may mean freeing ourselves from the grip of all the petty forces that keep us living in smaller worlds. What is asked of us, in other words, is quite literally that we learn to live large, and, in so doing, open up the space in which others might do the same—until each of us learns to live well in the more rarefied air of the great wide open.

THEO HORESH
Leeds, United Kingdom

BIBLIOGRAPHY - BOOKS

Abouzeid, Rania. No Turning Back: Life, Loss, and Hope in Wartime Syria. W.W. Norton and Company. 2019.

Acemoglu, Daron and Robinson, James. *Why Nations Fail: The Origins of Power, Prosperity, and Poverty.* Currency. 2013.

Acemoglu, Daren and Robinson, James A. *The Narrow Corridor: States, Societies, and the Fate of Liberty.* Penguin Press. 2019.

Ackerman, Bruce and Ayres, Ian. *Voting With Dollars: A New Paradigm for Campaign Finance.* Yale University Press. 2004.

Adorno, Theodore W. *The Authoritarian Personality.* Harper and Row. 1950.

Akerlof, George A. and Shiller, Robert J. *Animal Spirits: How Human Psychology Drives the Economy, and Why It Matters for Global Capitalism.* Princeton University Press. 2010.

Aly, Gotz. *Hitler's Beneficiaries: Plunder, Racial War, and the Nazi Welfare State.* Verso. 2016.

Anderson, Benedict. *Imagined Communities: Reflections on the Origin and Spread of Nationalism.* Verso. 1983.

Appiah, Kwame Anthony. *Cosmopolitanism: Ethics in a World of Strangers.* W.W. Norton and Company. 2007.

Applebaum, Anne. *Red Famine: Stalin's War on Ukraine.* Penguin Books. 2018.

Arendt, Hannah. *The Origins of Totalitarianism.* Harcourt, Inc. 1966.

Arendt, Hannah. *Eichmann in Jerusalem: A Report on the Banality of Evil.* Viking. 1968.

Armstrong, Karen. *The Case for God.* Anchor. 2010.

Aristotle and Sinclair, T.R. trans. *The Politics.* Penguin Classics. 1981.

Aristotle and Thomson, J.A.K. trans. *The Nicomachean Ethics.* Penguin Classics. 2004.

Armstrong, Karen. *A History of God: The 4,000-Year Quest of Judaism, Christianity, and Islam.* Ballantine Books. 1994.

Austin, J.L. *How to Do Things with Words.* Oxford University Press. 1962.

Baer, Elizabeth. *The Genocidal Gaze: From German Southeast Africa to the Third Reich.* Wayne State University Press. 2017.

Barzun, Jacques. *From Dawn to Decadence: 1500 to the Present, 500 Years of Western Cultural Life.* Harper Perennial. 2001.

Bates, Robert H. *When Things Fell Apart: State Failure in Late-Century Africa.* Cambridge University Press. 2015.

Baudrillard, Jean. *America.* Verso. 2010.

Bauman, Zygmunt. *Liquid Modernity.* Polity Press. 2000.

Bauman, Zygmunt. *Liquid Times: Living in an Age of Uncertainty.* Polity. 2006.

Baumol, William J. *The Free market Innovation Machine: Analyzing the Growth Miracle of Capitalism.* Princeton University Press. 2002.

Beck, Don and Cowan, Christopher C. *Spiral Dynamics: Mastering*

Values, Leadership, and Change. Blackwell Publishing Ltd. 1996

Beck, Ulrich. *World Risk Society.* Polity Press. 1999.

Beck, Ulrich. *Cosmopolitan Vision.* Polity Press. 2006.

Becker, Ernest. *The Denial of Death.* The Free Press. 1973.

Bellamy, Alex J. *World Peace: And How We Can Achieve It.* Oxford University Press. 2019.

Bell, Daniel. *The Coming of Postindustrial Society: A Venture in Social Forecasting.* Basic Books. 1973.

Benkler, Yochai. *The Penguin and the Leviathan: How Cooperation Triumphs Over Self-Interest.* Crown Business. 2011.

Berlin, Isaiah. *Four Essays on Liberty.* Oxford University Press. 1990.

Boorstin, Daniel J. *The Americans: The Democratic Experience.* Vintage. 1974.

Boucek, Christopher and Ottawa, Marina. *Yemen on the Brink.* Brookings Institution Press. 2010.

Bremmer, Ian. *Every Nation for Itself: Winners and Loser in a G-Zero World.* Penguin Books. 2013.

Broome, John. *Climate Matters: Ethics in a Warming World.* W.W. Norton and Company. 2012.

Browning Christopher. *Ordinary Men: Reserve Police Battalion 101 and the Final Solution in Poland.* Northwestern University Press. 1991.

Burke, Edmund. *Reflections on the Revolution in France.* J. Dodsley in Pall Mall. 1790.

Campbell, Joseph and Moyers, Bill. *The Power of Myth.* Anchor. 1991.

Campbell, Joseph. *The Hero's Journey: Joseph Campbell on His Life and Work.* New World Library. 2014.

Carlin, Dan. *The End is Always Near.* William Collins Books. 2019.

Chandler, David. *Peacebuilding: The Twenty Years' Crisis, 1997–2017.* Palgrave Macmillan. 2017.

Cicero and Walsh, P.G. *On Obligations.* Oxford University Press. 2008.

Cohen, G.A. *Karl Marx's Theory of History.* Princeton University Press. 2000.

Cohn, Norman. *The Pursuit of the Millennium: Revolutionary Millenarians and Mystical Anarchists of the Middle Ages.* Paladin. 1972.

Collier, Paul. *Exodus: How Migration is Changing the World.* Oxford University Press. 2015.

Confucius. *The Analects.* Penguin Classics. 1998.

Connerton, Paul. *How Modernity Forgets.* Cambridge University Press. 2009.

Dahl, Robert. *On Democracy.* Yale University Press. 2000.

Darwin, John. *After Tamerlane: The Rise and Fall of Global Empires, 1400–2000.* Bloomsbury Press. 2009.

De Botton, Allan. *Status Anxiety.* Vintage. 2005.

De Soto, Hernando. *The Mystery of Capital. Why Capitalism Triumphs in the West and Fails Everywhere Else.* Basic Books. 2003.

Debord, Guy. *Society of the Spectacle.* MIT Press. 1967.

Derrida, Jacques and Spivak, Gayatri Chakravorty trans. *Of Gram-*

matology. Johns Hopkins University Press. 2016.

Dewey, John. *Democracy and Education: An Introduction to the Philosophy of Education.* Free Press. 1916.

Dewey, John. *The Quest for Certainty: A Study of the Relation of Knowledge and Action.* Kessinger Publishing. 1929.

Diamond, Jared. *The Third Chimpanzee: On the Evolution and Future of the Human Animal.* Harper Collins. 1992.

Diamond, Jared. *Evolution and the Future of the Human Animal.* Harper Perennial. 2006

Diamond, Larry. *The Spirit of Democracy: The Struggle to Build Free Societies Throughout the World.* Henry Holt and Company. 2008.

Diamond, Larry. *Ill Winds: Saving Democracy from Russian Rage, Chinese Ambition, and American Complacency.* Penguin Press. 2019.

Dikotter, Frank. *Mao's Great Famine: The History of China's Most Devastating Catastrophe, 1958–1962.* Walker and Company. 2010.

Dikotter, Frank. *The Cultural Revolution: A People's History, 1962–1976.* Bloomsbury Paperbacks. 2017.

Dimitrov, Georgi. *Selected Works, Vol. 2.* Sofia Press. 1972.

Dionne, E.J. Jr. and Ornstein, Norman J. et al. *One Nation After Trump.* St. Martin's Press. 2017.

Dobbins, James and Jones, Seth G. *The UN's Role in Nation-Building: From Congo to Iraq.* Rand Corporation. 2005.

Doyle, Michael. *Ways of War and Peace: Realism, Liberalism, and Socialism.* W.W. Norton and Company. 1997.

Doyle, Michael. *Making War and Building Peace: United Nations*

Peace Operations. Princeton University Press. 2006.

Doyle, Michael. *Liberal Peace: Selected Essays.* Routledge. 2012.

Drucker, Peter. *Innovation and Entrepreneurship.* Butterworth Heinemann. 1985.

Drucker, Peter. *Post-Capitalist Society.* Harper Business. 1993.

Duggan, Christopher. *Fascist Voices: An Intimate History of Mussolini's Italy.* Vintage. 2013.

Eagleton, Terry. *On Evil.* Yale University Press. 2011.

Eatwell, Roger and Goodwin, Matthew. *National Populism: The Revolt Against Liberal Democracy.* Penguin Random House. 2018.

Elias, Norbert. *The Civilizing Process: Sociogenetic and Psychogenetic Investigations.* Basil Blackwell Ltd. 1982.

Evans, Richard J. *The Coming of the Third Reich: How the Nazis Destroyed Democracy and Seized Power in Germany.* Penguin. 2004.

Ferriss, Timothy. *The 4-Hour Workweek: Escape 9–5, Live Anywhere and Join the New Rich.* Crown Publishers. 2007.

Finkelstein, Norman G. *The Holocaust Industry: Reflections on the Exploitation of Jewish Suffering.* Verso. 2015.

Fogel, Robert W. *The Fourth Great Awakening: And the Future of Egalitarianism.* University of Chicago Press. 2000.

Foucault, Michael. *Madness and Civilization: A History of Insanity in the Age of Reason.* Random House, Inc. 1965.

Frank, Thomas. *What's the Matter with Kansas: How Conservatives Won the Heart of America.* Picador. 2005.

Frank, Thomas. *Listen, Liberal: Or, Whatever Happened to the Party of the People?* Picador. 2017.

Franklin, Benjamin. *The Autobiography of Benjamin Franklin.* J.P. Lippincott and Company. 1868.

Friere, Paolo and Ramos, Myra Bergman. *Pedagogy of the Oppressed.* Continuum International Publishing Group Ltd. 2001.

Freud, Sigmund. *Civilization and Its Discontents.* Internationaler Psychoanalytischer Verlag. 1930.

Fritzsche, Peter. *Life and Death in the Third Reich.* Belknap Press. 2008.

Fritzsche, Peter. *An Iron Wind: Europe Under Hitler.* Basic Books. 2016.

Fromm, Erich. *Escape from Freedom.* Farrar and Rinehart. 1941.

Fukuyama, Francis. *The End of History and the Last Man.* The Free Press. 1992.

Fukuyama, Francis. *Trust: The Social Virtues and the Creation of Prosperity.* The Free Press. 1996.

Fukuyama, Francis. *The Great Disruption: Human Nature and the Reconstitution of Social Order.* Profile Books Ltd. 2006.

Gandesha, Samir. *Spectres of Fascism: Historical, Theoretical, and International Perspectives.* Pluto Press. 2020.

Gay, Peter. *Weimar Culture: The Outsider as Insider.* W.W. Norton and Company. 1968.

Gardiner, Stephen M. *The Perfect Moral Storm: The Ethical Tragedy of Climate Change.* Oxford University Press. 2013.

Gessen, Masha. *The Future is History: How Totalitarianism Reclaimed Russia.* Granta Books. 2017.

Ghemawat, Pankaj. *World 3.0: World Prosperity and How to Achieve It*. Harvard Business Review Press. 2011.

Giddens, Anthony. *Modernity and Self-Identity: Self and Society in the Late Modern Age*. Polity Press. 1991.

Giddens, Anthony. *The Consequences of Modernity*. Stanford University Press. 1991.

Goldhagen, Daniel Jonah. *Worse Than War: Genocide, Eliminationism, and the Ongoing Assault on Humanity*. Public Affairs. 2009.

Goodhart, David. *The Road to Somewhere: The Populist Revolt and the Future of Politics*. C. Hurst and Co. Publishers. 2017.

Gordon, John Steele. *An Empire of Wealth: The Epic History of American Economic Power*. Harper Perennial. 2005.

Greene, Joshua. *Moral Tribes: Emotion, Reason, and the Gap Between Us and Them*. Atlantic Books. 2015.

Griffin, Roger. *The Nature of Fascism*. Routledge. 1993.

Griffin, Roger. *Modernism and Fascism: The Sense of Beginning Under Mussolini and Hitler*. Palgrave Macmillan. 2007.

Grossman, Dave. *On Killing: The Psychological Cost of Learning to Kill in War*. Back Bay Books. 2009.

Gutmann, Amy. *Democratic Education. Princeton* University Press. 1999.

Haas, Richard. *A World in Disarray: American Foreign Policy and the Crisis of the Old Order*. Penguin Books. 2017.

Habermas, Jurgen. *The Theory of Communicative Action: Reason and the Rationalization of Society*. Beacon Press. 1984.

Habermas, Jurgen. *Legitimation Crisis.* Beacon Press. 1975.

Habermas, Jurgen and McCarthy, Thomas trans. *Communication and the Evolution of Society.* Beacon Press. 1979.

Habermas, Jurgen. *The Philosophical Discourse of Modernity.* Polity Press. 1990

Habermas, Jurgen. *Between Facts and Norms.* Polity Press. 1996.

Haidt, Jonathan. *The Righteous Mind: Why Good People Are Divided By Politics and Religion.* Vintage Books. 2013.

Hamilton, Alexander and Madison, James, et al. *The Federalist Papers.* Penguin Classics. 1987.

Harding, Luke. *Collusion: How Russia Helped Trump Win the House.* Guardian Faber Publishing. 2017.

Harvey, David. *A Brief History of Neoliberalism.* Oxford University Press. 2007.

Hastings, Adrian. *The Construction of Nationhood: Ethnicity, Religion, and Nationalism.* Cambridge University Press. 1997.

Hayek, Friedrich A. *The Road to Serfdom.* Routledge Press. 1944.

Hedges, Chris. *American Fascists: The Christian Right and the War on America.* Free Press. 2008.

Hegel, G.W.F. *Introduction to the Philosophy of History.* Hackett Publishing Company. 1988.

Held, David. *Cosmopolitanism: Ideals and Realities.* Polity Press. 2010.

Herman, Judith L. *Trauma and Recovery: The Aftermath of Violence—From Domestic Abuse to Political Terror.* Basic Books. 1992.

Hobsbawm, Eric. *The Age of Extremes: A History of the World, 1914–1991.* Vintage. 1996.

Hochschild, Arlie Russell. *Strangers in Their Land: Anger and Mourning on the American Right.* The New Press. 2018.

Hoffer, Eric. *The Passionate State of Mind: And Other Aphorisms.* Hopewell Publications. 1954.

Hoffer, Eric. *The Ordeal of Change.* Hopewell Publications, Llc. 1963.

Hoffer, Eric. *The True Believer: Thoughts on the Nature of Mass Movements.* Perennial. 1966.

Hofstadter, Richard. *Anti-Intellectualism in American Life.* Vintage Books. 1962.

Horesh, Theo. *Convergence: The Globalization of Mind.* Bauu Institute. 2014.

Horesh, Theo. *The Inner Climate: Global Warming from the Inside Out.* Bauu Institute. 2016.

Horesh, Theo. *The Holocausts We All Deny.* Bauu Institute Press. 2018.

Horkheimer, Max. *Eclipse of Reason.* Oxford University Press. 1947.

Houellebecq, Michel. *Submission: A Novel.* Picador. 2016.

Howe, Neil and Strauss, William. *Millennials Rising: The Next Great Generation.* Vintage Books. 2000.

Hume, David. *An Enquiry Concerning the Principle of Morals.* Hackett Publishing Company. 1983.

Huntington, Samuel P. *Political Order in Changing Societies.* Yale

University Press. 1956.

Huntington, Samuel P. *The Third Wave: Democratization in the Late Twentieth Century.* University of Oklahoma Press. 1993.

Ikenberry, John G. Liberal Leviathan: *The Origins, Crisis, and Transformation of the American World Order.* Princeton University Press. 2012.

Ingelhart, Ronald F. *Modernization, Cultural Change, and Democracy: The Human Development Sequence.* Cambridge University Press. 2005.

Inglehart, Ronald F. *Cultural Evolution: People's Motivations are Changing, and Reshaping the World.* Cambridge University Press. 2018.

Jamieson, Dale. *Reason in a Dark Time: Why the Struggle Against Climate Change Failed and What It Means for Our Future.* Oxford University Press. 2014.

Johnson, Paul. *A History of the American People.* HarperCollins Publishers. 1998

Joyce, James. *Ulysses.* Shakespeare and Company. 1922.

Judah, Tim. *In Wartime: Stories from Ukraine.* Penguin Books. 2016.

Judis, John B. *The Populist Explosion: How the Great Recession Transformed American and European Politics.* Columbia Global Reports. 2016.

Judt, Tony. *Postwar: A History of Europe Since 1945.* Penguin Books. 2006.

Kagan, Robert. *The Jungle Grows Back: America and Our Imperiled World.* Vintage Books. 2019.

Kaldor, Mary. *Global Civil Society: An Answer to War.* Polity Press. 2003.

Kant, Immanuel and Gregor, Mary et al. trans. *Groundwork of the Metaphysic of Morals*. Cambridge University Press. 2012.

Kasparov, Garry. *Winter is Coming: Why Vladimir Putin and the Enemies of the Free World Must Be Stopped*. Atlantic Books. 2016.

Kedourie, Elie. *Nationalism*. Hutchinson. 1960.

Kegan, Robert. *The Evolving Self: Problem and Process in Human Development*. Harvard University Press. 1982.

Keneally, Thomas. *Three Famines: Starvation and Politics*. Public Affairs. 2011.

Kenny, Charles. *Getting Better: Why Global Development Is Succeeding—And How We Can Improve the World Even More*. Basic Books. 2011.

Keohane, Robert O. *After Hegemony: Cooperation and Discord in the World Political Economy*. Princeton University Press. 2005.

Kershaw, Ian. *The Hitler Myth: Image and Reality in the Third Reich*. Oxford University Press. 2001.

Kershaw, Ian. *To Hell and Back: Europe, 1914–1949*. Penguin. 2016.

Kessler, Glenn and The Washington Post Fact Checker Staff. *Donald Trump and His Assault on Truth: The President's Falsehoods, Misleading Claims, and Flat-Out Lies*. Scribner. 2020.

Keynes, John Maynard. *The Economic Consequences of the Peace*. Penguin Classics. 1995.

Khalidi, Rashid. *The Iron Cage: The Story of the Palestinian Struggle for Statehood*. Beacon Press. 2007.

Kimmerling, Baruch and Migdal, Joel S. *The Palestinian People: A History*. Harvard University Press. 2003.

Kirchick, James. *The End of Europe: Dictators, Demagogues, and the Coming Dark Age.* Yale University Press. 2017.

Kirk, Russell. *The Conservative Mind: From Burke to Eliot.* Gateway Editions. 2001.

Kissinger, Henry. *World Order: Reflections on the Character of Nations and the Course of History.* Penguin Books. 2015.

Klemperer, Victor. *The Language of the Third Reich.* Bloomsbury Academic. 2013.

Krastev, Ivan. *Democracy Disrupted: The Politics of Global Protest.* University of Pennsylvania Press. 2014.

Krastev, Ivan. *After Europe.* University of Pennsylvania Press. 2017.

Kristol, Irving. *Reflections of a Neoconservative.* Basic Books. 1983.

Kurlantzick, Joshua. *Charm Offensive: How China's Soft Power is Transforming the World.* Yale University Press. 2008.

Lackner, Helen. *Yemen in Crisis: The Road to War.* Verso. 2019.

Lakoff, George and Johnson, Mark. *Metaphors We Live By.* University of Chicago Press. 1980.

Lakoff, George. *Moral Politics: How Liberals and Conservatives Think.* University of Chicago Press. 1996.

Lakoff, George. *Don't Think of an Elephant: Know Your Values and Frame the Debate.* Chelsea Green Publishing. 2014.

Lappé, Frances Moore. *EcoMind: Changing the Way We Think, to Create the World We Want.* Perseus Books. 2011.

Lasch, Christopher. *The Culture of Narcissism: American Life in an Age of Diminishing Expectations.* W.W. Norton and Company. 1979.

Lessig, Lawrence. *Republic Lost 2.0.* Machete Book Group. 2015.

Levitsky, Steven and Ziblatt, Daniel. *How Democracies Die.* Broadway Books. 2019.

Lilla, Mark. *The Once and Future Liberal.* Harper Collins, Inc. 2017.

Locke, John. *A Letter Concerning Toleration.* Hackett Publishing Company. 1983.

Lukács, George. *History and Class Consciousness: Studies in Marxist Dialectics.* The Merlin Press Ltd. 1975.

MacIntyre, Alisdair. *After Virtue: A Study in Moral Theory.* University of Notre Dame Press. 1984.

Mann, Michael. *Fascists.* Cambridge University Press. 2004.

Marcuse, Herbert. *One-Dimensional Man: Studies in the Ideology of Advanced Industrial Society.* Beacon Press. 1964.

Marx, Karl. *The Eighteenth Brumaire of Louis Bonaparte.* International. 1969.

Marx, Karl and Engels, Fredrick. *The Economic and Philosophic Manuscripts and the Communist Manifesto.* Prometheus Books. 1988.

Marx, Karl and Engels, Friedrich. *The German Ideology.* Prometheus Books. 1998.

Marx, Karl. *Capital: Volume 1.* Penguin Classics. 1990.

Marx, Karl and Engels, Friedrich. *The Communist Manifesto.* Penguin Classics. 2002.

Massumi, Brian. *A User's Guide to Capitalism and Schizophrenia: Deviations from Deleuze and Guattari.* MIT Press. 1992.

McLuhan, Marshall. *Understanding Media: The Extensions of Man.* Routledge. 1964.

McNeill, William H. *Keeping Together in Time: Dance and Drill in Human History.* Harvard University Press. 1995.

Mead, Margaret. *Coming of Age in Samoa: A Psychological Study of Primitive Youth for Western Civilization.* William Morrow and Company. 1930.

Mead, Walter Russell. *Power, Terror, Peace, and War: America's Grand Strategy in a World at War.* Vintage Books. 2005.

Mearsheimer, John J. *The Tragedy of Great Power Politics.* W.W. Norton and Company. 2003.

Mearsheimer, John J. and Walt, Stephen M. *The Israel Lobby and U.S. Foreign Policy.* Penguin Books. 2008.

Mearsheimer, John. *The Great Delusion: Liberal Dreams and International Realities.* Yale University Press. 2018.

Metzl, Jonathan M. *Dying of Whiteness: How the Politics of Radical Resentment is Killing America's Heartland.* Basic Books. 2019.

Mill, John Stuart. *On Liberty.* Hackett Publishing Company. 1978.

Mill, John Stuart. *Utilitarianism.* Hackett Publishing Company, Inc. 2001.

Mindell, Arnold. *Sitting in the Fire: Large Group Transformation Using Conflict and Diversity.* Deep Democracy Exchange. 1995.

Mishra, Pankaj. *The Age of Anger: A History of the Present.* Picador. 2018.

Montaigne, Michele de and Screech, M.A. trans. *The Essays: A Selection.* Penguin Classics. 1994.

Morris, Benny. *Righteous Victims: A History of the Zionist-Arab Conflict, 1881–2001.* Vintage. 2001.

Mounk, Yascha. *The People vs. Democracy: Why Our Freedom is in Danger and How to Save It.* Harvard University Press. 2018.

Müller, Jan Werner. *What is Populism?* University of Pennsylvania Press. 2016.

Myers, Steven Lee. *The New Tsar: The Rise and Reign of Vladimir Putin.* Simon and Schuster. 2016

Murray, Charles. *Coming Apart: The State of White America: 1960–2010.* Crown Publishing Group. 2012.

Murray, Douglas. *The Strange Death of Europe: Immigration, Identity, Islam.* Bloomsbury Continuum. 2017.

Nathan, Stoltzfus. *Hitler's Compromises: Coercion and Consensus in Nazi Germany.* Yale University Press. 2016.

Nietzsche, Friedrich and Scarpitti, Michael A. trans. *On the Genealogy of Morals.* Penguin Classics. 2013.

Nussbaum, Martha. *Frontiers of Justice: Disability, Nationality, Species Membership.* Belknap Press. 2007.

Nussbaum, Martha. *Not for Profit: Why Democracy Needs the Humanities.* Princeton University Press. 2010.

Nussbaum, Martha. *Creating Capabilities: The Human Development Approach.* Belknap Press. 2013.

Nussbaum, Martha. *Anger and Forgiveness: Resentment, Generosity, and Justice.* Oxford University Press. 2016.

Nussbaum, Martha C. *The Cosmopolitan Tradition: A Noble but Flawed Ideal.* Harvard University Press. 2019.

Nye Jr., Joseph S. *Soft Power: The Means to Success in World Politics.* Public Affairs. 2005.

Ostrovsky, Arkady. *The Invention of Russia: The Journey from Gorbachev's Freedom to Putin's War.* Atlantic Books. 2016.

Paris, Roland. *At War's End: Building Peace After Civil Conflict.* Cambridge University Press. 2004.

Passmore, Kevin. *Fascism: A Very Short Introduction.* Oxford University Press. 2014.

Paxton, Robert O. *The Anatomy of Fascism.* Penguin. 2005.

Pappé, Ilan. *The Ethnic Cleansing of Palestine.* Oneworld Publications. 2007.

Payne, Stanley G. *A History of Fascism, 1914–1945.* University of Wisconsin Press. 1995.

Pearlman, Wendy. *We Crossed a Bridge and It Trembled: Voices from Syria.* Custom House. 2018.

Peter, Laurence J. and Hull, Raymond. *The Peter Principle: Why Things Always Go Wrong.* Pan Books. 1971.

Peterson, Jordan B. *12 Rules for Life: An Antidote to Chaos.* Random House. 2018.

Piketty, Thomas and Goldhammer, Arthur trans. *Capital in the Twenty-First Century.* Belknap Press. 2014.

Pinker, Steven. *The Better Angels of Our Nature: Why Violence Has Declined.* Penguin Books. 2012.

Pitzer, Andrea. *One Long Night: A Global History of Concentration Camps.* Back Bay Books. 2017.

Plato. *The Republic.* Penguin Classics. 2007.

Polakow-Saransky, Sasha. *Go Back to from Where You Came: The Backlash Against Immigration and the Fate of Western Democracy.* Nation Books. 2017.

Pomerantsev, Peter. *Nothing is True and Everything is Possible: Adventures in Modern Russia.* Faber and Faber. 2017.

Power, Samantha. *A Problem from Hell: America and the Age of Genocide.* Basic Books. 2013.

Proudhon, P.J. *General Idea of the Revolution in the Nineteenth Century.* University Press of the Pacific. 2004.

Putnam, Robert D. *Bowling Alone: The Collapse and Revival of American Community.* Simon and Schuster. 2000.

Putnam, Robert D. *E Pluribus Unum: Diversity and Community in the Twenty-First Century.* Johan Skytte Prize Lecture. 2006.

Rajan, Menon and Rumer, Eugene B et al. *Conflict in Ukraine: The Unwinding of the Post-Cold War Order.* MIT Press. 2015.

Rand, Ayn. *The Virtue of Selfishness.* Ayn Rand. 1961.

Rawls, John. *A Theory of Justice.* Belknap Press. 1971.

Rawls, John. *Political Liberalism.* Columbia University Press. 1993.

Reich, Wilhelm. *The Mass Psychology of Fascism.* Mary Boyd Higgins. 1946.

Ridley, Jasper. *Mussolini.* Constable. 1997.

Rodrik, Dani. *The Globalization Paradox: Democracy and the Future of the World Economy.* W.W. Norton and Company. 2012.

Rolston III, Holmes. *A New Environmental Ethics: The Next Millen-*

nium for Life on Earth. Routledge. 2011.

Rorty, Richard. *Achieving Our Country: Leftist Thought in Twenti-eth-Century America.* Harvard University Press. 1999.

Rousseau, Jean Jacques. *Emilé, or on Education.* Penguin Classics. 1991.

Rousseau, Jean Jacques. *Discourse on the Origin of Inequality.* Hackett Publishing Company. 2012.

Sachs, Jeffrey. *The End of Poverty: Economic Possibilities of Our Times.* Penguin Books. 2006.

Said, Edward W. *The Question of Palestine.* Vintage Books. 1992.

Saleh, Yassin Al-Haj. *Impossible Revolution: Making Sense of the Syrian Tragedy.* C. Hurst and Co. 2017.

Sandel, Michael. *What Money Can't Buy: The Moral Limits of Markets.* Farrar, Straus, and Giroux. 2013.

Scanlon, T.M. *What We Owe to Each Other.* Harvard University Press. 2000.

Schelling, Thomas C. *The Strategy of Conflict.* Harvard University Press. 1960.

Scott, Walter. *The Lay of the Last Minstrel.* Franklin Classics. 2018.

Scruton, Roger. *The Meaning of Conservatism.* Macmillan. 1980.

Sen, Amartya. *Development as Freedom.* Anchor. 2000.

Singer, Peter. *Expanding the Circle: Ethics, Evolution, and Moral Progress.* Princeton University Press. 1981.

Singer, Peter. *One World: The Ethics of Globalization.* Yale University Press. 2004.

Sisk, Timothy. *State Building*. Polity. 2013.

Slaughter, Anne-Marie. *A New World Order.* Princeton University Press. 2004.

Smith, Adam. *Wealth of Nations*. Oxford University Press. 2008.

Smith, Adam. *The Theory of Moral Sentiments*. Penguin Classics. 2010.

Snyder, Timothy. *Bloodlands: Europe Between Hitler and Stalin*. Vintage Books. 2010.

Snyder, Timothy. *On Tyranny: Twenty Lessons from the Twentieth Century.* Bodley Head. 2017.

Snyder, Timothy. *The Road to Unfreedom: Russia, Europe, America.* Tim Duggan Books. 2018.

Sowell, Thomas. *A Conflict of Visions: Ideological Origins of Political Struggles.* Basic Books. 1987.

Stanley, Jason. *How Fascism Works: The Politics of Us and Them.* Random House. 2018.

Stiglitz, Joseph. *Globalization and Its Discontents.* W.W. Norton and Company. 1994.

Stoltenberg, John. *Refusing to be a Man: Essays on Sex and Justice.* Plume. 1990.

Stone, Christopher D. *Earth and Other Ethics: The Case for Moral Pluralism.* Harper and Row. 1987.

Sunstein, Cass. *Infotopia: How Many Minds Produce Knowledge.* Oxford University Press. 2008.

Sunstein, Cass R. *Can It Happen Here?: Authoritarianism in America.* Dey Street Books. 2018.

Takaki, Ronald. *A Different Mirror: A History of Multicultural America*. Back Bay Books. 2008.

Tamir, Yael. *Why Nationalism*. Princeton University Press. 2019.

Taylor, Charles. *A Secular Age*. Belknap Press. 2018.

Tilly, Charles. *Coercion, Capital, and European States: A.D. 990 to 1990*. Wiley-Blackwell. 1993.

Tocqueville, Alexis de and Bevan, Gerald. *Democracy in America*. Penguin Classics. 2003.

Traverso, Enzo. *The New Faces of Fascism: Populism and the Far Right*. Verso. 2019.

Turner, Frederick Jackson. *The Significance of the Frontier in American History*. Martino Fine Books. 2014.

Van Dam, Nikolaos. *The Struggle for Power in Syria: Politics and Society Under Asad and the Ba'ath Party*. I.B. Taurus. 2011.

Vance, J.D. *Hillbilly Elegy: A Memoir of a Family and Culture in Crisis*. HarperCollins Publishers, Inc. 2016.

Veblen, Thorstein. *Theory of the Leisure Class*. Macmillan. 1899.

Waal, Frans de. *The Age of Empathy: Nature's Lessons for a Kinder Society*. Three Rivers Press. 2009.

Weber Eugen. *Varieties of Fascism*. Van Nostrand Reinhold Inc. 1964.

Whitman, Walt. *Democratic Vistas and Other Papers*. Franklin Classics. 2018.

Wilber, Ken. *Sex, Ecology, Spirituality: The Spirit of Evolution*. Shambhala Publications, Inc. 1995.

Wilber, Ken. *Integral Psychology: Consciousness, Spirit, Psycholo-*

gy, Therapy. Shambhala Publications, Inc. 2000.

Wilber, Ken. *Trump and a Post-Truth World.* Shambhala Publications, Inc. 2017.

Wilkinson, Richard and Pickett, Kate. *The Spirit Level: Why Greater Equality Makes Societies Stronger.* Bloomsbury Press. 2009.

Will, George. *The Conservative Sensibility.* Hachette Books. 2020.

Wilson, James Q. *The Moral Sense.* The Free Press. 1993.

Wright, Robert. *Nonzero: The Logic of Human Destiny.* Vintage Books. 2001.

Wu, Tim. *The Master Switch: The Rise and Fall of Information Empires.* Atlantic Books. 2012

Yassin-Kassab, Robin and Al-Shami, Leila. *Burning Country: Syrians in Revolution and War.* Pluto Press. 2016.

Yunus, Muhammad. *A World Without Poverty: Social Business and the Future of Capitalism.* Public Affairs. 2005.

Zakaria, Fareed. *The Future of Freedom: Illiberal Democracy at Home and Abroad.* W.W. Norton and company. 2007.

Zakaria, Fareed. *In Defense of a Liberal Education.* W.W. Norton and Company. 2015.

Zhu Xi and Nguyen Due Lan trans. *Explanation of the Four Books.* Vietnam Culture and Publishing House. 1998.

Zinn, Howard. *A People's History of the United States.* HarperCollins Publishers. 1980.

ARTICLES AND INSTITUTIONAL STATEMENTS

Allen, Kate. *Raqqa is in ruins like a modern Dresden. This is not 'precision' bombing.* The Guardian. May 2019.

Almosawa, Shuaib and Fahim, Kareem. *Airstrikes in Yemen Hit Wedding Party, Killing Dozens.* The New York Times. September 28, 2015.

American Heritage. *Dictionary of the English Language, Fifth Edition.* Houghton Mifflin. 2015.

Associated Press in Cetinje. *Montenegro ratifies Nato membership in historic shift to western alliance.* The Guardian. April 28, 2017.

Blake, Aaron. *'The only good Democrat is a dead Democrat.' 'When the looting starts, the shooting starts.' Twice in 25 hours, Trump tweets conspicuous allusions to violence.* The Washington Post. May 2020.

Brown, John. *Supreme Court Rules Against Exposing Israel's Role in Bosnian Genocide.* 972 Magazine. December 2016.

Browning, Christopher R. *The Suffocation of Democracy.* The New York Review of Books. October 2018.

Chin, Josh and Bürge, Clément. *Twelve Days in Xinjiang: How China's Surveillance State Overwhelms Daily Life.* The Wall Street Journal. December 2017.

Cortellessa, Eric. *Why Are Pro-Israel Groups Boosting a Far-Right, Anti-Muslim U.K. Extremist?* The Times of Israel. January 24, 2019.

Csaky, Zselyke. *Nations in Transition 2020: Dropping the Democratic Facade.* Freedom House. 2020.

Dunst, Charles. *Israel's Shameful Role in Myanmar's Genocidal Campaign Against Rohingya.* Haaretz. December 2019.

Food and Agricultural Organization of the United Nations. *FAO warns of rapidly deteriorating food security in Yemen.* January 28, 2016.

Freedom House. *Freedom in the World 2017: Freedom Decline Continues Amid Rising Populism and Autocracy.* January 2017.

Flynn, Meagan. *Detained migrant children got no toothbrush, no soap, no sleep. It's no problem, government argues.* The Washington Post. June 21, 2019.

Gettleman, Jeffrey. *Rohingya Recount Atrocities: 'They Threw My Baby Into a Fire.* The New York Times. October 2017.

Haag, Matthew. *Thousands of Immigrant Children Said They Were Sexually Abused in U.S. Detention Centers, Report Says.* The New York Times. February 27, 2019.

Helm, Sara. *"Will he lose his leg?": Thousands of Gaza protesters facing life-altering injuries from Israeli high-velocity bullets.* The Independent. Love 11, 2018.

Hubbard Ben. *U.S. Fingerprints on Obliterating Yemen's Economy.* The New York Times. November 13, 2016.

Human Rights Watch. *'All of My Body Was Pain:' Sexual Violence against Rohingya Women and Girls in Burma.* November 2017.

Itkowitz, Colby. *1 in every 4 circuit court judges is now a Trump appointee.* The Washington Post. December 21, 2019.

Legum, Judd. *9 terrifying things Trump has said about nuclear weapons.* Think Progress. August 2016.

Matthews, Dylan. *I asked 5 fascism experts whether Donald Trump is a fascist. Here's what they said.* Vox. May 2016.

Mitchell, Anna and Diamond, Larry. *China's Surveillance State Should Scare Everyone.* The Atlantic. February 2018.

Moraes, Claude. *The Far Right is Organized and Growing: Those Nazi Salutes are Serious.* The Guardian. June 14, 2018.

Mukherjee, Mayuri. *How Israel made friends in India.* Jerusalem Post. October 2018.

Open Democracy. *Jair Bolsonaro accused of inciting genocide before the International Criminal Court.* November 2019.

Oxfam International. *Oxfam Condemns Coalition Bombing of a Warehouse Containing Vital Humanitarian Aid.* April 18, 2015.

Pompa, Cynthia. *Immigrant Kids Keep Dying in CBP Detention Centers, and DHS Won't Take Accountability.* American Civil Liberties Union. June 24, 2019.

Pasha-Robinson, Lucy. *Donald Trump appears to shove world leader out of the way at Nato summit.* The Independent. May 25, 2017.

Pils, Eva and Zhang, Taisu, et al. *China's New Age of Fear.* Foreign Policy. February 2018.

Qin, Amy. *In China's crackdown on Muslims, children have not been spared.* The New York Times. February. 2020.

Rappleye, Hannah and Seville, Lisa Riordan. *24 migrants have died in ICE custody during administration.* NBC News. June 9. 2019.

Reuters. *Philippines president Roderigo Duterte likens himself to Hitler.* The Guardian. September 30, 2016.

Save the Children. *Starvation in Yemen: 85,000 Children May Have Died of Hunger.* November 21, 2018.

Scruton, Roger. *The Limits of Liberty.* The American Spectator. December 2008.

Stephen, Chris. *Gaddafi Files Show Evidence of Murderous Intent.* The Guardian. June 2011.

Stewart, Phil and Strobel, Warren. *U.S. to halt some arms sales to Saudi, citing civilian deaths in Yemen campaign.* Reuters. December 13, 2016.

Stockholm International Peace Research Institute. *World Military Expenditure Grows 1.8 Trillion in 2018.* April 29, 2019.

Stockholm International Peace Research Institute. *Nuclear weapon modernization continues but the outlook for arms control is bleak.* June 2020.

Sullivan, Eileen. *Trump Questions the Core of Nato: Mutual Defense, Including Montenegro.* The New York Times. July 18, 2018.

Taylor, Matthew. *"White Europe": 60,000 Nationalists March on Poland's Independence Day.* The Guardian. November 12, 2017.

Tharoor, Ishaan. *Before and after images reveal the huge destruction in Mosul.* The Washington Post. July 2017.

Tharoor, Ishaan. *Netanyahu and Orban Meet in Summit of Illiberal Nationalists.* The Washington Post. July 19, 2018.

Transparency International. *Corruption Perceptions Index.* 2016.

United Nations High Commissioner for Refugees. *Global forced dis-*

placement vastly more widespread in 2019. 2020.

United Nations Office for the Coordination of Humanitarian Affairs. *Yemen: We Are Losing the Fight Against Famine.* Sept. 21, 2018.

Walker, Shaun. *Alleged Russian spies sentenced to jail over Montenegro "coup plot."* The Guardian. May 9, 2019.

The Carter Center. *Countering the Islamophobia Industry: Toward More Effective Strategies.* May 2018.

The Washington Post. *The Mueller Report.* Scribner. 2019

Way, Lucan Ahmed and Casey, Adam. *Russia has been meddling in foreign elections for decades. Has it made a difference?* The Washington Post. January 8, 2018.

Wayne, Carly and Valentino, Nicholas et al. *How Sexism Drives Support for Donald Trump.* The Washington Post. October 2016.

Yasir, Sameer et al. *Inside Kashmir, Cut Off from the World: 'A Living Hell' of Anger and Fear.* The New York Times. August 2019.

Zengerle, Patricia. *Defying Congress, Trump sets $8 billion-plus in weapons sales to Saudi, UAE.* Reuters. May 24, 2019.

ENDNOTES

SPECIAL THANKS

1 Passmore, Kevin. *Fascism: A Very Short Introduction.* Oxford University Press. 2014.

2 Tocqueville, Alexis de and Bevan, Gerald. *Democracy in America.* Penguin Classics. 2003.

PROLOGUE

1 Burke, Edmund. *Reflections on the Revolution in France.* J. Dodsley in Pall Mall. 1790.

2 Fritzsche, Peter. *Life and Death in the Third Reich.* Belknap Press. 2008.

3 Arendt, Hannah. *Eichmann in Jerusalem: A Report on the Banality of Evil.* Viking. 1968.

4 Blake, Aaron. *'The only good Democrat is a dead Democrat.' 'When the looting starts, the shooting starts.' Twice in 25 hours, Trump tweets conspicuous allusions to violence.* The Washington Post. May 2020.

5 Kershaw, Ian. *The Hitler Myth: Image and Reality in the Third Reich.* Oxford University Press. 2001.

6 Browning Christopher. *Ordinary Men: Reserve Police Battalion 101 and the Final Solution in Poland.* Northwestern University Press. 1991.

7 Snyder, Timothy. *On Tyranny: Twenty Lessons from the Twentieth Century.* Bodley Head. 2017.

8 Sunstein, Cass R. *Can It Happen Here?: Authoritarianism in America.* Dey Street Books. 2018.

9 Rorty, Richard. *Achieving Our Country: Leftist Thought in Twentieth Century America.* Harvard University Press. 1999.

10 Eatwell, Roger and Goodwin, Matthew. *National Populism: The Revolt Against Liberal Democracy.* Penguin Random House. 2018.

[11] Fritzsche, Peter. *An Iron Wind: Europe Under Hitler.* Basic Books. 2016.

[12] Runciman, David. *How Democracy Ends.* Profile Books. 2017.

[13] Diamond, Larry. *Ill Winds: Saving Democracy from Russian Rage, Chinese Ambition, and American Complacency.* Penguin Press. 2019.

[14] Reich, Wilhelm. *The Mass Psychology of Fascism.* Mary Boyd Higgins. 1946.

[15] Fromm, Erich. *Escape from Freedom.* Farrar and Rinehart. 1941.

[16] Matthews, Dylan. *I asked 5 fascism experts whether Donald Trump is a fascist. Here's what they said.* Vox. May 2016.

[17] Müller, Jan Werner. *What is Populism?* University of Pennsylvania Press. 2016.

[18] Diamond, Larry. *Ill Winds: Saving Democracy from Russian Rage, Chinese Ambition, and American Complacency.* Penguin Press. 2019; Levitsky, Steven and Ziblatt, Daniel. *How Democracies Die.* Broadway Books. 2019; Mounk, Yascha. *The People vs. Democracy: Why Our Freedom is in Danger and How to Save It.* Harvard University Press. 2018.

[19] Blake, Aaron. *'The only good Democrat is a dead Democrat.' 'When the looting starts, the shooting starts.' Twice in 25 hours, Trump tweets conspicuous allusions to violence.* The Washington Post. May 2020.

[20] Browning, Christopher R. *The Suffocation of Democracy.* New York Review of Books. October 2018; Snyder, Timothy. *On Tyranny: Twenty Lessons from the Twentieth Century.* Bodley Head. 2017.

[21] Van Dam, Nikolaos. *The Struggle for Power in Syria: Politics and Society Under Asad and the Ba'ath Party.* I.B. Taurus. 2011.

[22] Saleh, Yassin Al-Haj. *Impossible Revolution: Making Sense of the Syrian Tragedy.* C. Hurst and Co. 2017.

[23] Yassin-Kassab, Robin and Al-Shami, Leila. *Burning Country: Syrians in Revolution and War.* Pluto Press. 2016.

24 Paxton, Robert O. *The Anatomy of Fascism*. Penguin. 2005.

25 Browning, Christopher R. *The Suffocation of Democracy*. The New York Review of Books. October 2018; Snyder, Timothy. *On Tyranny: Twenty Lessons from the Twentieth Century*. Bodley Head. 2017.

26 Matthews, Dylan. *I asked 5 fascism experts whether Donald Trump is a fascist. Here's what they said*. Vox. May 2016.

27 Dimitrov, Georgi. *Selected Works, Vol. 2*. Sofia Press. 1972.

28 Griffin, Roger. *The Nature of Fascism*. Routledge. 1993.

29 Paxton, Robert O. *The Anatomy of Fascism*. Penguin. 2005.

INTRODUCTION

1 Marx, Karl. *The Eighteenth Brumaire of Louis Bonaparte*. International. 1969.

2 Payne, Stanley G. *A History of Fascism, 1914–1945*. University of Wisconsin Press. 1995.

3 Paxton, Robert O. *The Anatomy of Fascism*. Penguin. 2005.

4 Duggan, Christopher. *Fascist Voices: An Intimate History of Mussolini's Italy*. Vintage. 2013; Ridley, Jasper. *Mussolini*. Constable. 1997.

5 Evans, Richard J. *The Coming of the Third Reich: How the Nazis Destroyed Democracy and Seized Power in Germany*. Penguin. 2004.

6 Fromm, Erich. *Escape from Freedom*. Farrar and Rinehart. 1941.

7 Paxton, Robert O. *The Anatomy of Fascism*. Penguin. 2005.

8 Tamir, Yael. *Why Nationalism*. Princeton University Press. 2019.

9 Mann, Michael. *Fascists*. Cambridge University Press. 2004.

10 Kershaw, Ian. *The Hitler Myth: Image and Reality in the Third Reich*. Oxford University Press. 2001.

11 Stanley, Jason. *How Fascism Works: The Politics of Us and Them*. Random House. 2018.

12 Baudrillard, Jean. *America*. Verso. 2010.

13 Dionne, E.J. Jr. and Ornstein,

Norman J. et al. *One Nation After Trump*. St. Martin's Press. 2017; Harding, Luke. *Collusion: How Russia Helped Trump Win the House*. Guardian Faber Publishing. 2017; Snyder, Timothy. *The Road to Unfreedom: Russia, Europe, America*. Tim Duggan Books. 2018.

14 Mann, Michael. *Fascists*. Cambridge University Press. 2004; Payne, Stanley G. *A History of Fascism, 1914–1945*. University of Wisconsin Press. 1995; Paxton, Robert O. *The Anatomy of Fascism*. Penguin. 2005; Griffin, Roger. *The Nature of Fascism*. Routledge. 1993.

15 Passmore, Kevin. *Fascism: A Very Short Introduction*. Oxford University Press. 2014; Weber Eugen. *Varieties of Fascism*. Van Nostrand Reinhold Inc. 1964.

16 Haidt, Jonathan. *The Righteous Mind: Why Good People are Divided By Politics and Religion*. Vintage Books. 2013.

17 Stanley, Jason. *How Fascism Works: The Politics of Us and Them*. Random House. 2018.

18 Paxton, Robert O. *The Anatomy of Fascism*. Penguin. 2005.

19 Burke, Edmund. *Reflections on the Revolution in France*. J. Dodsley in Pall Mall. 1790.

20 Hayek, Friedrich A. *The Road to Serfdom*. Routledge Press. 1944.

21 Judis, John B. *The Populist Explosion: How the Great Recession Transformed American and European Politics*. Columbia Global Reports. 2016; Müller, Jan Werner. *What is Populism?* University of Pennsylvania Press. 2016.

22 Fromm, Erich. *Escape from Freedom*. Farrar and Rinehart. 1941.

23 Stanley, Jason. *How Fascism Works: The Politics of Us and Them*. Random House. 2018.

24 Snyder, Timothy. *The Road to Unfreedom: Russia, Europe, America*. Tim Duggan Books. 2018.

25 Gessen, Masha. *The Future is History: How Totalitarianism Reclaimed Russia*. Granta Books. 2017.

26 Runciman, David. *How Democracy Ends*. Profile Books. 2017.

[27] Horesh, Theo. *Convergence: The Globalization of Mind.* Bauu Institute. 2015.

SECTION I

THIS IS HOW FASCISM COMES TO AMERICA

[1] Hobsbawm, Eric. *The Age of Extremes: A History of the World, 1914–1991.* Vintage. 1996.

[2] Keynes, John Maynard. *The Economic Consequences of the Peace.* Penguin Classics. 1995.

[3] Fromm, Erich. *Escape from Freedom.* Farrar and Rinehart. 1941.

[4] Weber Eugen. *Varieties of Fascism.* Van Nostrand Reinhold Inc. 1964.

[5] Evans, Richard J. *The Coming of the Third Reich: How the Nazis Destroyed Democracy and Seized Power in Germany.* Penguin. 2004.

[6] Ridley, Jasper. *Mussolini.* Constable. 1997.

[7] Myers, Steven Lee. *The New Tsar: The Rise and Reign of Vladimir Putin.* Simon and Schuster. 2016; Ostrovsky, Arkady. *The Invention of Russia: The Journey from Gorbachev's Freedom to Putin's War.* Atlantic Books. 2016.

[8] Kasparov, Garry. *Winter is Coming: Why Vladimir Putin and the Enemies of the Free World Must Be Stopped.* Atlantic Books. 2016.

[9] Gessen, Masha. *The Future is History: How Totalitarianism Reclaimed Russia.* Granta Books. 2017.

[10] Kershaw, Ian. *To Hell and Back: Europe, 1914–1949.* Penguin. 2016.

[11] Hoffer, Eric. *The True Believer: Thoughts on the Nature of Mass Movements.* Perennial. 1966.

[12] Paxton, Robert O. *The Anatomy of Fascism.* Penguin. 2005.

[13] Snyder, Timothy. *Bloodlands: Europe Between Hitler and Stalin.* Vintage Books. 2010.

[14] Hoffer, Eric. *The Passionate State of Mind: And Other Aphorisms.* Hopewell Publications. 1954.

[15] Confucius. *The Analects.*

Penguin Classics. 1998.

[16] Yassin-Kassab, Robin and Al-Shami, Leila. *Burning Country: Syrians in Revolution and War.* Pluto Press. 2016.

[17] Muller, Jan-Werner. *What is Populism?* Penguin Press. 2017.

[18] Stanley, Jason. *How Fascism Works: The Politics of Us and Them.* Random House. 2018.

[19] Gandesha, Samir. *Spectres of Fascism: Historical, Theoretical, and International Perspectives.* Pluto Press. 2020.

[20] Traverso, Enzo. *The New Faces of Fascism: Populism and the Far Right.* Verso. 2019.

[21] Payne, Stanley G. *A History of Fascism, 1914–1945.* University of Wisconsin Press. 1995.

[22] Eatwell, Roger and Goodwin, Matthew. *National Populism: The Revolt Against Liberal Democracy.* Penguin Random House. 2018; Griffin, Roger. *The Nature of Fascism.* Routledge. 1993; Payne, Stanley G. *A History of Fascism, 1914–1945.* University of Wisconsin Press. 1995; Paxton, Robert O. *The Anatomy of Fascism.* Penguin. 2005.

[23] Paxton, Robert O. *The Anatomy of Fascism.* Penguin. 2005.

[24] Judt, Tony. *Postwar: A History of Europe Since 1945.* Penguin Books. 2006.

[25] Darwin, John. *After Tamerlane: The Rise and Fall of Global Empires, 1400–2000.* Bloomsbury Press. 2009.

[26] Finkelstein, Norman G. *The Holocaust Industry: Reflections on the Exploitation of Jewish Suffering.* Verso. 2015.

[27] Browning Christopher. *Ordinary Men: Reserve Police Battalion 101 and the Final Solution in Poland.* Northwestern University Press. 1991.

[28] Power, Samantha. *A Problem from Hell: America and the Age of Genocide.* Basic Books. 2013.

[29] Horesh, Theo. *The Holocausts We All Deny.* Bauu Institute Press. 2018.

[30] Gottfried, Paul. *Fascism: The Career of a Concept.* Northern Illinois University Press. 2017.

[31] Paxton, Robert O. *The Anatomy*

of Fascism. Penguin. 2005.

[32] Snyder, Timothy. *On Tyranny: Twenty Lessons from the Twentieth Century.* Bodley Head. 2017.

[33] Mann, Michael. *Fascists.* Cambridge University Press. 2004.

[34] Reich, Wilhelm. *The Mass Psychology of Fascism.* Mary Boyd Higgins. 1946.

[35] Arendt, Hannah. *The Origins of Totalitarianism.* Harcourt, Inc. 1966.

[36] Griffin, Roger. *The Nature of Fascism.* Routledge. 1993.

[37] Mishra, Pankaj. *The Age of Anger: A History of the Present.* Picador. 2018.

[38] Stanley, Jason. *How Fascism Works: The Politics of Us and Them.* Random House. 2018.

[39] Browning, Christopher R. *The Suffocation of Democracy.* New York Review of Books. October 2018; Snyder, Timothy. *On Tyranny: Twenty Lessons from the Twentieth Century.* Bodley Head. 2017.

[40] Evans, Richard J. *The Coming of the Third Reich: How the Nazis Destroyed Democracy and Seized*

Power in Germany. Penguin. 2004.

[41] Snyder, Timothy. *On Tyranny: Twenty Lessons from the Twentieth Century.* Bodley Head. 2017.

[42] Klemperer, Victor. *The Language of the Third Reich, pg.15.* Bloomsbury Academic. 2013.

[43] Duggan, Christopher. *Fascist Voices: An Intimate History of Mussolini's Italy.* Vintage. 2013; Ridley, Jasper. *Mussolini.* Constable. 1997.

[44] Adorno, Theodore W. *The Authoritarian Personality.* Harper and Row. 1950.

[45] Paxton, Robert O. *The Anatomy of Fascism.* Penguin. 2005.

[46] Sen, Amartya. *Development as Freedom.* Anchor. 2000.

[47] Huntington, Samuel P. *Political Order in Changing Societies.* Yale University Press. 1956; Mill, John Stuart. *On Liberty.* John W. Parker and Son. 1859.

[48] Hoffer, Eric. *The Ordeal of Change.* Hopewell Publications, Llc. 1963.

[49] Joyce, James. *Ulysses.*

Shakespeare and Company. 1922.

[50] Mead, Margaret. *Coming of Age in Samoa: A Psychological Study of Primitive Youth for Western Civilization.* William Morrow and Company. 1930.

[51] Gay, Peter. *Weimar Culture: The Outsider as Insider.* W.W. Norton and Company. 1968.

[52] Barzun, Jacques. *From Dawn to Decadence: 1500 to the Present, 500 Years of Western Cultural Life.* Harper Perennial. 2001.

[53] Burke, Edmund. *Reflections on the Revolution in France.* J. Dodsley in Pall Mall. 1790.

[54] Weber Eugen. *Varieties of Fascism.* Van Nostrand Reinhold Inc. 1964.

[55] Gay, Peter. *Weimar Culture: The Outsider as Insider.* W.W. Norton and Company. 1968.

[56] Evans, Richard J. *The Coming of the Third Reich: How the Nazis Destroyed Democracy and Seized Power in Germany.* Penguin. 2004.

[57] Gessen, Masha. *The Future is History: How Totalitarianism Reclaimed Russia.* Granta Books. 2017.

[58] Peterson, Jordan B. *12 Rules for Life: An Antidote to Chaos.* Random House. 2018.

[59] Stoltenberg, John. *Refusing to be a Man: Essays on Sex and Justice.* Plume. 1990.

[60] Mishra, Pankaj. *The Age of Anger: A History of the Present.* Picador. 2018.

[61] Saleh, Yassin Al-Haj. *Impossible Revolution: Making Sense of the Syrian Tragedy.* C. Hurst and Co. 2017.

[62] Reich, Wilhelm. *The Mass Psychology of Fascism.* Mary Boyd Higgins. 1946.

[63] Inglehart, Ronald F. *Cultural Evolution: People's Motivations are Changing, and Reshaping the World.* Cambridge University Press. 2018.

[64] Arendt, Hannah. *The Origins of Totalitarianism.* Harcourt, Inc. 1966.

[65] Confucius. *The Analects.* Penguin Classics. 1998.

[66] Burke, Edmund. *Reflections on the Revolution in France.* J. Dodsley in Pall Mall. 1790.

[67] Arendt, Hannah. *The Origins of Totalitarianism.* Harcourt, Inc. 1966.

[68] Frank, Thomas. *What's the Matter with Kansas: How Conservatives Won the Heart of America.* Picador. 2005.

[69] Debord, Guy. *Society of the Spectacle.* MIT Press. 1967.

[70] Griffin, Roger. *Modernism and Fascism: The Sense of Beginning Under Mussolini and Hitler.* Palgrave Macmillan. 2007.

[71] Hochschild, Arlie Russell. *Strangers in Their Land: Anger and Mourning on the American Right.* The New Press. 2018.

[72] Mishra, Pankaj. *The Age of Anger: A History of the Present.* Picador. 2018.

[73] Marx, Karl and Engels, Fredrick. *The Economic and Philosophic Manuscripts and the Communist Manifesto.* Prometheus Books. 1988.

[74] Fromm, Erich. *Escape from Freedom.* Farrar and Rinehart. 1941.

[75] Hoffer, Eric. *The True Believer: Thoughts on the Nature of Mass Movements.* Perennial. 1966.

[76] Fromm, Erich. *Escape from Freedom.* Farrar and Rinehart. 1941.

[77] Becker, Ernest. *The Denial of Death.* The Free Press. 1973.

[78] Freud, Sigmund. *Civilization and Its Discontents.* Internationaler Psychoanalytischer Verlag. 1930.

[79] Hoffer, Eric. *The True Believer: Thoughts on the Nature of Mass Movements.* Perennial. 1966.

[80] Bauman, Zygmunt. *Liquid Times: Living in an Age of Uncertainty.* Polity. 2006.

[81] Scruton, Roger. *The Limits of Liberty.* The American Spectator. December 2008.

[82] Freud, Sigmund and Reddick, John trans. *Beyond the Pleasure Principle: and Other Writings.* Penguin Modern Classics. 2003.

[83] Freud, Sigmund. *Civilization and Its Discontents.* Internationaler Psychoanalytischer Verlag. 1930.

[84] Kristol, Irving. *Reflections of a Neoconservative.* Basic Books. 1983.

85 Fogel, Robert W. *The Fourth Great Awakening: And the Future of Egalitarianism.* University of Chicago Press. 2000.

86 Wilber, Ken. *Sex, Ecology, Spirituality: The Spirit of Evolution.* Shambhala Publications, Inc. 1995.

87 Bell, Daniel. *The Coming of Postindustrial Society: A Venture in Social Forecasting.* Basic Books. 1973.

88 Drucker, Peter. *Post-Capitalist Society.* Harper Business. 1993.

89 Kristol, Irving. *Reflections of a Neoconservative.* Basic Books. 1983.

90 Putnam, Robert D. *Bowling Alone: The Collapse and Revival of American Community.* Simon and Schuster. 2000; Murray, Charles. *Coming Apart: The State of White America: 1960–2010.* Crown Publishing Group. 2012.

91 Lasch, Christopher. *The Culture of Narcissism: American Life in an Age of Diminishing Expectations.* W.W. Norton and Company. 1979.

92 Barzun, Jacques. *From Dawn to Decadence: 1500 to the Present, 500 Years of Western Cultural Life.* Harper Perennial. 2001.

93 Rousseau, Jean Jacques. *Discourse on the Origin of Inequality.* Hackett Publishing Company. 2012.

94 Kedourie, Elie. *Nationalism.* Hutchinson. 1960.

95 Anderson, Benedict. *Imagined Communities: Reflections on the Origin and Spread of Nationalism.* Verso. 1983

96 Lakoff, George and Johnson, Mark. *Metaphors We Live By.* University of Chicago Press. 1980.

97 Derrida, Jacques and Spivak, Gayatri Chakravorty trans. *Of Grammatology.* Johns Hopkins University Press. 2016; Foucault, Michael. *Madness and Civilization: A History of Insanity in the Age of Reason.* Random House, Inc. 1965.

98 Aristotle and Sinclair, T.R. Trans. *The Politics.* Penguin Classics. 1981.

99 Boorstin, Daniel J. The Americans: *The Democratic*

Experience. Vintage. 1974; Johnson, Paul. *A History of the American People.* HarperCollins Publishers. 1998; Gordon, John Steele. *An Empire of Wealth: The Epic History of American Economic Power.* Harper Perennial. 2005.

100 Zinn, Howard. *A People's History of the United States.* HarperCollins Publishers. 1980.

101 Rand, Ayn. *The Virtue of Selfishness.* Ayn Rand. 1961.

102 Aristotle and Sinclair, T.R. Trans. *The Politics.* Penguin Classics. 1981.

103 Habermas, Jurgen. *Between Facts and Norms.* Polity Press. 1996.

104 Giddens, Anthony. *Modernity and Self-Identity: Self and Society in the Late Modern Age.* Polity Press. 1991.

105 Giddens, Anthony. *The Consequences of Modernity.* Stanford University Press. 1991.

106 Burke, Edmund. *Reflections on the Revolution in France.* J. Dodsley in Pall Mall. 1790; Will, George F. *Statecraft as Soulcraft:*

What Government Does. Simon and Schuster. 1984.

107 Scruton, Roger. *The Meaning of Conservatism.* Macmillan. 1980.

108 Habermas, Jurgen. *Legitimation Crisis.* Beacon Press. 1975.

109 Aristotle and Sinclair, T.R. Trans. *The Politics.* Penguin Classics. 1981.

110 Habermas, Jurgen. *The Theory of Communicative Action: Reason and the Rationalization of Society.* Beacon Press. 1984.

111 Fromm, Erich. *Escape from Freedom.* Farrar and Rinehart. 1941.

112 Horesh, Theo. *Convergence: The Globalization of Mind.* Bauu Institute. 2015.

113 Habermas, Jurgen. *Between Facts and Norms.* Polity Press. 1996.

114 Fromm, Erich. *Escape from Freedom.* Farrar and Rinehart. 1941.

SECTION II

THE MORAL ORDER
HAS BEEN INVERTED

[1] Arendt, Hannah. *The Origins of Totalitarianism.* Harcourt, Inc. 1966.

[2] Scott, Walter. *The Lay of the Last Minstrel.* Franklin Classics. 2018.

[3] Lakoff, George. *Moral Politics: How Liberals and Conservatives Think.* University of Chicago Press. 1996.

[4] Mill, John Stuart. *Utilitarianism.* Hackett Publishing Company, Inc. 2001.

[5] Rawls, John. *A Theory of Justice.* Belknap Press. 1971.

[6] Taylor, Charles. *A Secular Age.* Belknap Press. 2018.

[7] Fukuyama, Francis. *Trust: The Social Virtues and the Creation of Prosperity.* The Free Press. 1996; Putnam, Robert. *Bowling Alone: The Collapse and Revival of American Community.* Simon and Schuster. 2001.

[8] Scanlon, T.M. *What We Owe to Each Other.* Harvard University Press. 2000.

[9] Rawls, John. *A Theory of Justice.* Belknap Press. 1971.

[10] Beitz, Charles. *Political Theory and International Relations.* Princeton University Press. 1979.

[11] Sowell, Thomas. *A Conflict of Visions: Ideological Origins of Political Struggles.* Basic Books. 1987.

[12] Burke, Edmund. *Reflections on the Revolution in France.* J. Dodsley in Pall Mall. 1790.

[13] Will, George. *The Conservative Sensibility.* Hachette Books. 2020.

[14] Rawls, John. *Political Liberalism.* Columbia University Press. 1993.

[15] Eagleton, Terry. *On Evil.* Yale University Press. 2011.

[16] Fritzsche, Peter. *Life and Death in the Third Reich.* Belknap Press. 2009; Nathan, Stoltzfus. *Hitler's Compromises: Coercion and Consensus in Nazi Germany.* Yale University Press. 2016.

[17] Fromm, Erich. *Escape from Freedom.* Farrar and Rinehart. 1941.

[18] Zubok, Vladislov M. *A Failed Empire: The Soviet Union in the Cold War from Stalin to Gorbachev.* University of North Carolina Press. 2007.

[19] Dionne Jr., E.J. and Ornstein, Norman J. et al. *One Nation After Trump: A Guide for the Perplexed, the Disillusioned, the Desperate, and the Not-Yet Deported.* St. Martin's Griffin. 2018; Frank, Thomas. *Listen, Liberal: Or, Whatever Happened to the Party of the People?* Picador. 2017.

[20] Hochschild, Arlie Russell. *Strangers in Their Land: Anger and Mourning on the American Right.* The New Press. 2018; Vance, J.D. *Hillbilly Elegy: A Memoir of a Family and Culture in Crisis.* HarperCollins Publishers, Inc. 2016.

[21] Frank, Thomas. *What's the Matter with Kansas: How Conservatives Won the Heart of America.* Holt Paperbacks. 2005.

[22] Haas, Richard. *A World in Disarray: American Foreign Policy and the Crisis of the Old Order.* Penguin Books. 2017. Kagan, Robert. *The Jungle Grows Back: America and Our Imperiled World.* Vintage Books. 2019. Kissinger, Henry. *World Order: Reflections on the Character of Nations and the Course of History.* Penguin Books. 2015.

[23] Mearsheimer, John J. *The Tragedy of Great Power Politics.* W.W. Norton and Company. 2003.

[24] Schelling, Thomas C. *The Strategy of Conflict.* Harvard University Press. 1960.

[25] Hoffer, Eric. *The True Believer: Thoughts on the Nature of Mass Movements.* Perennial. 1966.

[26] Hastings, Adrian. *The Construction of Nationhood: Ethnicity, Religion, and Nationalism.* Cambridge University Press. 1997.

[27] Kessler, Glenn and The Washington Post Fact Checker Staff. *Donald Trump and His Assault on Truth: The President's Falsehoods, Misleading Claims, and Flat-Out Lies.* Scribner. 2020.

[28] Greene, Joshua. *Moral Tribes: Emotion, Reason, and the Gap Between Us and Them.* Atlantic Books. 2015.

29 Hoffer, Eric. *The True Believer: Thoughts on the Nature of Mass Movements.* Perennial. 1966.

30 Fromm, Erich. *Escape from Freedom.* Farrar and Rinehart. 1941.

31 Pomerantsev, Peter. *Nothing is True and Everything is Possible: Adventures in Modern Russia.* Faber and Faber. 2017.

32 Debord, Guy. *Society of the Spectacle.* Black and Red. 2000.

33 Hofstadter, Richard. *Anti-Intellectualism in American Life.* Vintage Books. 1962.

34 Franklin, Benjamin. *The Autobiography of Benjamin Franklin.* J.P. Lippincott and Company. 1868.

35 Ferriss, Timothy. *The 4-Hour Workweek: Escape 9–5, Live Anywhere and Join the New Rich.* Crown Publishers. 2007.

36 Veblen, Thorstein. *Theory of the Leisure Class.* Macmillan. 1899.

37 Peter, Laurence J. and Hull, Raymond. *The Peter Principle: Why Things Always Go Wrong.* Pan Books. 1971.

38 Akerlof, George A. and Shiller, Robert J. *Animal Spirits: How Human Psychology Drives the Economy, and Why It Matters for Global Capitalism.* Princeton University Press. 2010.

39 Shiller, Robert J. *Irrational Exuberance.* Princeton University Press. 2005.

40 De Tocqueville, Alexis and Bevan, Gerald. *Democracy in America.* Penguin Classics. 2003.

41 Mishra, Pankaj. *The Age of Anger: A History of the Present.* Picador. 2018.

42 Horesh, Theo. *Convergence: The Globalization of Mind.* Bauu Institute. 2014.

43 Postman, Neil. *Amusing Ourselves to Death.* Methuen Publishing Ltd. 1987.

44 Sandel, Michael. *What Money Can't Buy: The Moral Limits of Markets.* Farrar, Straus, and Giroux. 2013.

45 Bauman, Zygmunt. *Liquid Modernity.* Polity Press. 2000.

46 Beck, Don and Cowan, Christopher C.. *Spiral Dynamics: Mastering Values, Leadership, and Change.*

Blackwell Publishing Ltd. 1996; Wilber, Ken. *Sex, Ecology, and Spirituality: The Spirit of Evolution.* Shambhala Publications, Inc. 1995.

[47] Sen, Amartya. *Development as Freedom.* Anchor. 2000.

[48] Kegan, Robert. *The Evolving Self: Problem and Process in Human Development.* Harvard University Press. 1982; Wilber, Ken. *Integral Psychology: Consciousness, Spirit, Psychology, Therapy.* Shambhala Publications, Inc. 2000.

[49] Wilber, Ken. *Trump and a Post-Truth World.* Shambhala Publications, Inc. 2017.

[50] Scruton, Roger. *The Meaning of Conservatism.* Palgrave Macmillan. 1984.

[51] Gay, Peter. *Weimar Culture: The Outsider as Insider.* W.W. Norton and Company. 1968.

[52] Burke, Edmund. *Reflections on the Revolution in France.* J. Dodsley in Pall Mall. 1790.

[53] De Botton, Allan. *Status Anxiety.* Vintage. 2005.

[54] Wilkinson, Richard and Pickett, Kate. *The Spirit Level: Why Greater Equality Makes Societies Stronger.* Bloomsbury Press. 2009.

[55] De Tocqueville, Alexis and Bevan, Gerald. *Democracy in America.* Penguin Classics. 2003.

[56] Horesh, Theo. *The Inner Climate: Global Warming from the Inside Out.* Bauu Institute. 2016.

[57] Mishra, Pankaj. *The Age of Anger: A History of the Present.* Farrar, Straus, and Giroux. 2017.

[58] Nietzsche, Friedrich and Scarpitti, Michael A. trans. *On the Genealogy of Morals.* Penguin Classics. 2013.

[59] Hoffer, Eric. *The True Believer: Thoughts on the Nature of Mass Movements.* Perennial. 1966.

[60] Mishra, Pankaj. *The Age of Anger: A History of the Present.* Farrar, Straus, and Giroux. 2017.

[61] Cohen, G.A. *Karl Marx's Theory of History.* Princeton University Press. 2000.

[62] Metzl, Jonathan M. *Dying of Whiteness: How the Politics of Resentment is Killing America's Heartland.* Basic Books. 2020.

SECTION III

WHEN DEMOCRACY DEVOLVES INTO TYRANNY

[1] Plato. *The Republic*. Penguin Classics. 2007.

[2] Burke, Edmund. *Reflections on the Revolution in France*. J. Dodsley in Pall Mall. 1790.

[3] Plato. *The Republic*. Penguin Classics. 2007.

[4] Judis, John B. *The Populist Explosion: How the Great Recession Transformed American and European Politics*. Columbia Global Reports. 2016.

[5] Aristotle and Sinclair, T.R. Trans. *The Politics*. Penguin Classics. 1981.

[6] Diamond, Larry. *Ill Winds: Saving Democracy from Russian Rage, Chinese Ambition, and American Complacency*. Penguin Press. 2019.

[7] Gessen, Masha. *The Future is History: How Totalitarianism Reclaimed Russia*. Granta Books. 2017.

[8] Beck, Don and Cowan, Christopher C. *Spiral Dynamics: Mastering Values, Leadership and Change*. Blackwell Publishing. 1996; Wilber, Ken. *Sex, Ecology, and Spirituality: The Spirit of Evolution*. Shambhala Publications Inc. 1996.

[9] Lessig, Lawrence. *Republic Lost 2.0*. Machete Book Group. 2015.

[10] Diamond, Larry. *Ill Winds: Saving Democracy from Russian Rage, Chinese Ambition, and American Complacency*. Penguin Press. 2019.

[11] Hamilton, Alexander and Madison, James, et al. *The Federalist Papers*. Penguin Classics. 1987.

[12] Habermas, Jurgen. *Between Facts and Norms*. Polity Press. 1996.

[13] Lilla, Mark. *The Once and Future Liberal*. Harper Collins, Inc. 2017.

[14] Diamond, Larry. *The Spirit of Democracy: The Struggle to Build Free Societies Throughout the World*. Henry Holt and Company. 2008.

[15] Freedom House. *Freedom in the World 2017: Freedom Decline*

Continues Amid Rising Populism and Autocracy. January 2017.

[16] Huntington, Samuel P. *The Third Wave: Democratization in the Late Twentieth Century.* University of Oklahoma Press. 1993.

[17] Acemoglu, Daron and Robinson, James. *Why States Fail: The Origins of Power, Prosperity, and Poverty.* Currency. 2013.

[18] Yassin-Kassab, Robin and Al-Shami, Leila. *Burning Country: Syrians in Revolution and War.* Pluto Press. 2016; Saleh, Yassin Al-Haj. *Impossible Revolution: Making Sense of the Syrian Tragedy.* C. Hurst and Co. 2017.

[19] Sunstein, Cass. *Infotopia: How Many Minds Produce Knowledge.* Oxford University Press. 2008.

[20] Nussbaum, Martha. *Not for Profit: Why Democracy Needs the Humanities.* Princeton University Press. 2010; Zakaria, Fareed. *In Defense of a Liberal Education.* W.W. Norton and Company. 2015.

[21] Kurlantzick, Joshua. *Charm Offensive: How China's Soft Power is Transforming the World.* Yale University Press. 2008.

[22] Diamond, Larry. *Ill Winds: Saving Democracy from Russian Rage, Chinese Ambition, and American Complacency.* Penguin Press. 2019.

[23] Tilly, Charles. *Coercion, Capital, and European States: A.D. 990 to 1990.* Wiley-Blackwell. 1993.

[24] Piketty, Thomas and Goldhammer, Arthur trans. *Capital in the Twenty-First Century.* Belknap Press. 2014.

[25] Zakaria, Fareed. *The Future of Freedom: Illiberal Democracy at Home and Abroad.* W.W. Norton and company. 2007.

[26] Gutmann, Amy. *Democratic Education.* Princeton University Press. 1999.

[27] Debord, Guy. *The Society of the Spectacle.* Black and Red. 2000.

[28] Harding, Luke. *Collusion: Secret Meetings, Dirty Money, and How Russia Helped Donald Trump Win.* Vintage. 2017.

[29] Gessen, Masha. *The Future is History: How Totalitarianism Reclaimed Russia.* Granta Books. 2017.

30 Kasparov, Garry. *Winter is Coming: Why Vladimir Putin and the Enemies of the Free World Must Be Stopped.* Public Affairs. 2016.

31 Acemoglu, Daron and Robinson, James. *Why States Fail: The Origins of Power, Prosperity, and Poverty.* Currency. 2013.

32 Acemoglu, Daren and Robinson, James A. *The Narrow Corridor: States, Societies, and the Fate of Liberty.* Penguin Press. 2019.

33 Sen, Amartya. *Development as Freedom.* Anchor. 2000.

34 Dewey, John. *Democracy and Education: An Introduction to the Philosophy of Education.* Macmillan. 2016; Friere, Paolo and Ramos, Myra Bergman. *Pedagogy of the Oppressed.* Continuum International Publishing Group Ltd. 2001; Gutmann, Amy. *Democratic Education.* Princeton University Press. 1999; Nussbaum, Martha. *Not for Profit: Why Democracy Needs the Humanities.* Princeton University Press. 2010: Rousseau, Jean Jacques. *Emilé, or on Education.* Penguin Classics. 1991.

35 Nussbaum, Martha. *Creating Capabilities: The Human Development Approach.* Belknap Press. 2013.

36 Habermas, Jurgen and McCarthy, Thomas trans. *Communication and the Evolution of Society.* Beacon Press. 1979.

37 Singer, Peter. *Expanding the Circle: Ethics, Evolution, and Moral Progress.* Princeton University Press. 1981.

38 Nussbaum, Martha C. *The Cosmopolitan Tradition: A Noble but Flawed Ideal.* Harvard University Press. 2019.

39 Plato. *The Republic.* Penguin Classics. 2007.

40 Mill, John Stuart. *On Liberty.* Hackett Publishing Company. 1978.

41 Zakaria, Fareed. *The Future of Freedom: Illiberal Democracy at Home and Abroad.* W.W. Norton and Company. 2007.

42 Acemoglu, Daron and Robinson, James. *Why States Fail: The Origins of Power,*

Prosperity, and Poverty. Currency. 2013.

[43] Lessig, Lawrence. *Republic Lost: How Money Corrupts Congress and a Plan to Stop It.* Twelve. 2011.

[44] Aristotle and Sinclair, T.R. Trans. *The Politics.* Penguin Classics. 1981.

[45] Transparency International. *Corruption Perceptions Index.* 2016.

[46] Rodrik, Dani. *The Globalization Paradox: Democracy and the Future of the World Economy.* W.W. Norton and Company. 2012.

[47] Wilkinson, Richard and Pickett, Kate. *The Spirit Level: Why Greater Equality Makes Societies Stronger.* Bloomsbury Press. 2009.

[48] Petit, Phillip. *Just Freedom: A Moral Compass for a Complex World.* W.W. Norton and Company. 2014.

[49] Rawls, John. *A Theory of Justice.* Belknap Press. 1971.

[50] Fromm, Erich. *Escape from Freedom.* Farrar and Rinehart. 1941.

[51] Arendt, Hannah. *The Origins of Totalitarianism.* Harcourt, Inc. 1966.

[52] Beck, Ulrich. *World Risk Society.* Polity Press. 1999.

[53] Slaughter, Anne-Marie. *A New World Order.* Princeton University Press. 2004.

[54] Pinker, Steven. *The Better Angels of Our Nature: Why Violence Has Declined.* Penguin Books. 2012.

[55] Diamond, Larry. *The Spirit of Democracy: The Struggle to Build Free Societies Throughout the World.* Henry Holt and Company. 2008.

[56] Bellamy, Alex J. *World Peace: And How We Can Achieve It.* Oxford University Press. 2019.

[57] Haas, Richard. *A World in Disarray: American Foreign Policy and the Crisis of the Old Order.* Penguin Books. 2017. Kagan, Robert. *The Jungle Grows Back: America and Our Imperiled World.* Vintage Books. 2019. Kissinger, Henry. *World Order: Reflections on the Character of Nations and the Course of History.* Penguin Books. 2015.

[58] Diamond, Larry. *The Spirit of Democracy: The Struggle to Build Free Societies Throughout the World.* St. Martin's Griffin. 2009.

[59] Dobbins, James and Jones, Seth G. *The UN's Role in Nation-Building: From Congo to Iraq.* Rand Corporation. 2005; Doyle, Michael. *Making War and Building Peace: United Nations Peace Operations.* Princeton University Press. 2006; Paris, Roland. *At War's End: Building Peace After Civil Conflict.* Cambridge University Press. 2004; Sisk, Timothy. *State Building.* Polity. 2013.

[60] Chandler, David. *Peacebuilding: The Twenty Years' Crisis, 1997–2017.* Palgrave Macmillan. 2017.

[61] Diamond, Larry. *Ill Winds: Saving Democracy from Russian Rage, Chinese Ambition, and American Complacency.* Penguin Press. 2019.

[62] Doyle, Michael. *Ways of War and Peace: Realism, Liberalism, and Socialism.* W.W. Norton and Company. 1997.

[63] Keohane, Robert O. *After Hegemony: Cooperation and Discord in the World Political Economy.* Princeton University Press. 2005; Nye Jr., Joseph S. *Soft Power: The Means to Success in World Politics.* Public Affairs. 2005.

[64] Kinzer, Stephen. *Overthrow: America's Century of Regime Change from Hawaii to Iraq.* Times Books. 2007.

[65] De Soto, Hernando. *The Mystery of Capital. Why Capitalism Triumphs in the West and Fails Everywhere Else.* Basic Books. 2003; Sachs, Jeffrey. *The End of Poverty: Economic Possibilities of Our Times.* Penguin Books. 2006; Yunus, Muhammad. *A World Without Poverty: Social Business and the Future of Capitalism.* Public Affairs. 2005.

[66] Fukuyama, Francis. *The End of History and the Last Man.* The Free Press. 1992.

[67] Csaky, Zselyke. *Nations in Transition 2020: Dropping the Democratic Facade.* Freedom House. 2020.

[68] Human Rights Watch. *'All of My Body Was Pain:' Sexual Violence against Rohingya*

Women and Girls in Burma.
November 2017.

[69] Gettleman, Jeffrey. *Rohingya Recount Atrocities: 'They Threw My Baby Into a Fire.'* The New York Times. October 2017.

[70] Stewart, Phil and Strobel, Warren. *U.S. to halt some arms sales to Saudi, citing civilian deaths in Yemen campaign.* Reuters. December 13, 2016.

[71] Zengerle, Patricia. *Defying Congress, Trump sets $8 billion-plus in weapons sales to Saudi, UAE.* Reuters. May 24, 2019.

[72] Summers, Hannah. *Yemen on the brink of 'world's worst famine in 100 years' if war continues.* The Guardian. October 2018.

[73] Qin, Amy. *In China's crackdown on Muslims, children have not been spared.* The New York Times. February. 2020.

[74] Open Democracy. *Jair Bolsonaro accused of inciting genocide before the International Criminal Court.* November 2019.

[75] Ratcliffe, Rebecca. *'A nightmarish mess:' Millions in Assam brace for a loss of*

citizenship. The Guardian. August 2019.

[76] Yasir, Sameer et al. *Inside Kashmir, Cut Off from the World: 'A Living Hell' of Anger and Fear.* The New York Times. August 2019.

[77] Helm, Sara. *"Will he lose his leg?": Thousands of Gaza protesters facing life altering injuries from Israeli high velocity bullets.* The Independent. Love 11, 2018.

[78] Bremmer, Ian. *Every Nation for Itself: Winners and Loser in a G-Zero World.* Penguin Books. 2013.

[79] Stockholm International Peace Research Institute. *Nuclear weapon modernization continues but the outlook for arms control is bleak.* June 2020.

[80] United Nations High Commissioner for Refugees. *Global forced displacement vastly more widespread in 2019.* 2020.

[81] Kershaw, Ian. *To Hell and Back: Europe, 1914–1949.* Penguin. 2016.

[82] McNeill, William H. *Keeping*

Together in Time: Dance and Drill in Human History. Harvard University Press. 1995.

[83] Connerton, Paul. *How Modernity Forgets.* Cambridge University Press. 2009.

[84] Grossman, Dave. *On Killing: The Psychological Cost of Learning to Kill in War.* Back Bay Books. 2009.

[85] Nye Jr., Joseph S. *Soft Power: The Means to Success in World Politics.* Public Affairs. 2005.

[86] Doyle, Michael. *Ways of War and Peace: Realism, Liberalism, and Socialism.* W.W. Norton and Company. 1997.

[87] Diamond, Jared. *Evolution and the Future of the Human Animal.* Harper Perennial. 2006; Dunbar, Robin. *Grooming, Gossip, and the Evolution of Language.* Harvard University Press. 1998.

[88] Smith, Adam. *The Theory of Moral Sentiments.* Penguin Classics. 2010.

[89] Aristotle and Thomson, J.A.K. trans. *The Nicomachean Ethics.* Penguin Classics. 2004; Aristotle and Sinclair, T.R. Trans. *The Politics.* Penguin Classics. 1981.

[90] Hamilton, Alexander and Madison, James, et al. *The Federalist Papers.* Penguin Classics. 1987.

[91] Snyder, Timothy. *Bloodlands: Europe Between Hitler and Stalin.* Vintage. 2011.

[92] Stockholm International Peace Research Institute. *World Military Expenditure Grows 1.8 Trillion in 2018.* April 29, 2019.

[93] Fritzsche, Peter. *Life and Death in the Third Reich.* Belknap Press. 2008.

[94] Allen, Kate. *Raqqa is in ruins like a modern Dresden. This is not 'precision' bombing.* The Guardian. May 2019.

[95] Tharoor, Ishaan. *Before and after images reveal the huge destruction in Mosul.* The Washington Post. July 2017.

[96] Ikenberry, John G. *Liberal Leviathan: The Origins, Crisis, and Transformation of the American World Order.* Princeton University Press. 2012.

[97] Helm, Sara. *"Will he lose his leg?": Thousands of Gaza*

protesters facing life altering injuries from Israeli high velocity bullets. The Independent. November 2018.

[98] Rappleye, Hannah and Seville, Lisa Riordan. *24 migrants have died in ICE custody during administration.* NBC News. June 9. 2019.

[99] Pompa, Cynthia. *Immigrant Kids Keep Dying in CBP Detention Centers, and DHS Won't Take Accountability.* American Civil Liberties Union. June 24, 2019.

[100] Haag, Matthew. *Thousands of Immigrant Children Said They Were Sexually Abused in U.S. Detention Centers, Report Says.* New York Times. February 27, 2019.

[101] Flynn, Meagan. *Detained migrant children got no toothbrush, no soap, no sleep. It's no problem, government argues.* Washington Post. June 21, 2019.

[102] Itkowitz, Colby. *1 in every 4 circuit court judges is now a Trump appointee.* Washington Post. December 21, 2019.

[103] American Heritage. *Dictionary of the English Language, Fifth Edition.* Houghton Mifflin. 2015.

[104] Pitzer, Andrea. *One Long Night: A Global History of Concentration Camps.* Back Bay Books. 2017.

[105] Fritzsche, Peter. *Life and Death in the Third Reich.* Belknap Press. 2008.

[106] Herman, Judith L. *Trauma and Recovery: The Aftermath of Violence—From Domestic Abuse to Political Terror.* Basic Books. 1992.

[107] Snyder, Timothy. *Bloodlands: Europe Between Hitler and Stalin.* Vintage Books. 2010.

[108] Aly, Gotz. *Hitler's Beneficiaries: Plunder, Racial War, and the Nazi Welfare State.* Verso. 2016.

[109] Fritzsche, Peter. *Life and Death in the Third Reich.* Belknap Press. 2008.

[110] Goldhagen, Daniel Jonah. *Worse Than War: Genocide, Eliminationism, and the Ongoing Assault on Humanity.* Public Affairs. 2009.

[111] United Nations Office for the

Coordination of Humanitarian Affairs. *Yemen: We Are Losing the Fight Against Famine.* Sept. 21, 2018.

[112] Boucek, Christopher and Ottawa, Marina. *Yemen on the Brink.* Brookings Institution Press. 2010.

[113] Lackner, Helen. *Yemen in Crisis: The Road to War.* Verso. 2019.

[114] Save the Children. *Starvation in Yemen: 85,000 Children May Have Died of Hunger.* November 21, 2018.

[115] Almosawa, Shuaib and Fahim, Kareem. *Airstrikes in Yemen Hit Wedding Party, Killing Dozens.* New York Times. September 28, 2015.

[116] Oxfam International. *Oxfam Condemns Coalition Bombing of a Warehouse Containing Vital Humanitarian Aid.* April 18, 2015.

[117] Hubbard Ben. *U.S. Fingerprints on Obliterating Yemen's Economy.* New York Times. November 13, 2016.

[118] Food and Agricultural Organization of the United Nations. *FAO warns of rapidly deteriorating food security in Yemen.* January 28, 2016.

[119] Applebaum, Anne. *Red Famine: Stalin's War on Ukraine.* Penguin Books. 2018.

[120] Keneally, Thomas. *Three Famines: Starvation and Politics.* Public Affairs. 2011.

[121] Stewart, Phil and Strobel, Warren. *U.S. to halt some arms sales to Saudi, citing civilian deaths in Yemen campaign.* Reuters. December 13, 2016.

[122] Zengerle, Patricia. *Defying Congress, Trump sets $8 billion-plus in weapons sales to Saudi, UAE.* Reuters. May 24, 2019.

[123] Dikotter, Frank. *Mao's Great Famine: The History of China's Most Devastating Catastrophe, 1958-1962.* Walker and Company. 2010.

[124] Keneally, Thomas. *Three Famines: Starvation and Politics.* Public Affairs. 2011.

SECTION IV

THIS LOVE AFFAIR WITH DICTATORS HAS GOT TO END

[1] Horkheimer, Max. *Eclipse of Reason.* Oxford University Press. 1947.

[2] Massumi, Brian. *A User's Guide to Capitalism and Schizophrenia: Deviations from Deleuze and Guattari.* MIT Press. 1992.

[3] Pasha-Robinson, Lucy. *Donald Trump appears to shove world leader out of the way at Nato summit.* Independent. May 25, 2017.

[4] Walker, Shaun. *Alleged Russian spies sentenced to jail over Montenegro "coup plot."* The Guardian. May 9, 2019.

[5] Associated Press in Cetinje. *Montenegro ratifies Nato membership in historic shift to western alliance.* The Guardian. April 28, 2017.

[6] Sullivan, Eileen. *Trump Questions the Core of Nato: Mutual Defense, Including Montenegro.* New York Times. July 18, 2018.

[7] Snyder, Timothy. *The Road to Unfreedom: Russia, Europe, America.* Tim Duggan Books. 2018.

[8] Rajan, Menon and Rumer, Eugene B et al. *Conflict in Ukraine: The Unwinding of the Post-Cold War Order.* MIT Press. 2015; Snyder, Timothy. *The Road to Unfreedom: Russia, Europe, America.* Bodley Head. 2018.

[9] Judah, Tim. *In Wartime: Stories from Ukraine.* Penguin Books. 2016.

[10] Way, Lucan Ahmed and Casey, Adam. *Russia has been meddling in foreign elections for decades. Has it made a difference?* Washington Post. January 8, 2018.

[11] Stephen, Chris. *Gaddafi Files Show Evidence of Murderous Intent.* The Guardian. June 2011.

[12] Diamond, Larry. *Ill Winds: Saving Democracy from Russian Rage, Chinese Ambition, and American Complacency.* Penguin Press. 2019.

[13] Doyle, Michael. *Liberal Peace: Selected Essays.* Routledge. 2012.

[14] Diamond, Larry. *The Spirit of*

Democracy: The Struggle to Build Free Societies Throughout the World. St. Martin's Griffin. 2009.

[15] Diamond, Larry. *Ill Winds: Saving Democracy from Russian Rage, Chinese Ambition, and American Complacency.* Penguin Press. 2019.

[16] Acemoglu, Daron and Robinson, James. *Why Nations Fail: The Origins of Power, Prosperity, and Poverty.* Currency. 2013.

[17] Fromm, Erich. *Escape from Freedom.* Farrar and Rinehart. 1941.

[18] Mishra, Pankaj. *The Age of Anger: A History of the Present.* Picador. 2018.

[19] Müller, Jan Werner. *What is Populism?* University of Pennsylvania Press. 2016.

[20] Reuters. *Philippines president Roderigo Duterte likens himself to Hitler.* The Guardian. September 30, 2016.

[21] Power, Samantha. *A Problem from Hell: America and the Age of Genocide.* Basic Books. 2013.

[22] Kagan, Robert. *The Jungle Grows Back: America and Our Imperiled World.* Vintage Books. 2019.

[23] Diamond, Larry. *Ill Winds: Saving Democracy from Russian Rage, Chinese Ambition, and American Complacency.* Penguin Press. 2019.

[24] Marx, Karl and Engels, Friedrich. *The Communist Manifesto.* Penguin Classics. 2002.

[25] Csaky, Zselyke. *Nations in Transition 2020: Dropping the Democratic Facade.* Freedom House. 2020.

[26] Mann, Michael. *Fascists.* Cambridge University Press. 2004.

[27] Houellebecq, Michel. *Submission: A Novel.* Picador. 2016; Kirchik, James. *The End of Europe: Dictators, Demagogues, and the Coming Dark Age.* Yale University Press. 2017; Murray, Douglas. *The Strange Death of Europe: Immigration, Identity, Islam.* Bloomsbury Continuum. 2017.

[28] Mindell, Arnold. *Sitting in the Fire: Large Group*

Transformation Using Conflict and Diversity. Deep Democracy Exchange. 1995.

29 Krastev, Ivan. *After Europe.* University of Pennsylvania Press. 2017.

30 Eatwell, Roger and Goodwin, Matthew. *National Populism: The Revolt Against Liberal Democracy.* Penguin Random House. 2018.

31 Polakow-Saransky, Sasha. *Go Back to from Where You Came: The Backlash Against Immigration and the Fate of Western Democracy.* Nation Books. 2017.

32 Judt, Tony. P*ostwar: A History of Europe Since 1945.* Penguin Books. 2006.

33 Krastev, Ivan. *After Europe.* University of Pennsylvania Press. 2017.

34 Baer, Elizabeth. *The Genocidal Gaze: From German Southeast Africa to the Third Reich.* Wayne State University Press. 2017.

35 Snyder, Timothy. *Bloodlands: Europe Between Hitler and Stalin.* Basic Books. 2012.

36 Collier, Paul. *Exodus: How Migration is Changing the World.* Oxford University Press. 2015.

37 Eatwell, Roger and Goodwin, Matthew. *National Populism: The Revolt Against Liberal Democracy.* Penguin Random House. 2018.

38 Armstrong, Karen. *A History of God: The 4,000-Year Quest of Judaism, Christianity, and Islam.* Ballantine Books. 1994.

39 Horesh, Theo. *The Holocausts We All Deny: Collective Trauma in the World Today.* Bauu Institute. 2018.

40 Finkelstein, Norman G. *The Holocaust Industry: Reflections on the Exploitation of Jewish Suffering.* Verso. 2015.

41 Pappé, Ilan. *The Ethnic Cleansing of Palestine.* Oneworld Publications. 2007; Khalidi, Rashid. *The Iron Cage: The Story of the Palestinian Struggle for Statehood.* Beacon Press. 2007; Kimmerling, Baruch and Migdal, Joel S. *The Palestinian People: A History.* Harvard University Press. 2003; Morris, Benny. *Righteous Victims: A History of the Zionist-Arab Conflict, 1881–*

2001. Vintage. 2001.

[42] Abouzeid, Rania. *No Turning Back: Life, Loss, and Hope in Wartime Syria.* W.W. Norton and Company. 2019.

[43] Pearlman, Wendy. *We Crossed a Bridge and It Trembled: Voices from Syria.* Custom House. 2018.

[44] Polakow-Saransky, Sasha. *Go Back to from Where You Came: The Backlash Against Immigration and the Fate of Western Democracy.* Nation Books. 2017.

[45] Mearsheimer, John J. and Walt, Stephen M. *The Israel Lobby and U.S. Foreign Policy.* Penguin Books. 2008.

[46] The Carter Center. *Countering the Islamophobia Industry: Toward More Effective Strategies.* May 2018.

[47] Brown, John. *Supreme Court Rules Against Exposing Israel's Role in Bosnian Genocide.* 972 Magazine. December 2016.

[48] Dunst, Charles. *Israel's Shameful Role in Myanmar's Genocidal Campaign Against Rohingya.* Haaretz. December 2019.

[49] Mukherjee, Mayuri. *How Israel made friends in India.* Jerusalem Post. October 2018.

[50] Said, Edward W. *The Question of Palestine.* Vintage Books. 1992.

[51] Proudhon, P.J. *General Idea of the Revolution in the Nineteenth Century.* University Press of the Pacific. 2004.

[52] Mitchell, Anna and Diamond, Larry. *China's Surveillance State Should Scare Everyone.* The Atlantic. February 2018; Pils, Eva and Zhang, Taisu, et al. *China's New Age of Fear.* Foreign Policy. February 2018.

[53] Chin, Josh and Bürge, Clément. *Twelve Days in Xinjiang: How China's Surveillance State Overwhelms Daily Life.* Wall Street Journal. December 2017.

[54] Dikotter, Frank. *The Cultural Revolution: A People's History, 1962–1976.* Bloomsbury Paperbacks. 2017.

[55] Diamond, Larry. *Ill Winds: Saving Democracy from Russian Rage, Chinese Ambition, and American Complacency.* Penguin Press. 2019.

56 Mill, John Stuart. *On Liberty.* Hackett Publishing Company. 1978.

57 Hoffer, Eric. *The True Believer: Thoughts on the Nature of Mass Movements.* Perennial. 1966.

58 Paxton, Robert O. *The Anatomy of Fascism.* Penguin. 2005.

59 Smith, Adam. *Wealth of Nations.* Oxford University Press. 2008.

60 Hayek, F.A. *The Road to Serfdom.* George Routledge and Sons. 1944.

61 Stoltzfus, Nathan. *Hitler's Compromises: Coercion and Consensus in Nazi Germany.* Yale University Press. 2016.

62 Berlin, Isaiah. *Four Essays on Liberty.* Oxford University Press. 1990.

63 Diamond, Larry. *Ill Winds: Saving Democracy from Russian Rage, Chinese Ambition, and American Complacency.* Penguin Press. 2019.

64 Acemoglu, Daron and Robinson, James. *Why States Fail: The Origins of Power, Prosperity, and Poverty.* Currency. 2013.

65 Mill, John Stuart. *On Liberty.* Hackett Publishing Company. 1978.

66 Huntington, Samuel P. *The Third Wave: Democratization in the Late Twentieth Century.* University of Oklahoma Press. 1993.

67 Piketty, Thomas and Goldhammer, Arthur trans. *Capital in the Twenty-First Century.* Belknap Press. 2014.

68 Müller, Jan Werner. *What is Populism?* University of Pennsylvania Press. 2016.

69 Aristotle and Sinclair, T.R. trans. *The Politics.* Penguin Classics. 1981.

70 Bates, Robert H. *When Things Fell Apart: State Failure in Late-Century Africa.* Cambridge University Press. 2015.

71 Putnam, Robert D. *E Pluribus Unum: Diversity and Community in the Twenty-First Century.* Johan Skytte Prize Lecture. 2006.

72 Dahl, Robert. *On Democracy.* Yale University Press. 2000.

73 Diamond, Larry. *Ill Winds: Saving Democracy from Russian Rage, Chinese Ambition, and*

American Complacency. Penguin Press. 2019.

[74] Levitsky, Steven and Ziblatt, Daniel. *How Democracies Die.* Broadway Books. 2019.

[75] Fromm, Erich. *Escape from Freedom.* Farrar and Rinehart. 1941.

[76] Horesh, Theo. *Convergence: The Globalization of Mind.* Bauu Institute. 2014.

[77] Krastev, Ivan. *Democracy Disrupted: The Politics of Global Protest.* University of Pennsylvania Press. 2014.

[78] Howe, Neil and Strauss, William. *Millennials Rising: The Next Great Generation.* Vintage Books. 2000.

[79] McLuhan, Marshall. *Understanding Media: The Extensions of Man.* Routledge. 1964.

[80] Fromm, Erich. *Escape from Freedom.* Farrar and Rinehart. 1941.

[81] Wu, Tim. *The Master Switch: The Rise and Fall of Information Empires.* Atlantic Books. 2012

[82] Fukuyama, Francis. *The Great Disruption: Human Nature and*

the Reconstitution of Social Order. The Free Press. 1999.

[83] Elias, Norbert. *The Civilizing Process: Sociogenetic and Psychogenetic Investigations.* Basil Blackwell Ltd. 1982.

[84] Eatwell, Roger and Goodwin, Matthew. *National Populism: The Revolt Against Liberal Democracy.* Penguin Random House. 2018; Mearsheimer, John. *The Great Delusion: Liberal Dreams and International Realities.* Yale University Press. 2018; Tamir, Yael. *Why Nationalism.* Princeton University Press. 2019;

[85] Ghemawat, Pankaj. *World 3.0: World Prosperity and How to Achieve It.* Harvard Business Review Press. 2011.

[86] Kaldor, Mary. *Global Civil Society: An Answer to War.* Polity Press. 2003.

[87] Beck, Ulrich. *Cosmopolitan Vision.* Polity Press. 2006.

[88] Dahl, Robert. *On Democracy.* Yale University Press. 2000.

[89] Marx, Karl. *Capital: Volume 1.* Penguin Classics. 1990.

[90] Lukács, George. *History and Class Consciousness: Studies in*

Marxist Dialectics. The Merlin Press Ltd. 1975.

[91] Singer, Peter. *The Expanding Circle: Ethics, Evolution, and Moral Progress*. Princeton University Press. 1981.

[92] Habermas, Jurgen. *Between Facts and Norms*. Polity Press. 1996.

[93] Mill, John Stuart. *On Liberty*. Hackett Publishing Company. 1978.

[94] Habermas, Jurgen. *The Theory of Communicative Action: Reason and the Rationalization of Society*. Beacon Press. 1984.

[95] Marcuse, Herbert. *One-Dimensional Man: Studies in the Ideology of Advanced Industrial Society*. Beacon Press. 1964.

[96] Pickett, Kate and Wilkinson, Richard. *The Spirit Level: Why Greater Equality Makes Societies Stronger*. Bloomsbury Press. 2010.

[97] Burke, Edmund. *Reflections on the Revolution in France*. J. Dodsley in Pall Mall. 1790.

[98] Sunstein, Cass. *Infotopia: How Many Minds Produce Knowledge*. Oxford University Press. 2006.

[99] Haidt, Jonathan. *The Righteous Mind: Why Good People Are Divided By Politics and Religion*. Vintage Books. 2013.

[100] Lakoff, George. *Moral Politics: How Liberals and Conservatives Think*. University of Chicago Press. 1996.

[101] Armstrong, Karen. *The Case for God*. Anchor. 2010.

[102] Taylor, Charles. *A Secular Age*. Belknap Press. 2018.

[103] MacIntyre, Alisdair. *After Virtue: A Study in Moral Theory*. University of Notre Dame Press. 1984.

[104] Dewey, John. *Democracy and Education: An Introduction to the Philosophy of Education*. Free Press. 1916; Dewey, John. *The Quest for Certainty: A Study of the Relation of Knowledge and Action*. Kessinger Publishing. 1929.

[105] Habermas, Jurgen. *Between Facts and Norms*. Polity Press. 1996.

[106] Held, David. *Cosmopolitanism: Ideals and Realities*. Polity Press. 2010.

SECTION V

UNLEASHING THE SPIRIT OF DEMOCRACY

[1] Rorty, Richard. *Achieving Our Country: Leftist Thought in Twentieth Century America.* Harvard University Press. 1999.

[2] Rorty, Richard. *Achieving Our Country: Leftist Thought in Twentieth-Century America.* Harvard University Press. 1999.

[3] Hegel, G.W.F. *Introduction to the Philosophy of History.* Hackett Publishing Company. 1988.

[4] De Tocqueville, Alexis and Bevan, Gerald. *Democracy in America.* Penguin Classics. 2003.

[5] Mead, Walter Russell. *Power, Terror, Peace, and War: America's Grand Strategy in a World at War.* Vintage Books. 2005.

[6] Drucker, Peter. *Innovation and Entrepreneurship.* Butterworth Heinemann. 1985.

[7] Baumol, William J. *The Free market Innovation Machine: Analyzing the Growth Miracle of Capitalism.* Princeton University Press. 2002.

[8] Takaki, Ronald. *A Different Mirror: A History of Multicultural America.* Back Bay Books. 2008.

[9] Whitman, Walt. *Democratic Vistas and Other Papers.* Franklin Classics. 2018.

[10] Turner, Frederick Jackson. *The Significance of the Frontier in American History.* Martino Fine Books. 2014.

[11] Rorty, Richard. *Achieving Our Country: Leftist Thought in Twentieth-Century America.* Harvard University Press. 1999.

[12] Whitman, Walt. *Democratic Vistas and Other Papers.* Franklin Classics. 2018.

[13] Scruton, Roger. *The Meaning of Conservatism.* Macmillan. 1980.

[14] Mill, John Stuart. *On Liberty.* Hackett Publishing Company. 1978.

[15] Kirk, Russell. *The Conservative Mind: From Burke to Eliot.* Gateway Editions. 2001.

[16] Rand, Ayn. *The Virtue of Selfishness.* Ayn Rand. 1961.

[17] The Washington Post. *The Mueller Report.* Scribner. 2019.

[18] Ackerman, Bruce and Ayres, Ian. *Voting With Dollars: A New Paradigm for Campaign Finance.* Yale University Press. 2004.

[19] Hamilton, Alexander and Madison, James, et al. *The Federalist Papers.* Penguin Classics. 1987.

[20] Locke, John. *A Letter Concerning Toleration.* Hackett Publishing Company. 1983.

[21] Mill, John Stuart. *On Liberty.* Hackett Publishing Company. 1978.

[22] Aristotle and Erwin, Terrence trans. *Nicomachean Ethics.* Hackett Publishing Company. 1999.

[23] Montaigne, Michele de and Screech, M.A. trans. *The Essays: A Selection.* Penguin Classics. 1994; Schaefer, David Lewis. *The Political Philosophy of Montaigne.* Cornell University. 1990.

[24] Rawls, John. *Political Liberalism.* Columbia University Press. 1993.

[25] Walzer, Michael. *On Toleration.* Yale University Press. 1999.

[26] Brown, Garrett Wallace. *Grounding Cosmopolitanism: From Kant to the Idea of a Cosmopolitan Constitution.* Edinburgh University Press. 2009; Held, David. *Cosmopolitanism: Ideals and Realities.* Polity Press. 2010.

[27] Nussbaum, Martha C. *The Cosmopolitan Tradition: A Noble but Flawed Ideal.* Harvard University Press. 2019.

[28] Appiah, Kwame Anthony. *Cosmopolitanism: Ethics in a World of Strangers.* W.W. Norton and Company. 2007.

[29] Stiglitz, Joseph. *Globalization and Its Discontents.* W.W. Norton and Company. 1994.

[30] Goodhart, David. *The Road to Somewhere: The Populist Revolt and the Future of Politics.* C. Hurst and Co. Publishers. 2017.

[31] Harvey, David. *A Brief History of Neoliberalism.* Oxford University Press. 2007.

[32] Haidt, Jonathan. *The Righteous Mind: Why Good People Are Divided By Politics and Religion.* Vintage Books. 2013.

[33] Kershaw, Ian. *To Hell and Back: Europe, 1914–1949.* Penguin. 2016.

[34] Polakow-Saransky, Sasha. *Go Back to From Where You Came: The Backlash Against Immigration and the Fate of Western Democracy.* Nation Books. 2017.

[35] De Tocqueville, Alexis and Bevan, Gerald. *Democracy in America.* Penguin Classics. 2003.

[36] Blake, Aaron. *'The only good Democrat is a dead Democrat.' 'When the looting starts, the shooting starts.' Twice in 25 hours, Trump tweets conspicuous allusions to violence.* The Washington Post. May 2020.

[37] Campbell, Joseph. *The Hero's Journey: Joseph Campbell on His Life and Work.* New World Library. 2014.

[38] Hume, David. *An Enquiry Concerning the Principle of Morals.* Hackett Publishing Company. 1983.

[39] Nussbaum, Martha. *Anger and Forgiveness: Resentment, Generosity, and Justice.* Oxford University Press. 2016.

[40] Benkler, Yochai. *The Penguin and the Leviathan: How Cooperation Triumphs Over Self-Interest.* Crown Business. 2011; Waal, Frans de. *The Age of Empathy: Nature's Lessons for a Kinder Society.* Three Rivers Press. 2009; Wilson, James Q. *The Moral Sense.* The Free Press. 1993.

[41] Cicero and Walsh, P.G. *On Obligations.* Oxford University Press. 2008.

[42] Hedges, Chris. *American Fascists: The Christian Right and the War on America.* Free Press. 2008.

[43] Frank, Thomas. *What's the Matter with Kansas: How Conservatives Won the Heart of America.* Henry Holt and Company. 2004; Hochschild, Arlie Russell. *Strangers in their Own Land: Anger and Mourning on the American Right.* The New Press. 2016; Metzl, Jonathan M. *Dying of Whiteness: How the Politics of Radical Resentment is Killing America's Heartland.* Basic Books. 2019.

[44] Zhu Xi and Nguyen Due Lan trans. *Explanation of the Four*

Books. Vietnam Culture and Publishing House. 1998.

[45] Eatwell, Roger and Goodwin, Matthew. *National Populism: The Revolt Against Liberal Democracy.* Penguin Random House. 2018; Judis, John B. *The Populist Explosion: How the Great Recession Transformed American and European Politics.* Columbia Global Reports. 2016; Müller, Jan Werner. *What is Populism?* University of Pennsylvania Press. 2016; Polakow-Saransky, Sasha. *Go Back to from Where You Came: The Backlash Against Immigration and the Fate of Western Democracy.* Nation Books. 2017.

[46] Austin, J.L. *How to Do Things with Words.* Oxford University Press. 1962.

[47] Lakoff, George. *Don't Think of an Elephant: Know Your Values and Frame the Debate.* Chelsea Green Publishing. 2014.

[48] Marx, Karl and Engels, Friedrich. *The German Ideology.* Prometheus Books. 1998.

[49] Moraes, Claude. *The Far Right is Organized and Growing: Those Nazi Salutes are Serious.* The Guardian. June 14, 2018.

[50] Cortellessa, Eric. *Why Are Pro-Israel Groups Boosting a Far-Right, Anti-Muslim U.K. Extremist?* The Times of Israel. January 24, 2019.

[51] Tharoor, Ishaan. *Netanyahu and Orban Meet in Summit of Illiberal Nationalists.* Washington Post. July 19, 2018.

[52] Taylor, Matthew. *"White Europe": 60,000 Nationalists March on Poland's Independence Day.* The Guardian. November 12, 2017.

[53] Snyder, Timothy. *The Road to Unfreedom: Russia, Europe, America.* Tim Duggan Books. 2018.

[54] Diamond, Larry. *Ill Winds: Saving Democracy from Russian Rage, Chinese Ambition, and American Complacency.* Penguin Press. 2019.

[55] Kissinger, Henry. *World Order: Reflections on the Character of Nations and the Course of History.* Penguin Books. 2015.

[56] Snyder, Timothy. *The Road*

to Unfreedom: Russia, Europe, America. Tim Duggan Books. 2018.

[57] Snyder, Timothy. *On Tyranny: Twenty Lessons from the Twentieth Century.* Bodley Head. 2017.

[58] Ingelhart, Ronald F. *Modernization, Cultural Change, and Democracy: The Human Development Sequence.* Cambridge University Press. 2005.

[59] Singer, Peter. *The Expanding Circle: Ethics, Evolution, and Moral Progress.* Princeton University Press. 1981.

[60] Habermas, Jurgen. *The Theory of Communicative Action: Reason and the Rationalization of Society.* Beacon Press. 1984; Rawls, John. *A Theory of Justice.* Belknap Press. 1971.

[61] Nussbaum, Martha. *Frontiers of Justice: Disability, Nationality, Species Membership.* Belknap Press. 2007.

[62] Appiah, Kwame Anthony. *Cosmopolitanism: Ethics in a World of Strangers. W.W.* Norton and Company. 2007.

[63] Appiah, Kwame Anthony. *Cosmopolitanism: Ethics in a World of Strangers.* W.W. Norton and Company. 2007; Singer, Peter. *One World: The Ethics of Globalization.* Yale University Press. 2004.

[64] Rolston III, Holmes. *A New Environmental Ethics: The Next Millennium for Life on Earth.* Routledge. 2011; Stone, Christopher D. *Earth and Other Ethics: The Case for Moral Pluralism.* Harper and Row. 1987.

[65] De Waal, Franz. *The Age of Empathy: Nature's Lessons for a Kinder Society.* Broadway Books. 2010.

[66] Broome, John. *Climate Matters: Ethics in a Warming World.* W.W. Norton and Company. 2012; Gardiner, Stephen M. *The Perfect Moral Storm: The Ethical Tragedy of Climate Change.* Oxford University Press. 2013; Jamieson, Dale. *Reason in a Dark Time: Why the Struggle Against Climate Change Failed and What It Means for Our Future.* Oxford University Press. 2014.

[67] Fukuyama, Francis. *The Great Disruption: Human Nature and*

the Reconstitution of Social Order. Profile Books Ltd. 2006; Kristol, Irving. *Reflections of a Neoconservative.* Basic Books. 1983.

[68] Jurgen Habermas. *The Philosophical Discourse of Modernity.* Polity Press. 1990; Wilber, Ken. *Trump and the Post-Truth World.* Shambhala Publications, Inc. 2017.

[69] Habermas, Jurgen. *Between Facts and Norms.* Polity Press. 1996.

[70] Nussbaum. *Not for Profit: Why Democracy Needs the Humanities.* Princeton University Press. 2010.

[71] Judt, Tony. *Postwar: A History of Europe Since 1945.* The Penguin Press. 2005.

[72] Horesh, Theo. *The Inner Climate: Global Warming from the Inside Out.* Bauu Institute. 2015.

[73] Lakoff, George. *Metaphors We Live By.* University of Chicago Press. 2003.

[74] Kant, Immanuel and Gregor, Mary et al. trans. *Groundwork*

of the Metaphysic of Morals. Cambridge University Press. 2012.

[75] Cohn, Norman. *The Pursuit of the Millennium: Revolutionary Millenarians and Mystical Anarchists of the Middle Ages.* Paladin. 1972.

[76] Foucault, Michel. *Madness and Civilization: A History of Insanity in the Age of Reason.* Random House. 1965.

[77] Rorty, Richard. *Achieving Our Country: Leftist Thought in Twentieth-Century America.* Harvard University Press. 1999.

[78] Fukuyama, Francis. *The End of History and the Last Man.* The Free Press. 1992.

[79] Wilber, Ken. *Sex, Ecology, Spirituality: The Spirit of Evolution.* Shambhala Publications, Inc. 1995.

[80] Wright, Robert. *Nonzero: The Logic of Human Destiny.* Vintage Books. 2001.

[81] Fukuyama, Francis. *The End of History and the Last Man.* The Free Press. 1992.

[82] Pinker, Steven. *The Better*

Angels of Our Nature: Why Violence Has Declined. Penguin Books. 2012.

[83] Nussbaum, Martha. *Frontiers of Justice: Disability, Nationality, and Species Membership.* Harvard university Press. 2007.

[84] Lakoff, George and Johnson, Mark. *Metaphors We Live By.* University of Chicago Press. 1980.

[85] Lappé, Frances Moore. *EcoMind: Changing the Way We Think, to Create the World We Want.* Perseus Books. 2011.

[86] Horesh, Theo. *Convergence: The Globalization of Mind.* Bauu Institute Press. 2014.

[87] Pinker, Steven. *The Better Angels of Our Nature: Why Violence Has Declined.* Penguin Books. 2012.

[88] Bellamy, Alex J. *World Peace: And How We Can Achieve It.* Oxford University Press. 2019;

Kenny, Charles. *Getting Better: Why Global Development Is Succeeding—And How We Can Improve the World Even More.* Basic Books. 2011.

FTERWARD

THE FASCIST MOMENT AND THE FATE OF THE EARTH

[1] Evans, Richard J. *The Coming of the Third Reich: How the Nazis Destroyed Democracy and Seized Power in Germany.* Penguin. 2004.

[2] Diamond, Jared. *The Third Chimpanzee: On the Evolution and Future of the Human Animal.* Harper Collins. 1992.

[3] Carlin, Dan. *The End is Always Near.* William Collins Books. 2019.

[4] Rorty, Richard. *Achieving Our Country: Leftist Thought in Twentieth-Century America.* Harvard University Press. 1999.